MERA
QUEEN OF ATLANTIS

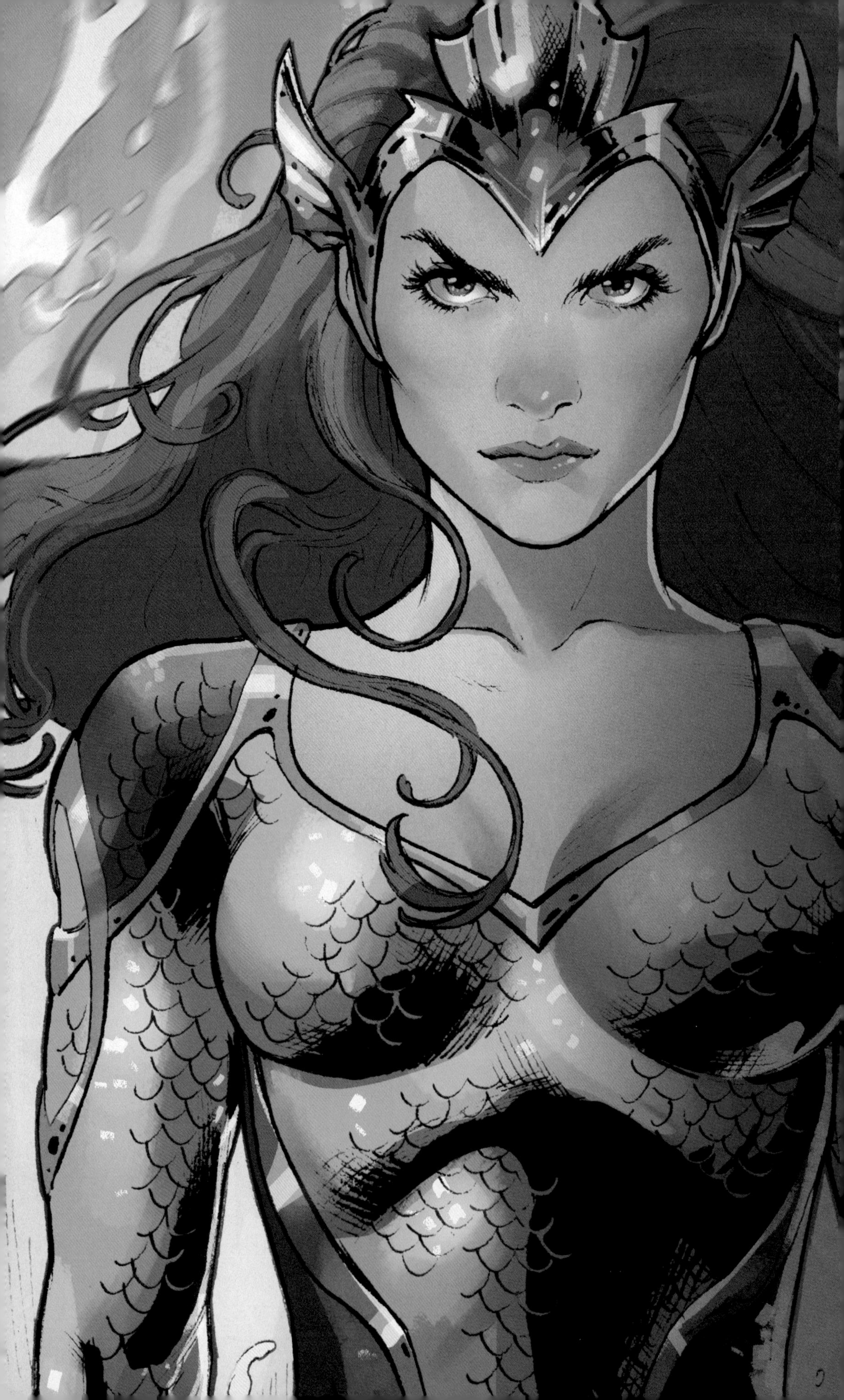

MERA
QUEEN OF ATLANTIS

DAN ABNETT writer   LAN MEDINA penciller
NORM RAPMUND RICHARD FRIEND inkers
VERONICA GANDINI colorist   SIMON BOWLAND letterer
NICOLA SCOTT and ROMULO FAJARDO JR. series cover artists
STANLEY "ARTGERM" LAU collection cover artist

SUPERMAN created by JERRY SIEGEL and JOE SHUSTER
By special arrangement with the Jerry Siegel family

ALEX ANTONE Editor – Original Series
BRITTANY HOLZHERR Associate Editor – Original Series
ANDREA SHEA Assistant Editor – Original Series
JEB WOODARD Group Editor – Collected Editions
ERIKA ROTHBERG Editor – Collected Edition
STEVE COOK Design Director – Books
LOUIS PRANDI Publication Design

BOB HARRAS Senior VP – Editor-in-Chief, DC Comics
PAT McCALLUM Executive Editor, DC Comics

DAN DiDIO Publisher
JIM LEE Publisher & Chief Creative Officer
AMIT DESAI Executive VP – Business & Marketing Strategy, Direct to Consumer & Global Franchise Management
BOBBIE CHASE VP & Executive Editor, Young Reader & Talent Development
MARK CHIARELLO Senior VP – Art, Design & Collected Editions
JOHN CUNNINGHAM Senior VP – Sales & Trade Marketing
BRIAR DARDEN VP – Business Affairs
ANNE DePIES Senior VP – Business Strategy, Finance & Administration
DON FALLETTI VP – Manufacturing Operations
LAWRENCE GANEM VP – Editorial Administration & Talent Relations
ALISON GILL Senior VP – Manufacturing & Operations
JASON GREENBERG VP – Business Strategy & Finance
HANK KANALZ Senior VP – Editorial Strategy & Administration
JAY KOGAN Senior VP – Legal Affairs
NICK J. NAPOLITANO VP – Manufacturing Administration
LISETTE OSTERLOH VP – Digital Marketing & Events
EDDIE SCANNELL VP – Consumer Marketing
COURTNEY SIMMONS Senior VP – Publicity & Communications
JIM (SKI) SOKOLOWSKI VP – Comic Book Specialty Sales & Trade Marketing
NANCY SPEARS VP – Mass, Book, Digital Sales & Trade Marketing
MICHELE R. WELLS VP – Content Strategy

MERA: QUEEN OF ATLANTIS

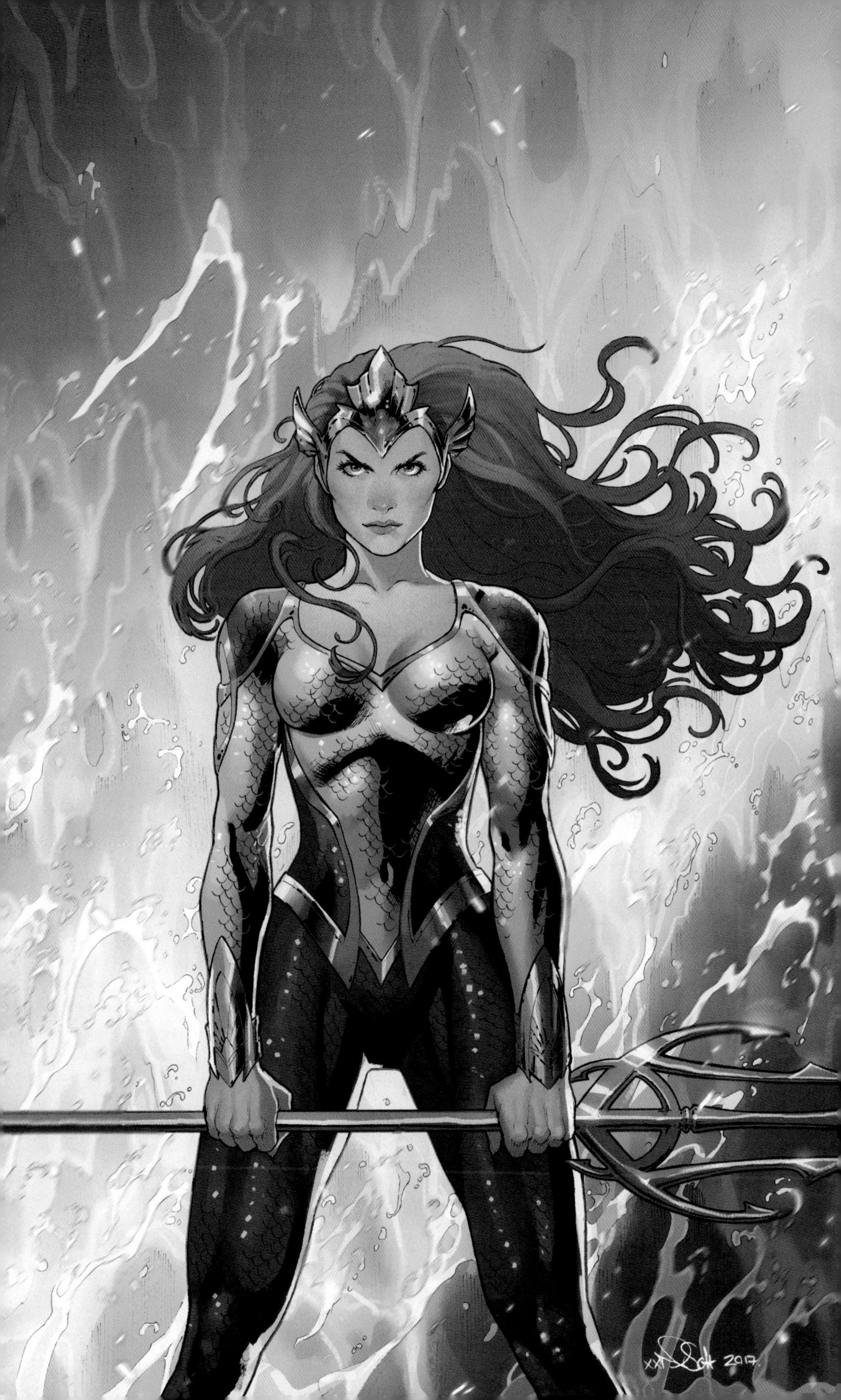

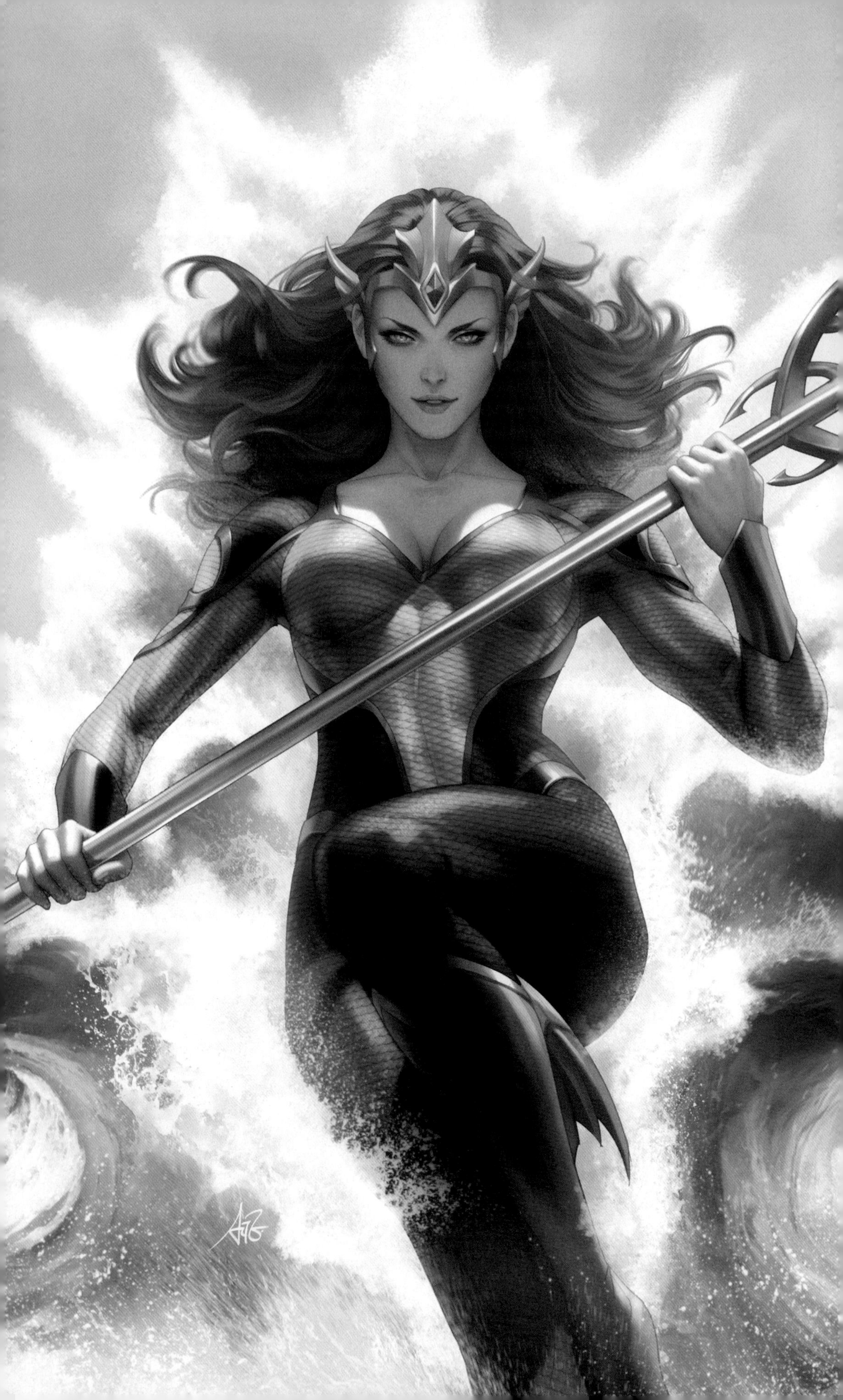

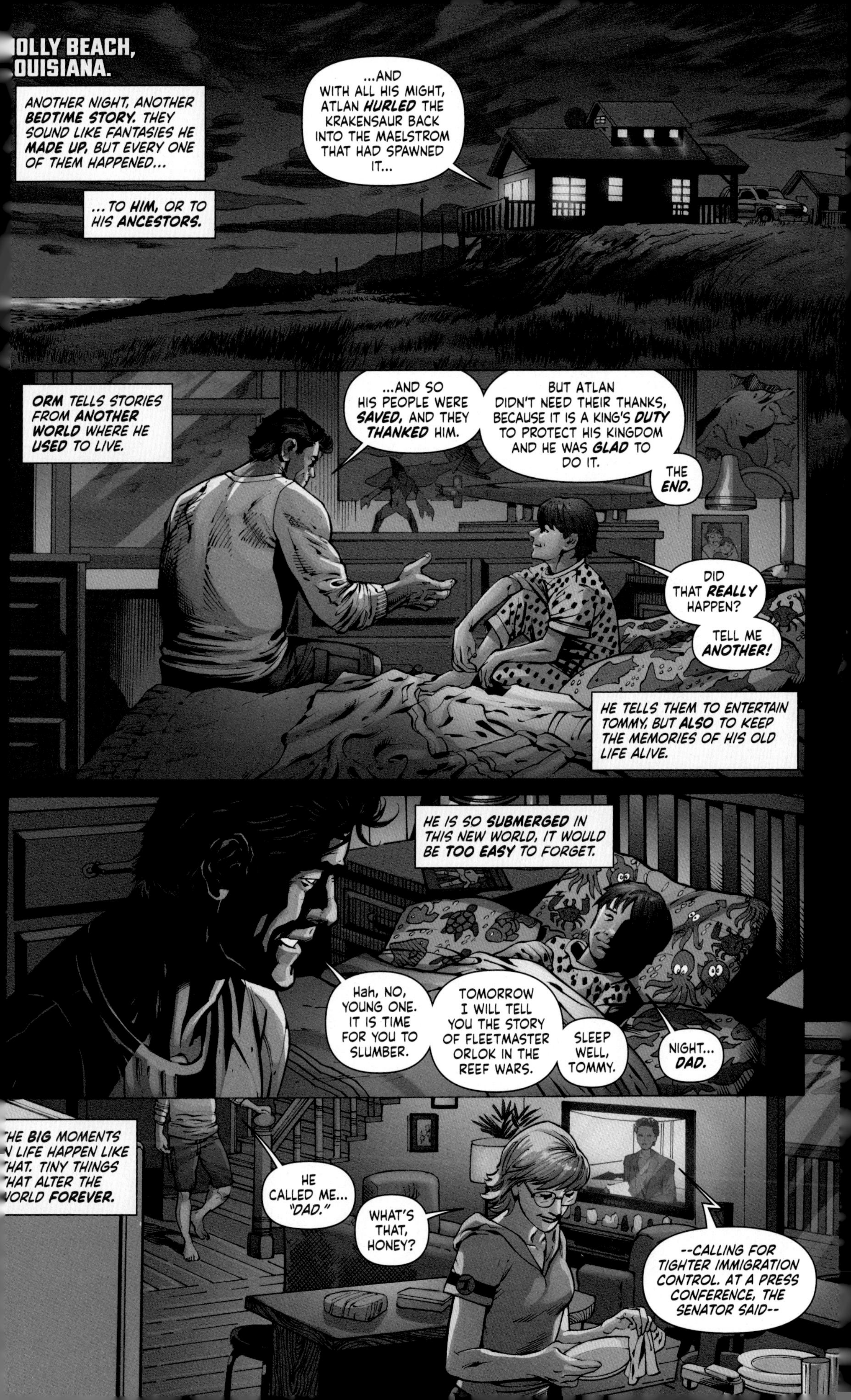
OLLY BEACH,
OUISIANA.
ANOTHER NIGHT, ANOTHER BEDTIME STORY. THEY SOUND LIKE FANTASIES HE MADE UP, BUT EVERY ONE OF THEM HAPPENED...
...TO HIM, OR TO HIS ANCESTORS.
...AND WITH ALL HIS MIGHT, ATLAN HURLED THE KRAKENSAUR BACK INTO THE MAELSTROM THAT HAD SPAWNED IT...
ORM TELLS STORIES FROM ANOTHER WORLD WHERE HE USED TO LIVE.
...AND SO HIS PEOPLE WERE SAVED, AND THEY THANKED HIM.
BUT ATLAN DIDN'T NEED THEIR THANKS, BECAUSE IT IS A KING'S DUTY TO PROTECT HIS KINGDOM AND HE WAS GLAD TO DO IT.
THE END.
DID THAT REALLY HAPPEN?
TELL ME ANOTHER!
HE TELLS THEM TO ENTERTAIN TOMMY, BUT ALSO TO KEEP THE MEMORIES OF HIS OLD LIFE ALIVE.
HE IS SO SUBMERGED IN THIS NEW WORLD, IT WOULD BE TOO EASY TO FORGET.
Hah, NO, YOUNG ONE. IT IS TIME FOR YOU TO SLUMBER.
TOMORROW I WILL TELL YOU THE STORY OF FLEETMASTER ORLOK IN THE REEF WARS.
SLEEP WELL, TOMMY.
NIGHT... DAD.
HE BIG MOMENTS N LIFE HAPPEN LIKE HAT. TINY THINGS HAT ALTER THE VORLD FOREVER.
HE CALLED ME... "DAD."
WHAT'S THAT, HONEY?
--CALLING FOR TIGHTER IMMIGRATION CONTROL. AT A PRESS CONFERENCE, THE SENATOR SAID--

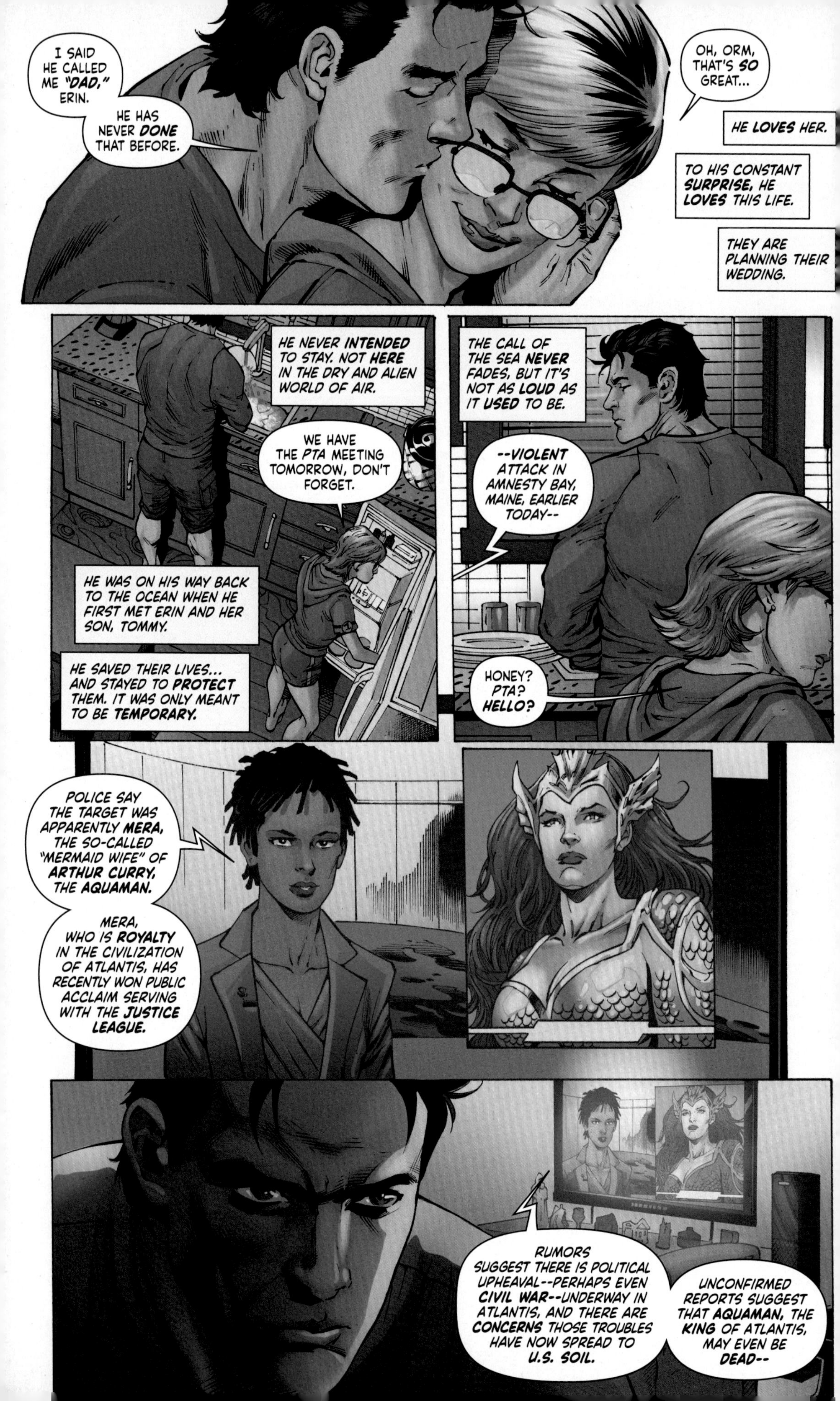
I SAID HE CALLED ME "DAD," ERIN.
HE HAS NEVER DONE THAT BEFORE.
OH, ORM, THAT'S SO GREAT...
HE LOVES HER.
TO HIS CONSTANT SURPRISE, HE LOVES THIS LIFE.
THEY ARE PLANNING THEIR WEDDING.
HE NEVER INTENDED TO STAY. NOT HERE IN THE DRY AND ALIEN WORLD OF AIR.
WE HAVE THE PTA MEETING TOMORROW, DON'T FORGET.
HE WAS ON HIS WAY BACK TO THE OCEAN WHEN HE FIRST MET ERIN AND HER SON, TOMMY.
HE SAVED THEIR LIVES... AND STAYED TO PROTECT THEM. IT WAS ONLY MEANT TO BE TEMPORARY.
THE CALL OF THE SEA NEVER FADES, BUT IT'S NOT AS LOUD AS IT USED TO BE.
--VIOLENT ATTACK IN AMNESTY BAY, MAINE, EARLIER TODAY--
HONEY? PTA? HELLO?
POLICE SAY THE TARGET WAS APPARENTLY MERA, THE SO-CALLED "MERMAID WIFE" OF ARTHUR CURRY, THE AQUAMAN.
MERA, WHO IS ROYALTY IN THE CIVILIZATION OF ATLANTIS, HAS RECENTLY WON PUBLIC ACCLAIM SERVING WITH THE JUSTICE LEAGUE.
RUMORS SUGGEST THERE IS POLITICAL UPHEAVAL--PERHAPS EVEN CIVIL WAR--UNDERWAY IN ATLANTIS, AND THERE ARE CONCERNS THOSE TROUBLES HAVE NOW SPREAD TO U.S. SOIL.
UNCONFIRMED REPORTS SUGGEST THAT AQUAMAN, THE KING OF ATLANTIS, MAY EVEN BE DEAD--

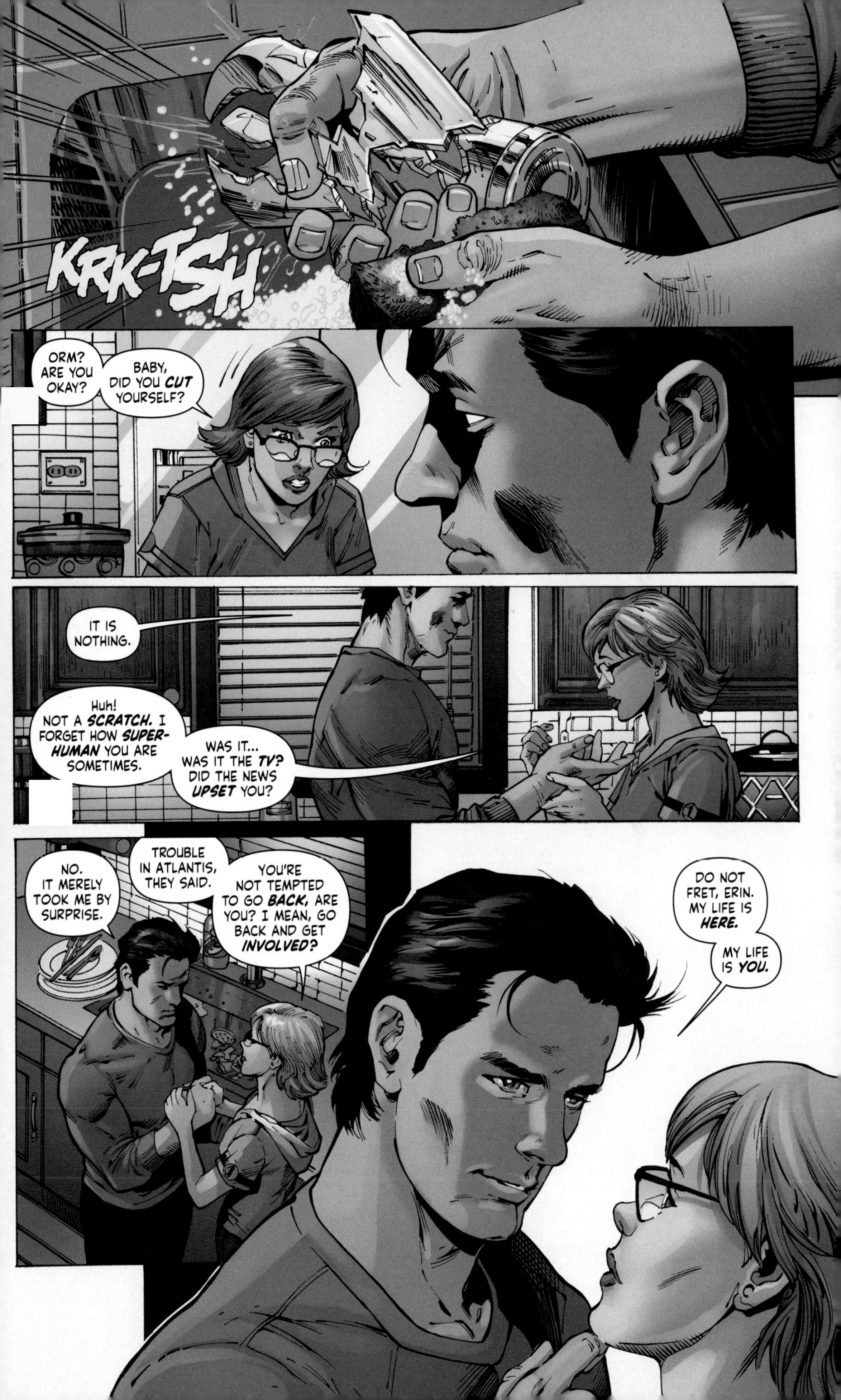
KRK-TSH
ORM? ARE YOU OKAY?
BABY, DID YOU CUT YOURSELF?
IT IS NOTHING.
Huh! NOT A SCRATCH. I FORGET HOW SUPER-HUMAN YOU ARE SOMETIMES.
WAS IT... WAS IT THE TV? DID THE NEWS UPSET YOU?
NO. IT MERELY TOOK ME BY SURPRISE.
TROUBLE IN ATLANTIS, THEY SAID.
YOU'RE NOT TEMPTED TO GO BACK, ARE YOU? I MEAN, GO BACK AND GET INVOLVED?
DO NOT FRET, ERIN. MY LIFE IS HERE.
MY LIFE IS YOU.

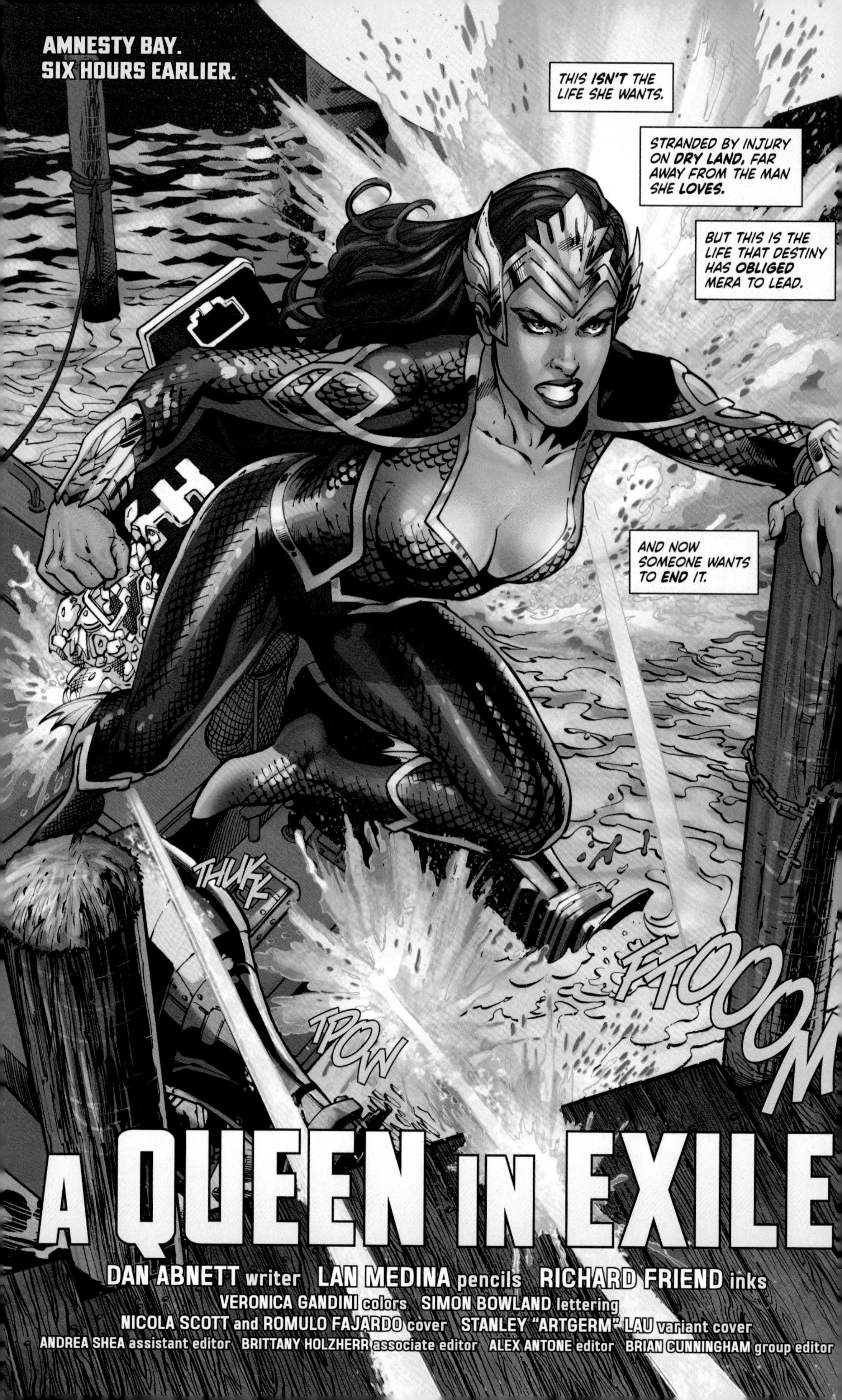
AMNESTY BAY.
SIX HOURS EARLIER.
THIS ISN'T THE LIFE SHE WANTS.
STRANDED BY INJURY ON DRY LAND, FAR AWAY FROM THE MAN SHE LOVES.
BUT THIS IS THE LIFE THAT DESTINY HAS OBLIGED MERA TO LEAD.
AND NOW SOMEONE WANTS TO END IT.
THUKK
FTOOOM
TPOW
A QUEEN IN EXILE
DAN ABNETT writer LAN MEDINA pencils RICHARD FRIEND inks
VERONICA GANDINI colors SIMON BOWLAND lettering
NICOLA SCOTT and ROMULO FAJARDO cover STANLEY "ARTGERM" LAU variant cover
ANDREA SHEA assistant editor BRITTANY HOLZHERR associate editor ALEX ANTONE editor BRIAN CUNNINGHAM group editor

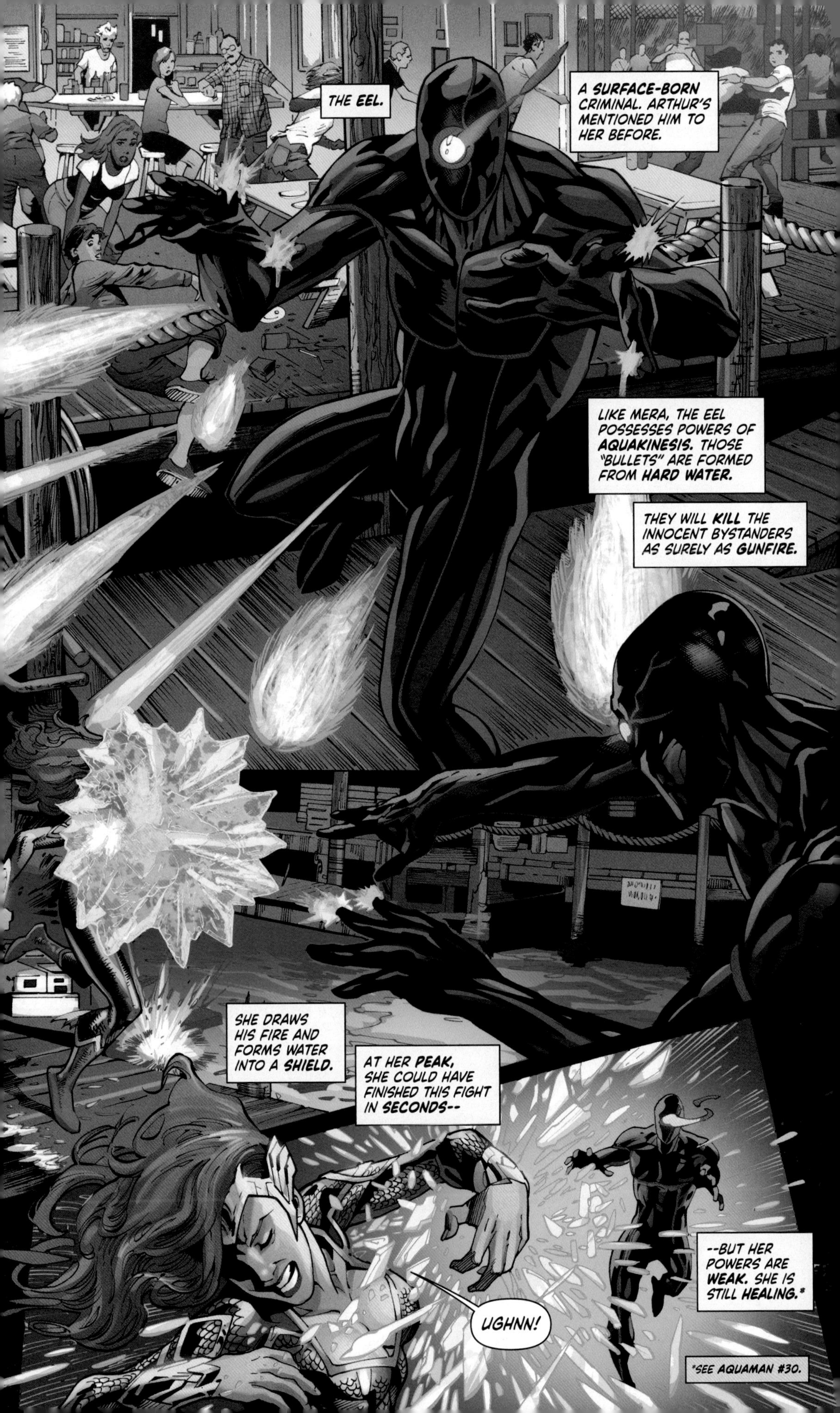
THE EEL.
A SURFACE-BORN CRIMINAL. ARTHUR'S MENTIONED HIM TO HER BEFORE.
LIKE MERA, THE EEL POSSESSES POWERS OF AQUAKINESIS. THOSE "BULLETS" ARE FORMED FROM HARD WATER.
THEY WILL KILL THE INNOCENT BYSTANDERS AS SURELY AS GUNFIRE.
SHE DRAWS HIS FIRE AND FORMS WATER INTO A SHIELD.
AT HER PEAK, SHE COULD HAVE FINISHED THIS FIGHT IN SECONDS--
--BUT HER POWERS ARE WEAK. SHE IS STILL HEALING.*
UGHNN!
*SEE AQUAMAN #30.

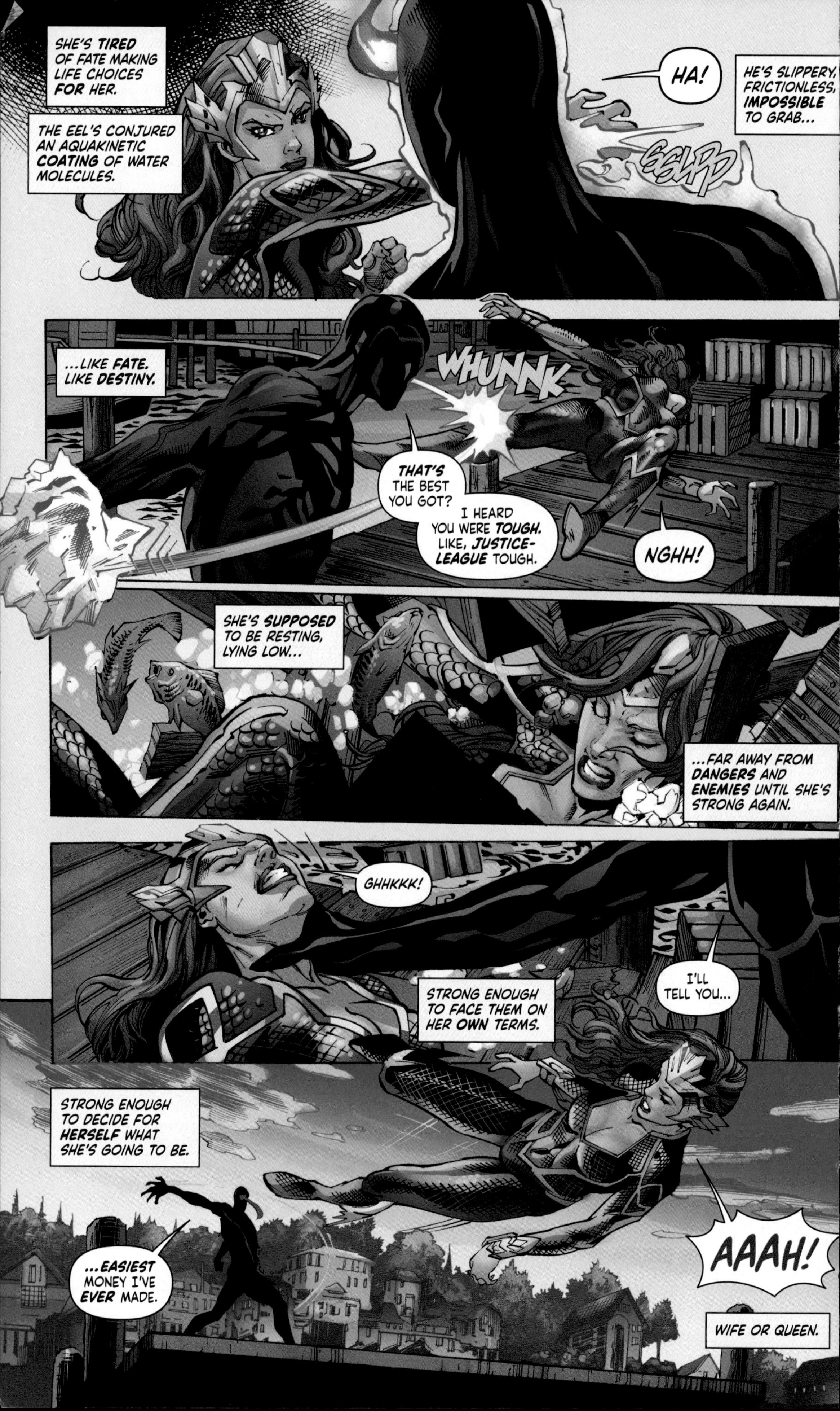
SHE'S TIRED OF FATE MAKING LIFE CHOICES FOR HER.
THE EEL'S CONJURED AN AQUAKINETIC COATING OF WATER MOLECULES.
HA!
HE'S SLIPPERY, FRICTIONLESS, IMPOSSIBLE TO GRAB...
SSLPP
...LIKE FATE. LIKE DESTINY.
WHUNNK
THAT'S THE BEST YOU GOT?
I HEARD YOU WERE TOUGH. LIKE, JUSTICE-LEAGUE TOUGH.
NGHH!
SHE'S SUPPOSED TO BE RESTING, LYING LOW...
...FAR AWAY FROM DANGERS AND ENEMIES UNTIL SHE'S STRONG AGAIN.
GHHKKK!
I'LL TELL YOU...
STRONG ENOUGH TO FACE THEM ON HER OWN TERMS.
STRONG ENOUGH TO DECIDE FOR HERSELF WHAT SHE'S GOING TO BE.
...EASIEST MONEY I'VE EVER MADE.
AAAH!
WIFE OR QUEEN.

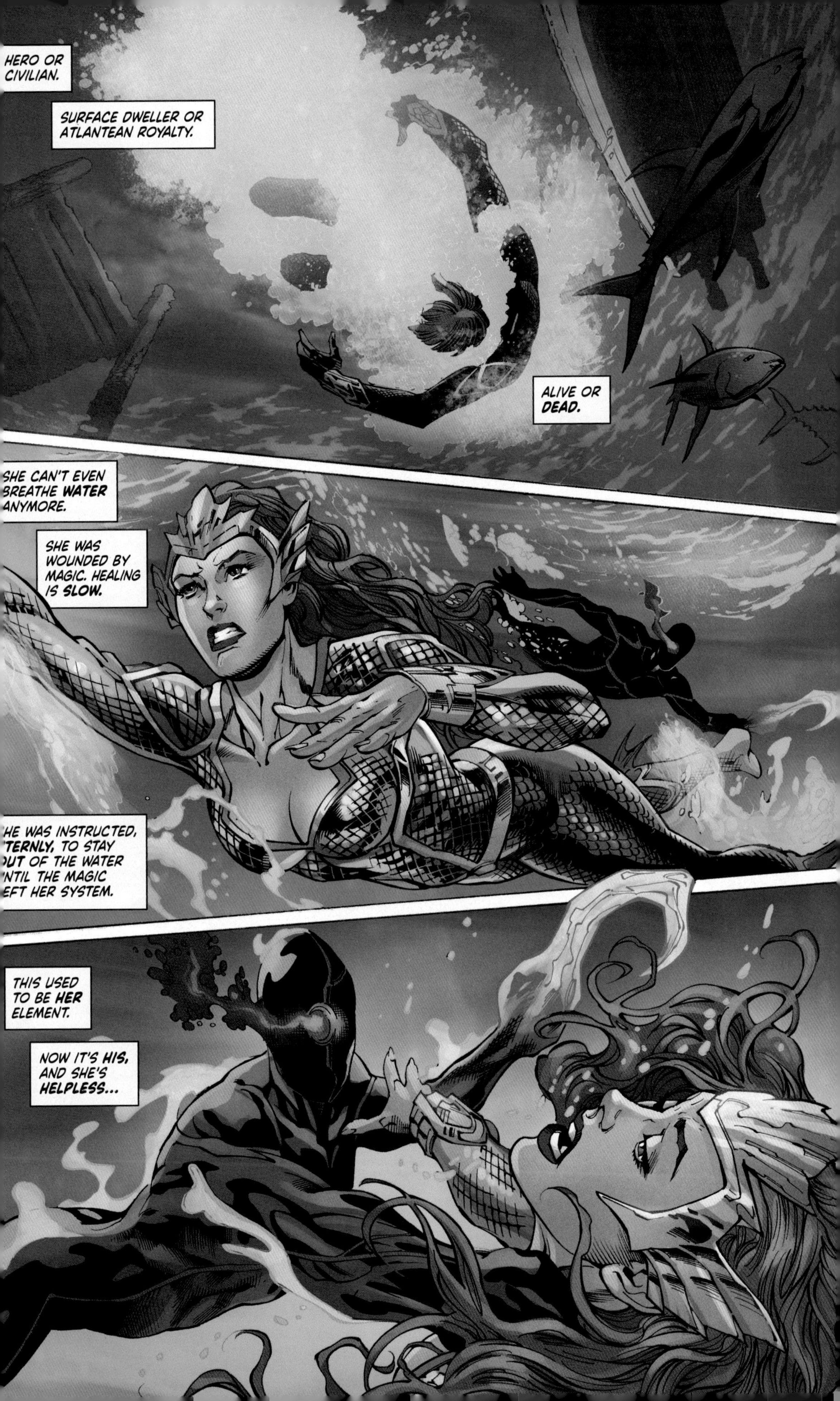
HERO OR CIVILIAN.
SURFACE DWELLER OR ATLANTEAN ROYALTY.
ALIVE OR DEAD.
SHE CAN'T EVEN BREATHE WATER ANYMORE.
SHE WAS WOUNDED BY MAGIC. HEALING IS SLOW.
HE WAS INSTRUCTED, TERNLY, TO STAY OUT OF THE WATER NTIL THE MAGIC EFT HER SYSTEM.
THIS USED TO BE HER ELEMENT.
NOW IT'S HIS, AND SHE'S HELPLESS...

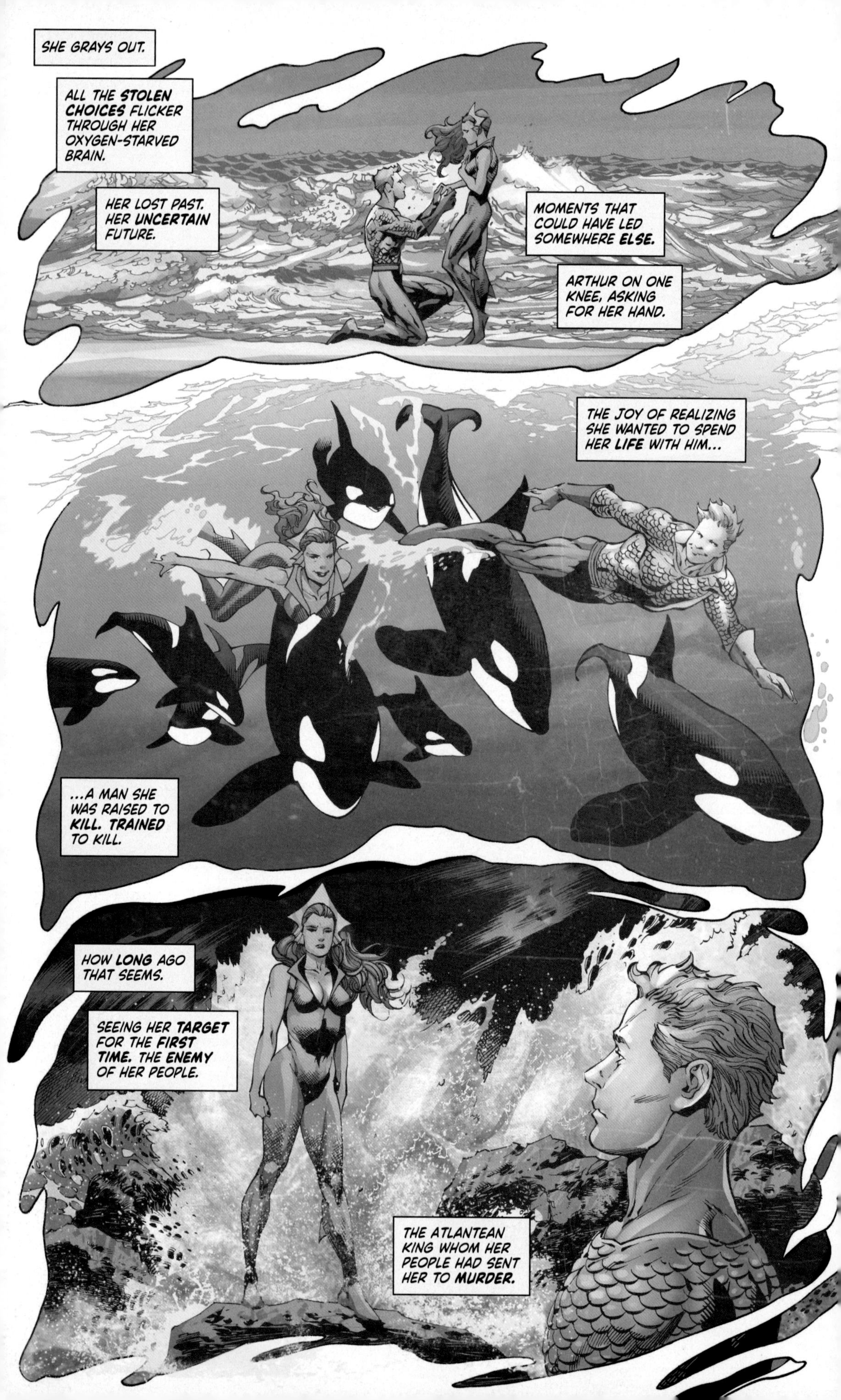
SHE GRAYS OUT.
ALL THE STOLEN CHOICES FLICKER THROUGH HER OXYGEN-STARVED BRAIN.
HER LOST PAST. HER UNCERTAIN FUTURE.
MOMENTS THAT COULD HAVE LED SOMEWHERE ELSE.
ARTHUR ON ONE KNEE, ASKING FOR HER HAND.
THE JOY OF REALIZING SHE WANTED TO SPEND HER LIFE WITH HIM...
...A MAN SHE WAS RAISED TO KILL. TRAINED TO KILL.
HOW LONG AGO THAT SEEMS.
SEEING HER TARGET FOR THE FIRST TIME. THE ENEMY OF HER PEOPLE.
THE ATLANTEAN KING WHOM HER PEOPLE HAD SENT HER TO MURDER.

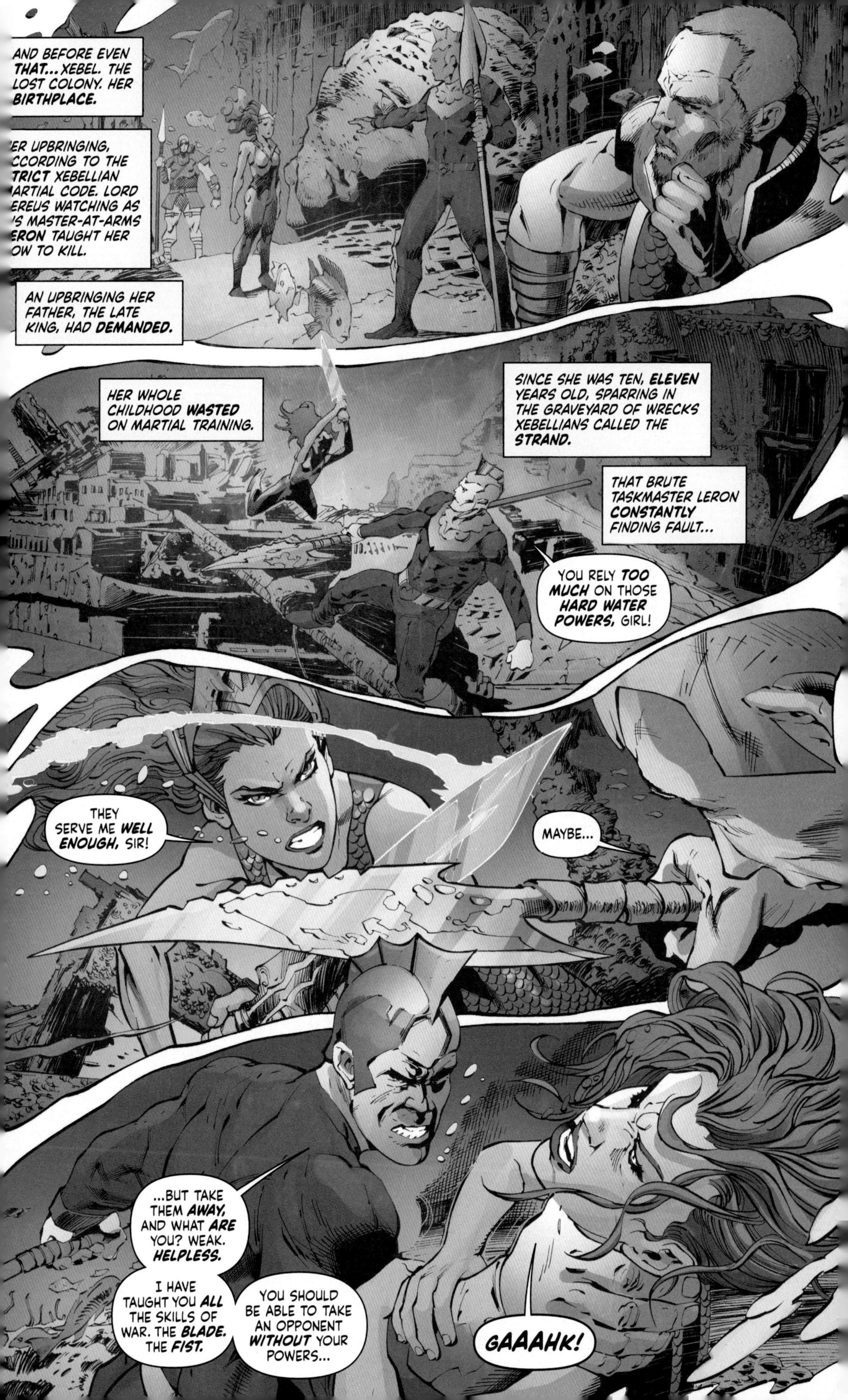
AND BEFORE EVEN THAT... XEBEL. THE LOST COLONY. HER BIRTHPLACE.
ER UPBRINGING, CCORDING TO THE TRICT XEBELLIAN MARTIAL CODE. LORD EREUS WATCHING AS 'S MASTER-AT-ARMS ERON TAUGHT HER OW TO KILL.
AN UPBRINGING HER FATHER, THE LATE KING, HAD DEMANDED.
HER WHOLE CHILDHOOD WASTED ON MARTIAL TRAINING.
SINCE SHE WAS TEN, ELEVEN YEARS OLD, SPARRING IN THE GRAVEYARD OF WRECKS XEBELLIANS CALLED THE STRAND.
THAT BRUTE TASKMASTER LERON CONSTANTLY FINDING FAULT...
YOU RELY TOO MUCH ON THOSE HARD WATER POWERS, GIRL!
THEY SERVE ME WELL ENOUGH, SIR!
MAYBE...
...BUT TAKE THEM AWAY, AND WHAT ARE YOU? WEAK. HELPLESS.
I HAVE TAUGHT YOU ALL THE SKILLS OF WAR. THE BLADE. THE FIST.
YOU SHOULD BE ABLE TO TAKE AN OPPONENT WITHOUT YOUR POWERS...
GAAAHK!

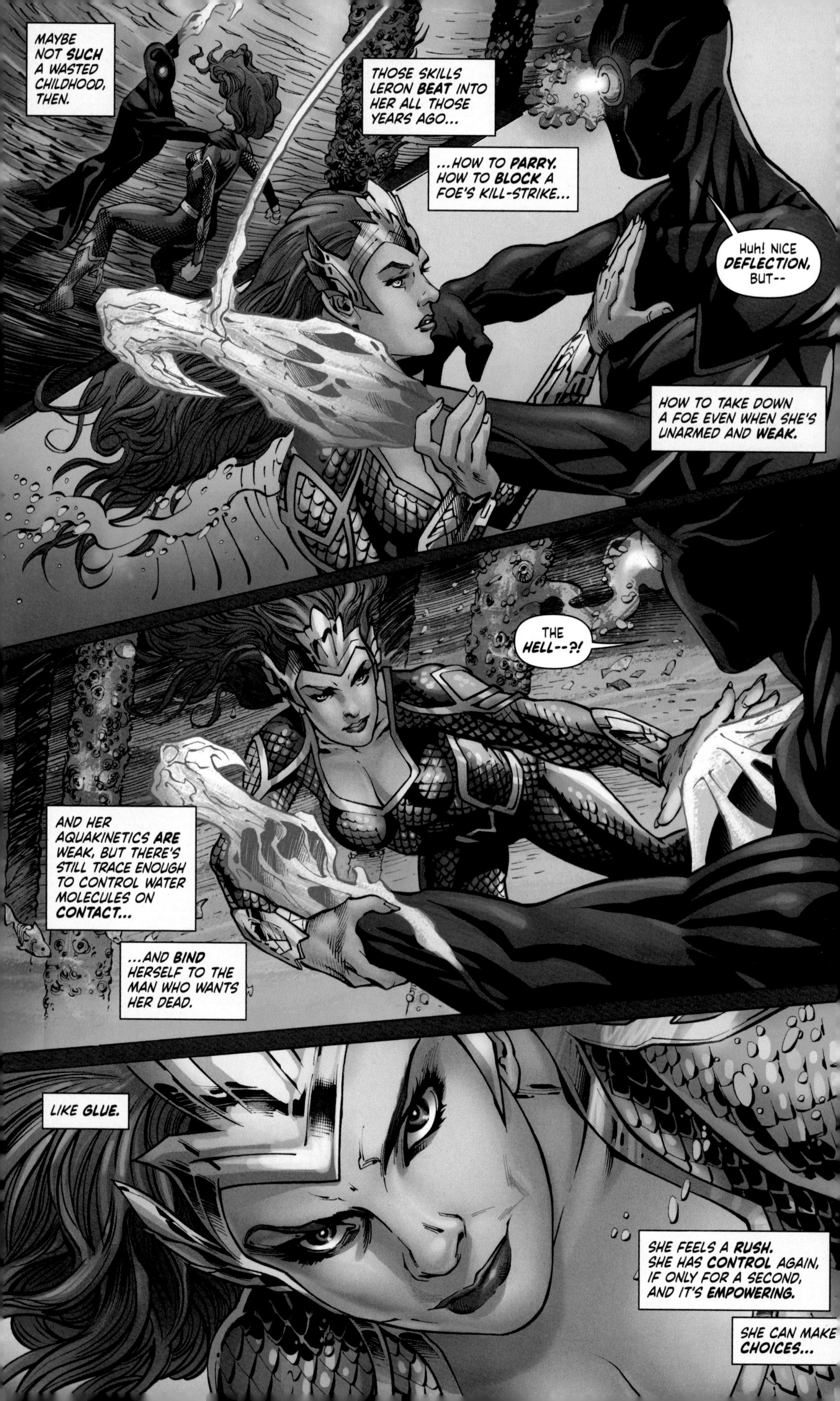
MAYBE NOT SUCH A WASTED CHILDHOOD, THEN.
THOSE SKILLS LERON BEAT INTO HER ALL THOSE YEARS AGO...
...HOW TO PARRY. HOW TO BLOCK A FOE'S KILL-STRIKE...
Huh! NICE DEFLECTION, BUT--
HOW TO TAKE DOWN A FOE EVEN WHEN SHE'S UNARMED AND WEAK.
THE HELL--?!
AND HER AQUAKINETICS ARE WEAK, BUT THERE'S STILL TRACE ENOUGH TO CONTROL WATER MOLECULES ON CONTACT...
...AND BIND HERSELF TO THE MAN WHO WANTS HER DEAD.
LIKE GLUE.
SHE FEELS A RUSH. SHE HAS CONTROL AGAIN, IF ONLY FOR A SECOND, AND IT'S EMPOWERING.
SHE CAN MAKE CHOICES...

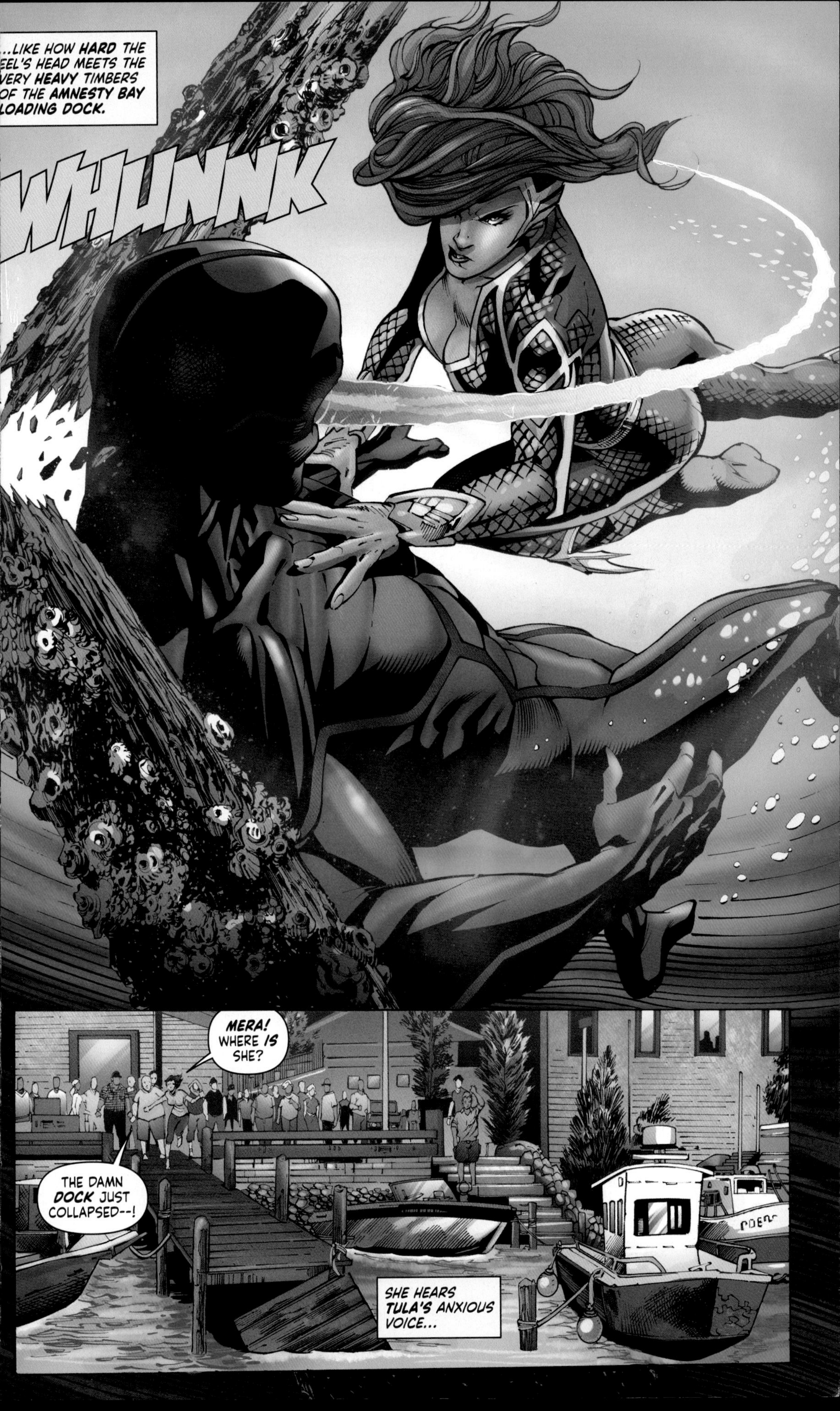
...LIKE HOW HARD THE EEL'S HEAD MEETS THE VERY HEAVY TIMBERS OF THE AMNESTY BAY LOADING DOCK.
WHUNNK
MERA! WHERE IS SHE?
THE DAMN DOCK JUST COLLAPSED--!
SHE HEARS TULA'S ANXIOUS VOICE...

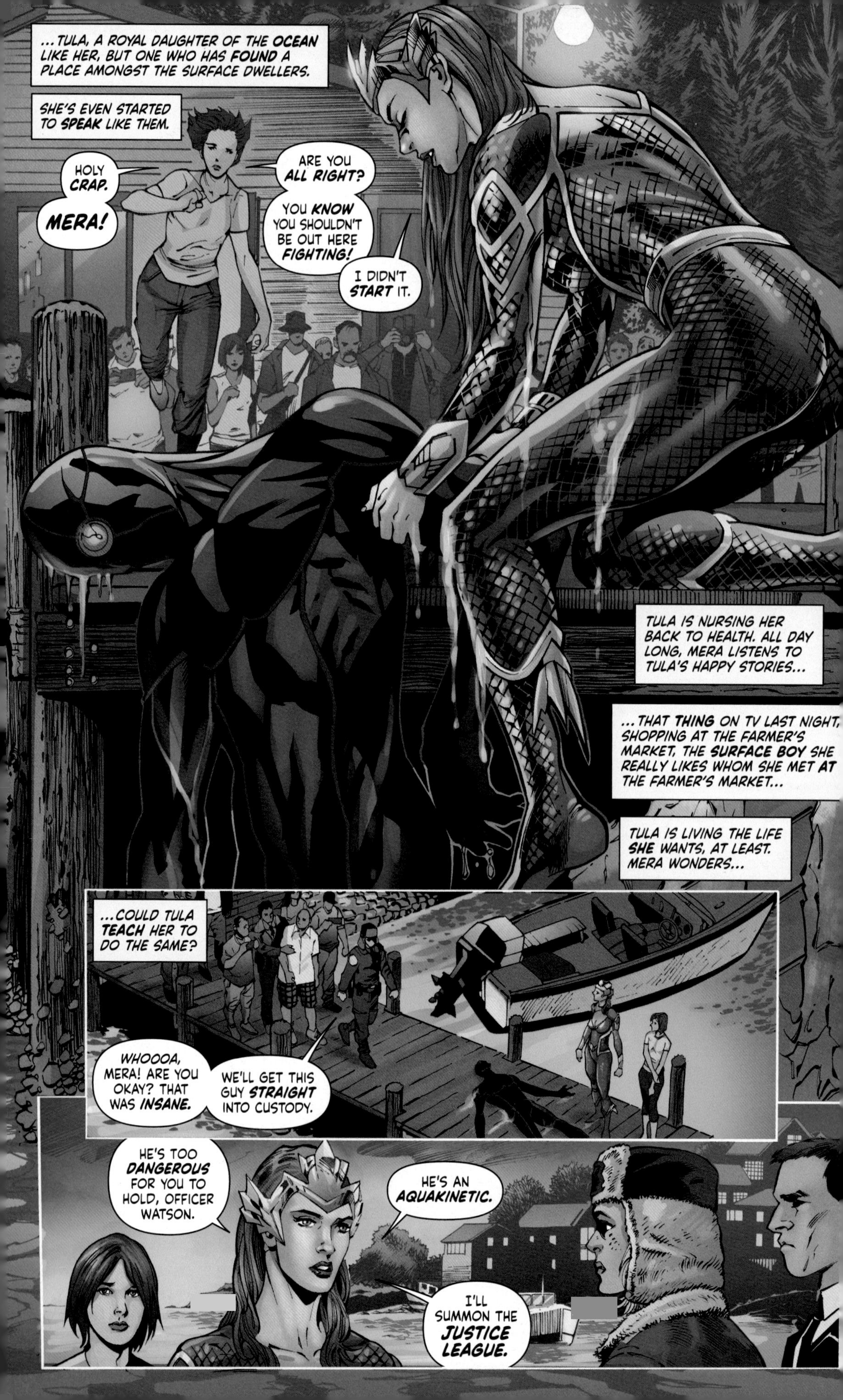

...TULA, A ROYAL DAUGHTER OF THE OCEAN LIKE HER, BUT ONE WHO HAS FOUND A PLACE AMONGST THE SURFACE DWELLERS.
SHE'S EVEN STARTED TO SPEAK LIKE THEM.
HOLY CRAP.
MERA!
ARE YOU ALL RIGHT?
YOU KNOW YOU SHOULDN'T BE OUT HERE FIGHTING!
I DIDN'T START IT.
TULA IS NURSING HER BACK TO HEALTH. ALL DAY LONG, MERA LISTENS TO TULA'S HAPPY STORIES...
...THAT THING ON TV LAST NIGHT, SHOPPING AT THE FARMER'S MARKET, THE SURFACE BOY SHE REALLY LIKES WHOM SHE MET AT THE FARMER'S MARKET...
TULA IS LIVING THE LIFE SHE WANTS, AT LEAST. MERA WONDERS...
...COULD TULA TEACH HER TO DO THE SAME?
WHOOOA, MERA! ARE YOU OKAY? THAT WAS INSANE.
WE'LL GET THIS GUY STRAIGHT INTO CUSTODY.
HE'S TOO DANGEROUS FOR YOU TO HOLD, OFFICER WATSON.
HE'S AN AQUAKINETIC.
I'LL SUMMON THE JUSTICE LEAGUE.

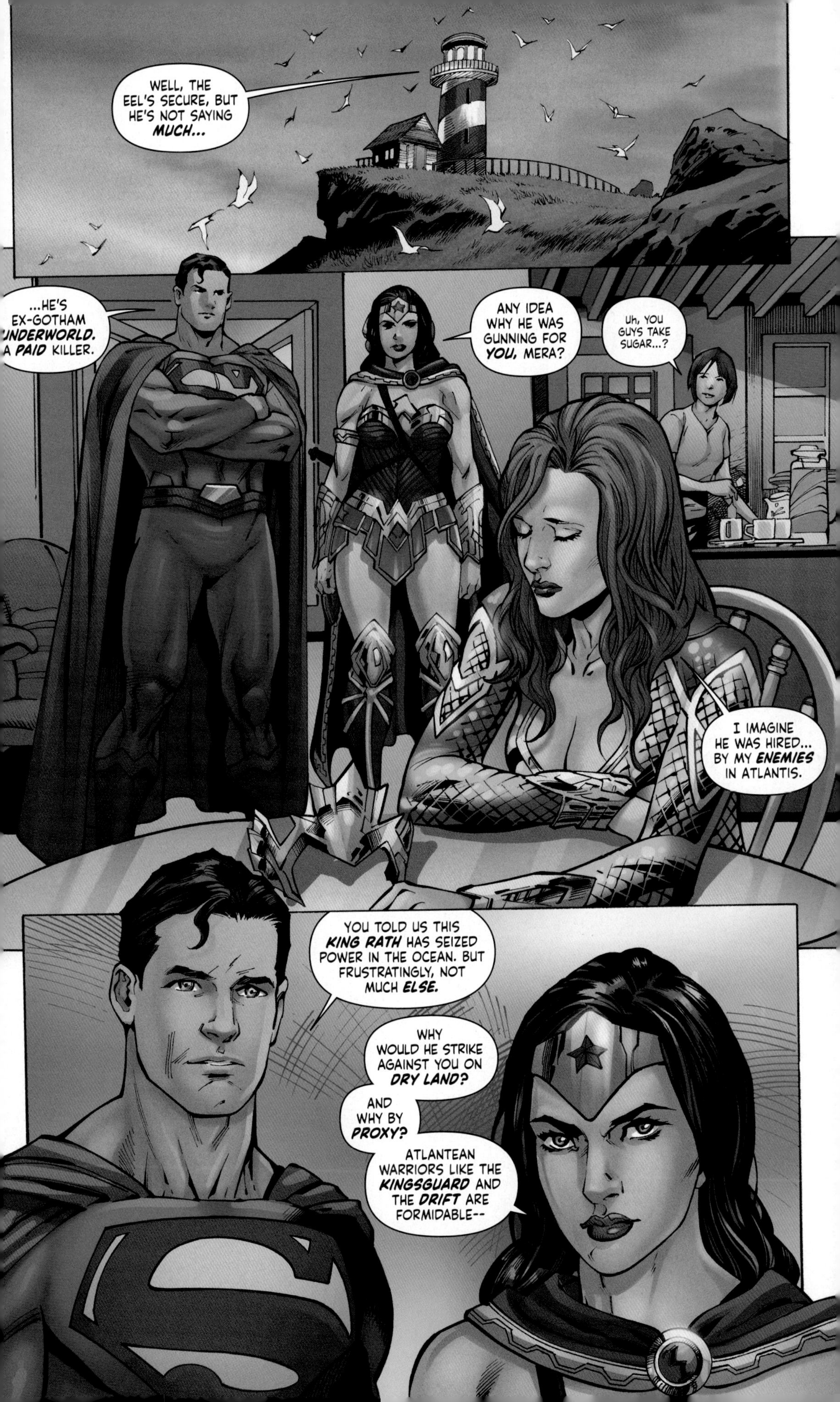

WELL, THE EEL'S SECURE, BUT HE'S NOT SAYING *MUCH...*
...HE'S EX-GOTHAM *UNDERWORLD.* A *PAID* KILLER.
ANY IDEA WHY HE WAS GUNNING FOR *YOU,* MERA?
UH, YOU GUYS TAKE SUGAR...?
I IMAGINE HE WAS HIRED... BY MY *ENEMIES* IN ATLANTIS.
YOU TOLD US THIS *KING RATH* HAS SEIZED POWER IN THE OCEAN. BUT FRUSTRATINGLY, NOT MUCH *ELSE.*
WHY WOULD HE STRIKE AGAINST YOU ON *DRY LAND?*
AND WHY BY *PROXY?*
ATLANTEAN WARRIORS LIKE THE *KINGSGUARD* AND THE *DRIFT* ARE FORMIDABLE--

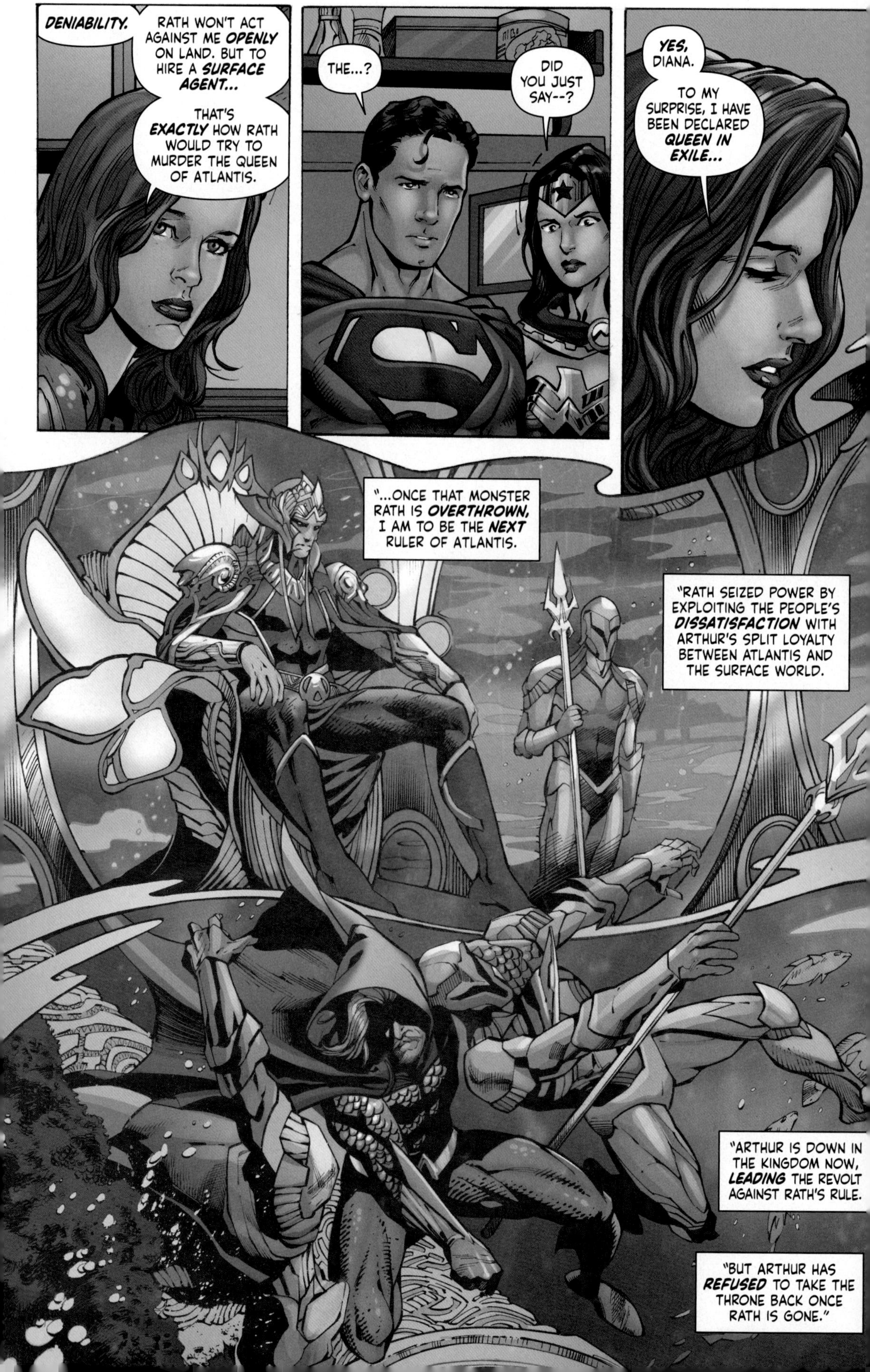
DENIABILITY.
RATH WON'T ACT AGAINST ME OPENLY ON LAND. BUT TO HIRE A SURFACE AGENT...
THAT'S EXACTLY HOW RATH WOULD TRY TO MURDER THE QUEEN OF ATLANTIS.
THE...?
DID YOU JUST SAY--?
YES, DIANA.
TO MY SURPRISE, I HAVE BEEN DECLARED QUEEN IN EXILE...
"...ONCE THAT MONSTER RATH IS OVERTHROWN, I AM TO BE THE NEXT RULER OF ATLANTIS.
"RATH SEIZED POWER BY EXPLOITING THE PEOPLE'S DISSATISFACTION WITH ARTHUR'S SPLIT LOYALTY BETWEEN ATLANTIS AND THE SURFACE WORLD.
"ARTHUR IS DOWN IN THE KINGDOM NOW, LEADING THE REVOLT AGAINST RATH'S RULE.
"BUT ARTHUR HAS REFUSED TO TAKE THE THRONE BACK ONCE RATH IS GONE."

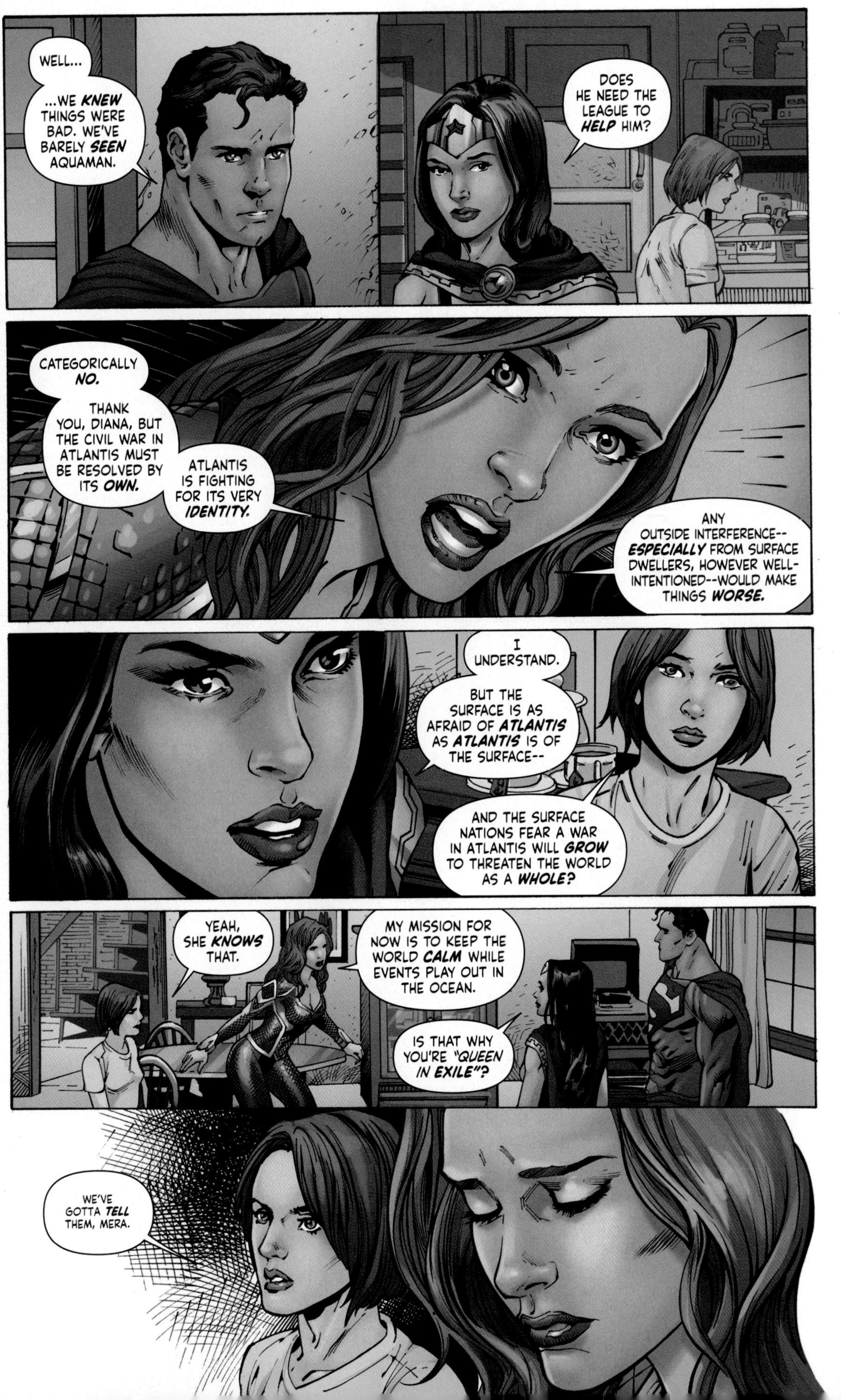

WELL...
...WE KNEW THINGS WERE BAD. WE'VE BARELY SEEN AQUAMAN.
DOES HE NEED THE LEAGUE TO HELP HIM?
CATEGORICALLY NO.
THANK YOU, DIANA, BUT THE CIVIL WAR IN ATLANTIS MUST BE RESOLVED BY ITS OWN.
ATLANTIS IS FIGHTING FOR ITS VERY IDENTITY.
ANY OUTSIDE INTERFERENCE--ESPECIALLY FROM SURFACE DWELLERS, HOWEVER WELL-INTENTIONED--WOULD MAKE THINGS WORSE.
I UNDERSTAND.
BUT THE SURFACE IS AS AFRAID OF ATLANTIS AS ATLANTIS IS OF THE SURFACE--
AND THE SURFACE NATIONS FEAR A WAR IN ATLANTIS WILL GROW TO THREATEN THE WORLD AS A WHOLE?
YEAH, SHE KNOWS THAT.
MY MISSION FOR NOW IS TO KEEP THE WORLD CALM WHILE EVENTS PLAY OUT IN THE OCEAN.
IS THAT WHY YOU'RE "QUEEN IN EXILE"?
WE'VE GOTTA TELL THEM, MERA.

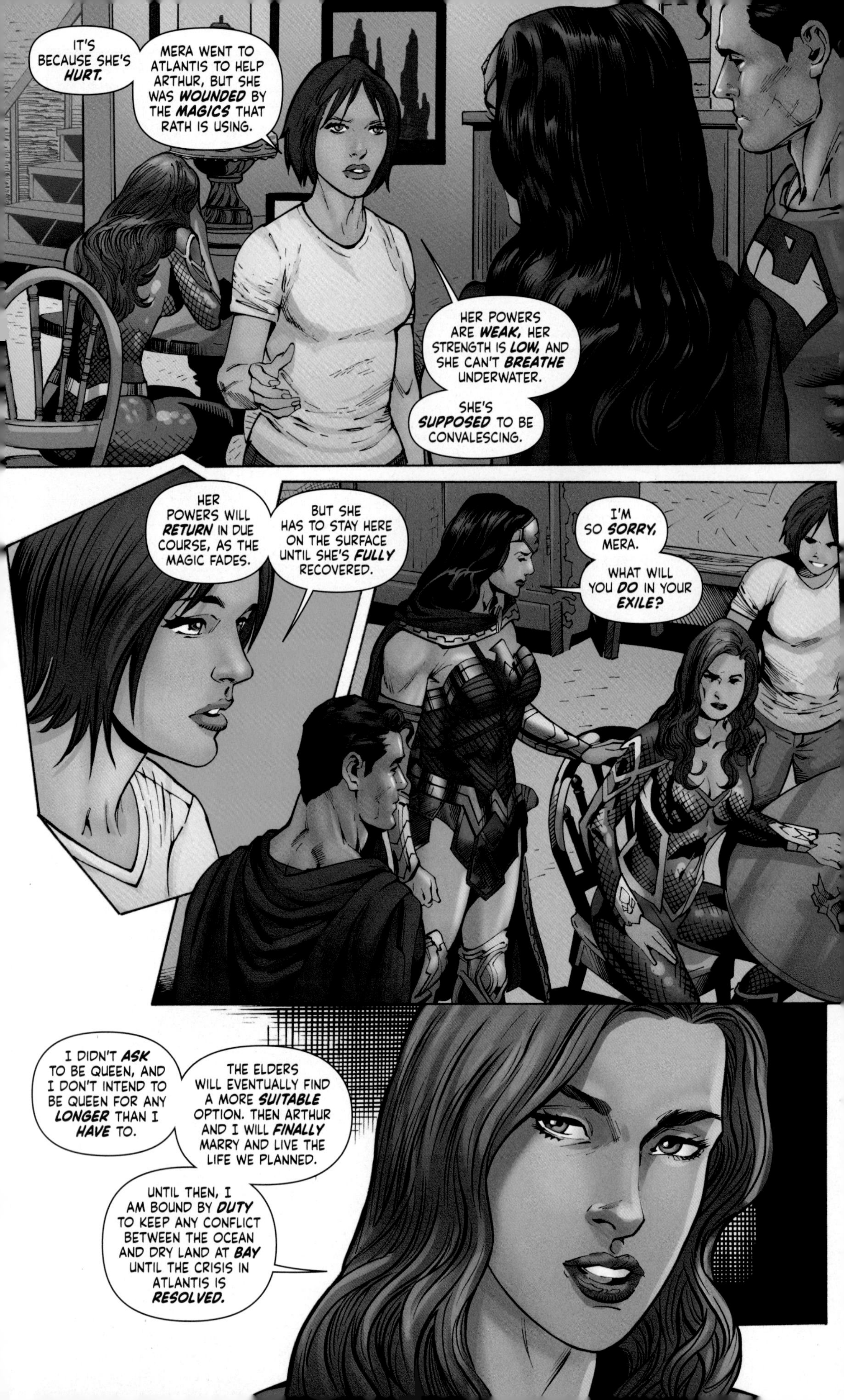
IT'S BECAUSE SHE'S HURT.
MERA WENT TO ATLANTIS TO HELP ARTHUR, BUT SHE WAS WOUNDED BY THE MAGICS THAT RATH IS USING.
HER POWERS ARE WEAK, HER STRENGTH IS LOW, AND SHE CAN'T BREATHE UNDERWATER.
SHE'S SUPPOSED TO BE CONVALESCING.
HER POWERS WILL RETURN IN DUE COURSE, AS THE MAGIC FADES.
BUT SHE HAS TO STAY HERE ON THE SURFACE UNTIL SHE'S FULLY RECOVERED.
I'M SO SORRY, MERA.
WHAT WILL YOU DO IN YOUR EXILE?
I DIDN'T ASK TO BE QUEEN, AND I DON'T INTEND TO BE QUEEN FOR ANY LONGER THAN I HAVE TO.
THE ELDERS WILL EVENTUALLY FIND A MORE SUITABLE OPTION. THEN ARTHUR AND I WILL FINALLY MARRY AND LIVE THE LIFE WE PLANNED.
UNTIL THEN, I AM BOUND BY DUTY TO KEEP ANY CONFLICT BETWEEN THE OCEAN AND DRY LAND AT BAY UNTIL THE CRISIS IN ATLANTIS IS RESOLVED.

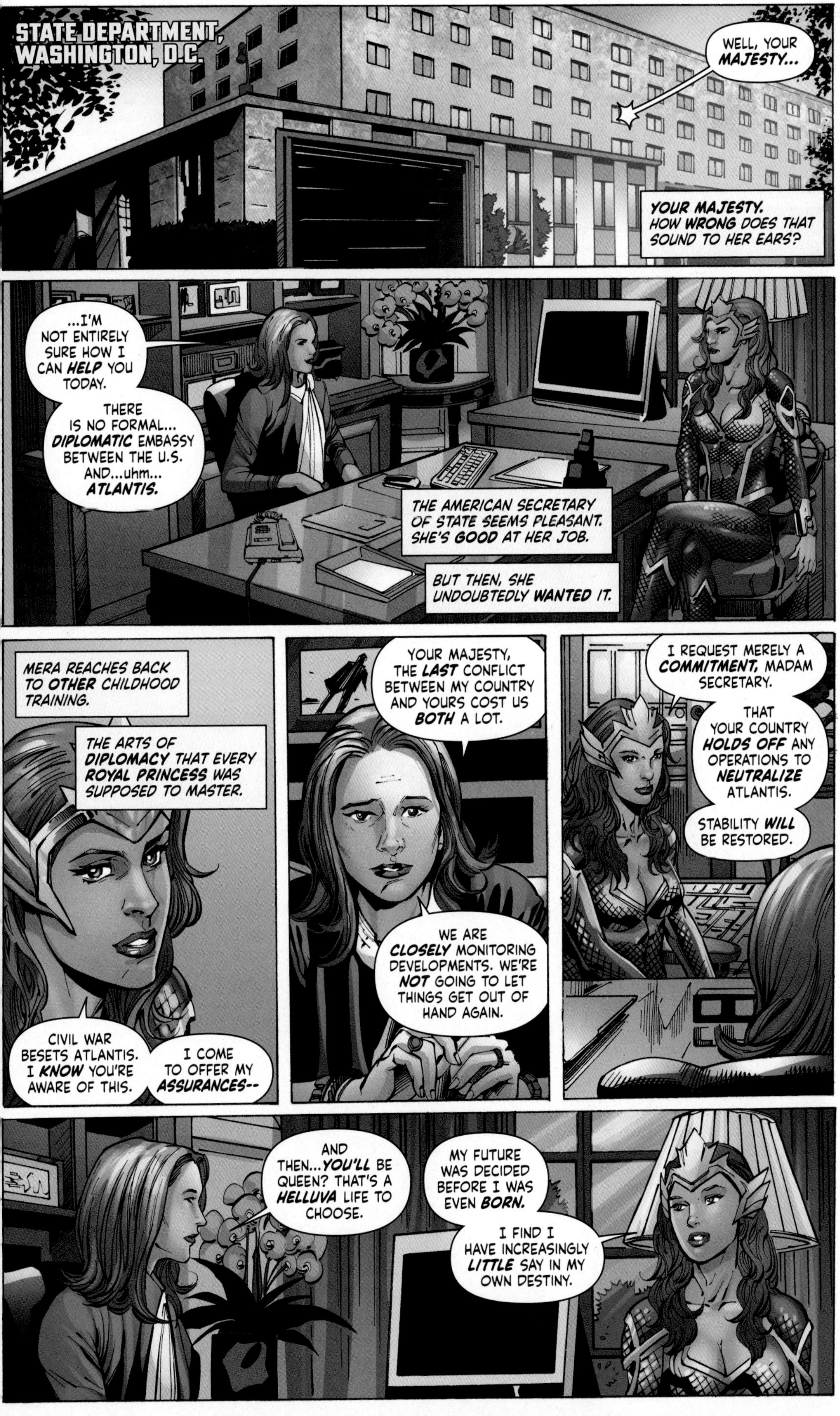
STATE DEPARTMENT, WASHINGTON, D.C.
WELL, YOUR MAJESTY...
YOUR MAJESTY. HOW WRONG DOES THAT SOUND TO HER EARS?
...I'M NOT ENTIRELY SURE HOW I CAN HELP YOU TODAY.
THERE IS NO FORMAL... DIPLOMATIC EMBASSY BETWEEN THE U.S. AND...uhm... ATLANTIS.
THE AMERICAN SECRETARY OF STATE SEEMS PLEASANT. SHE'S GOOD AT HER JOB.
BUT THEN, SHE UNDOUBTEDLY WANTED IT.
MERA REACHES BACK TO OTHER CHILDHOOD TRAINING.
THE ARTS OF DIPLOMACY THAT EVERY ROYAL PRINCESS WAS SUPPOSED TO MASTER.
CIVIL WAR BESETS ATLANTIS. I KNOW YOU'RE AWARE OF THIS.
I COME TO OFFER MY ASSURANCES--
YOUR MAJESTY, THE LAST CONFLICT BETWEEN MY COUNTRY AND YOURS COST US BOTH A LOT.
WE ARE CLOSELY MONITORING DEVELOPMENTS. WE'RE NOT GOING TO LET THINGS GET OUT OF HAND AGAIN.
I REQUEST MERELY A COMMITMENT, MADAM SECRETARY.
THAT YOUR COUNTRY HOLDS OFF ANY OPERATIONS TO NEUTRALIZE ATLANTIS.
STABILITY WILL BE RESTORED.
AND THEN...YOU'LL BE QUEEN? THAT'S A HELLUVA LIFE TO CHOOSE.
MY FUTURE WAS DECIDED BEFORE I WAS EVEN BORN.
I FIND I HAVE INCREASINGLY LITTLE SAY IN MY OWN DESTINY.

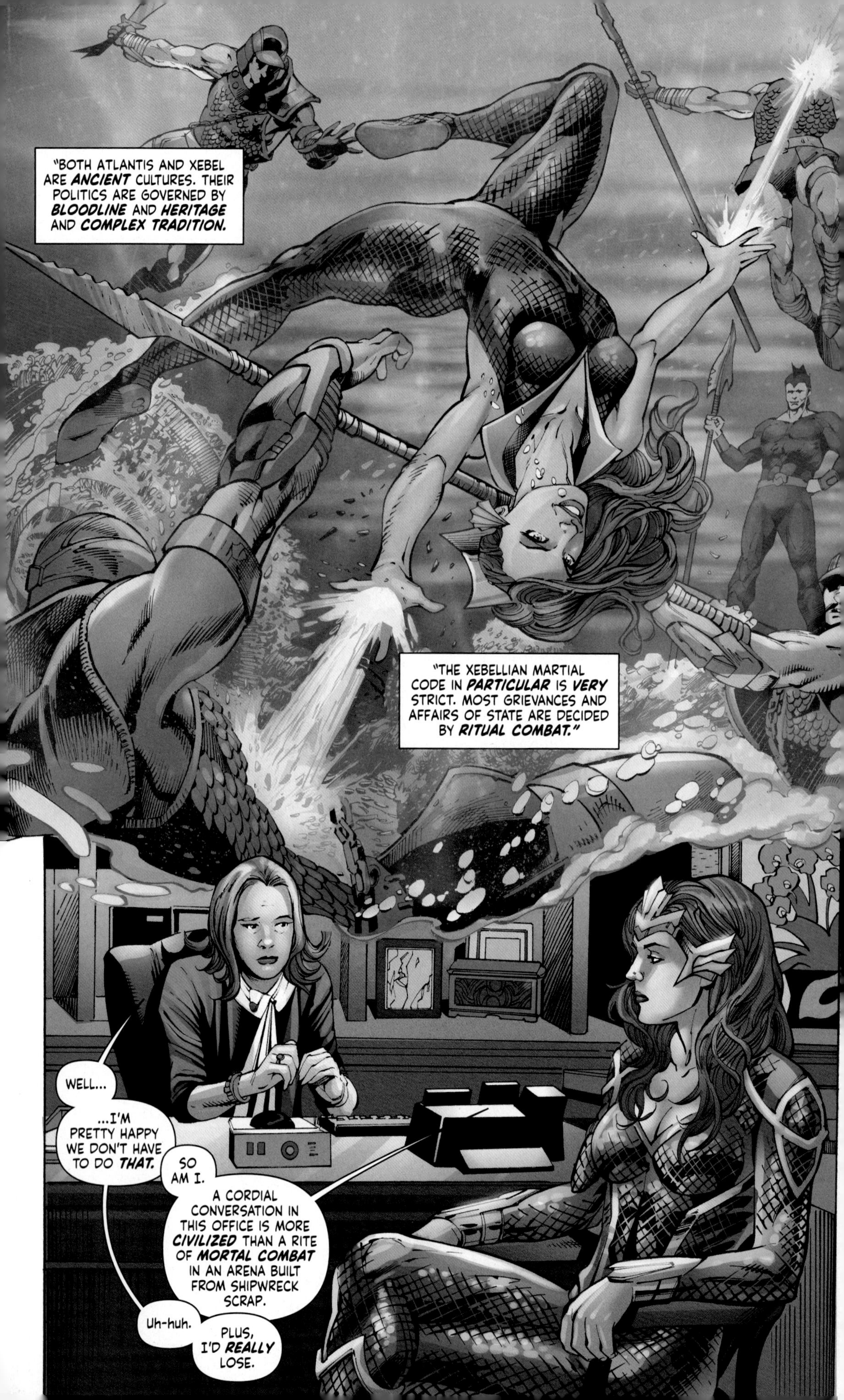

"BOTH ATLANTIS AND XEBEL ARE ANCIENT CULTURES. THEIR POLITICS ARE GOVERNED BY BLOODLINE AND HERITAGE AND COMPLEX TRADITION.
"THE XEBELLIAN MARTIAL CODE IN PARTICULAR IS VERY STRICT. MOST GRIEVANCES AND AFFAIRS OF STATE ARE DECIDED BY RITUAL COMBAT."
WELL...
...I'M PRETTY HAPPY WE DON'T HAVE TO DO THAT.
SO AM I.
A CORDIAL CONVERSATION IN THIS OFFICE IS MORE CIVILIZED THAN A RITE OF MORTAL COMBAT IN AN ARENA BUILT FROM SHIPWRECK SCRAP.
Uh-huh.
PLUS, I'D REALLY LOSE.

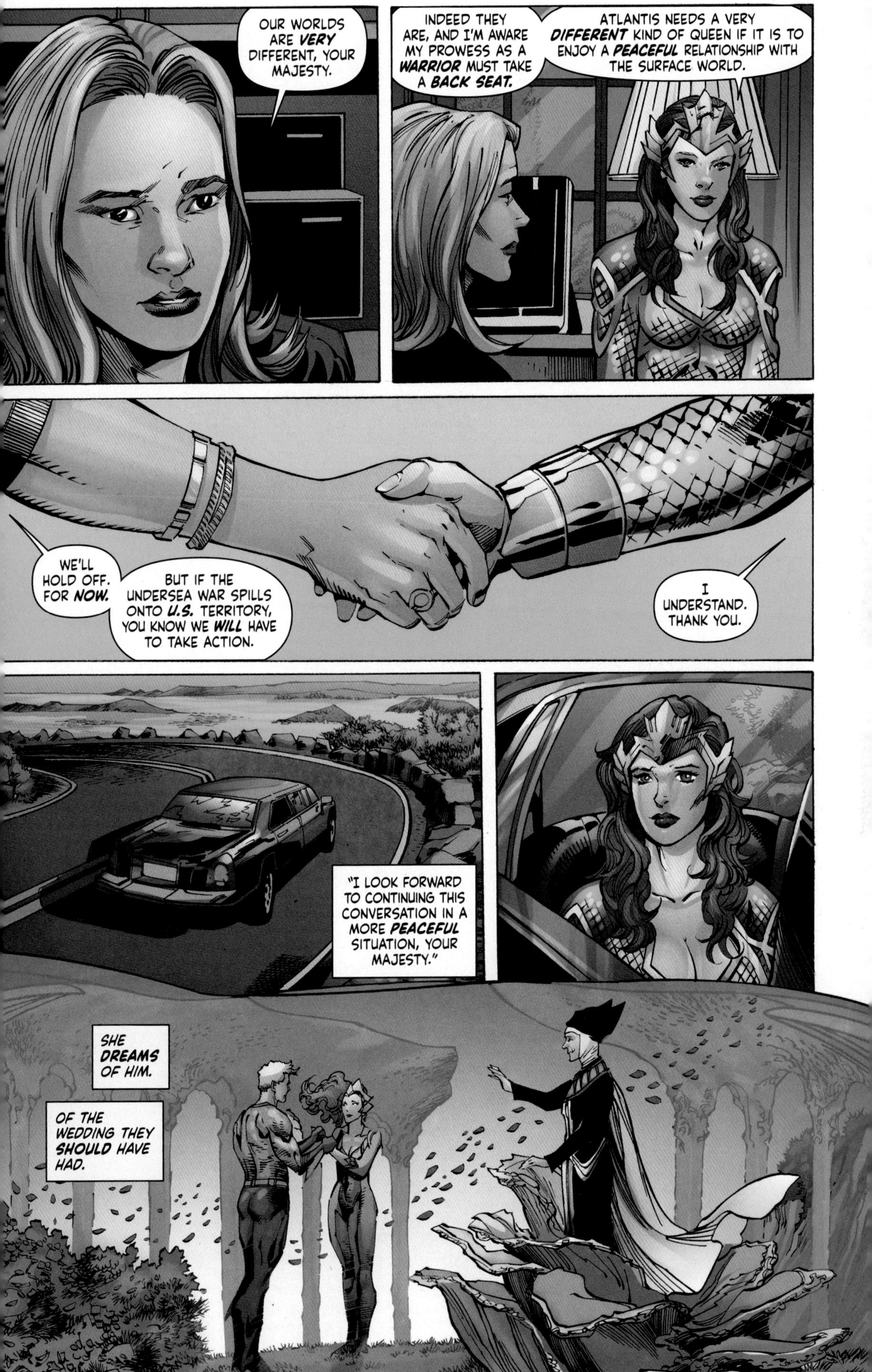

OUR WORLDS ARE VERY DIFFERENT, YOUR MAJESTY.
INDEED THEY ARE, AND I'M AWARE MY PROWESS AS A WARRIOR MUST TAKE A BACK SEAT.
ATLANTIS NEEDS A VERY DIFFERENT KIND OF QUEEN IF IT IS TO ENJOY A PEACEFUL RELATIONSHIP WITH THE SURFACE WORLD.
WE'LL HOLD OFF. FOR NOW.
BUT IF THE UNDERSEA WAR SPILLS ONTO U.S. TERRITORY, YOU KNOW WE WILL HAVE TO TAKE ACTION.
I UNDERSTAND. THANK YOU.
"I LOOK FORWARD TO CONTINUING THIS CONVERSATION IN A MORE PEACEFUL SITUATION, YOUR MAJESTY."
SHE DREAMS OF HIM.
OF THE WEDDING THEY SHOULD HAVE HAD.

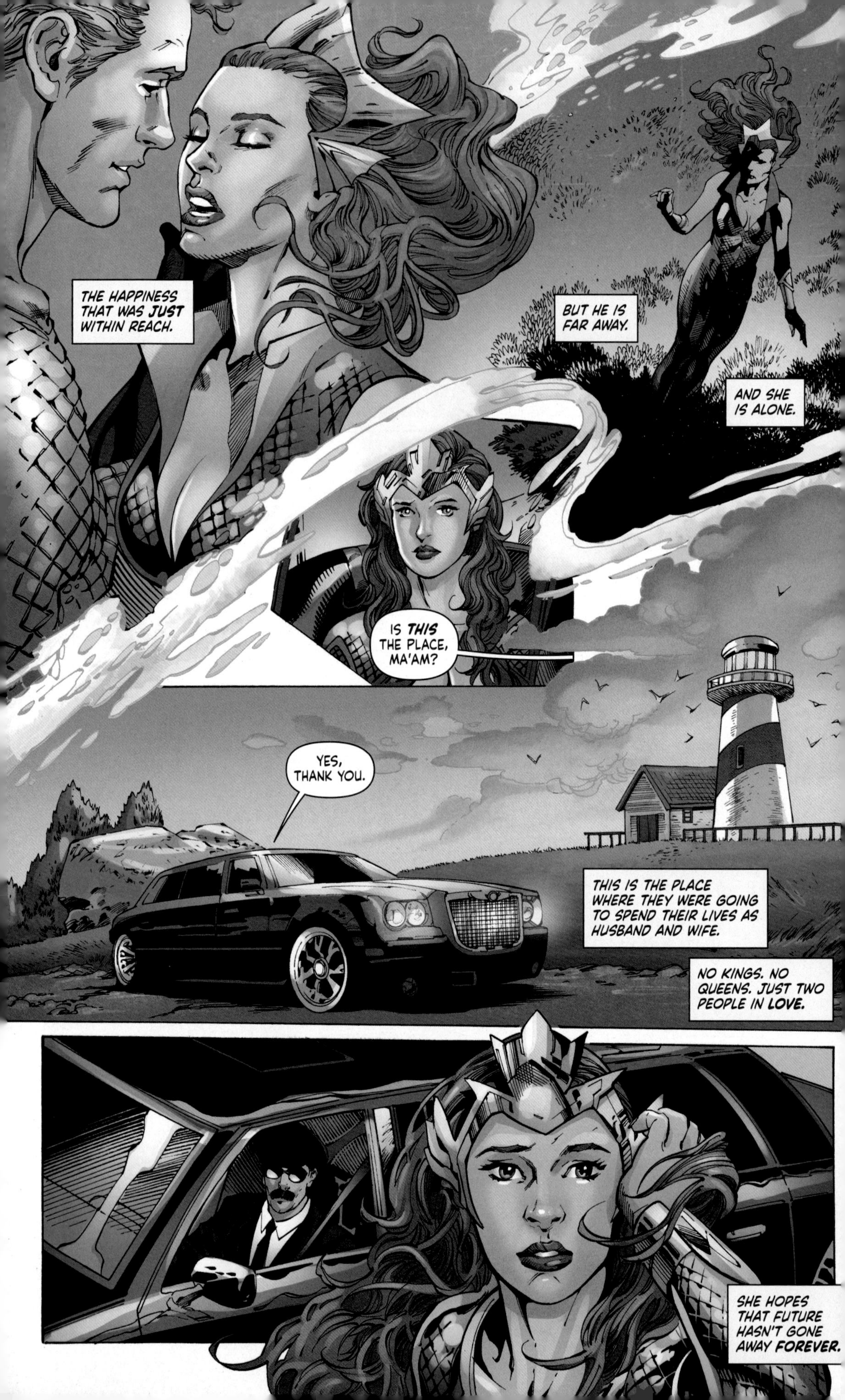
THE HAPPINESS THAT WAS JUST WITHIN REACH.
BUT HE IS FAR AWAY.
AND SHE IS ALONE.
IS THIS THE PLACE, MA'AM?
YES, THANK YOU.
THIS IS THE PLACE WHERE THEY WERE GOING TO SPEND THEIR LIVES AS HUSBAND AND WIFE.
NO KINGS. NO QUEENS. JUST TWO PEOPLE IN LOVE.
SHE HOPES THAT FUTURE HASN'T GONE AWAY FOREVER.

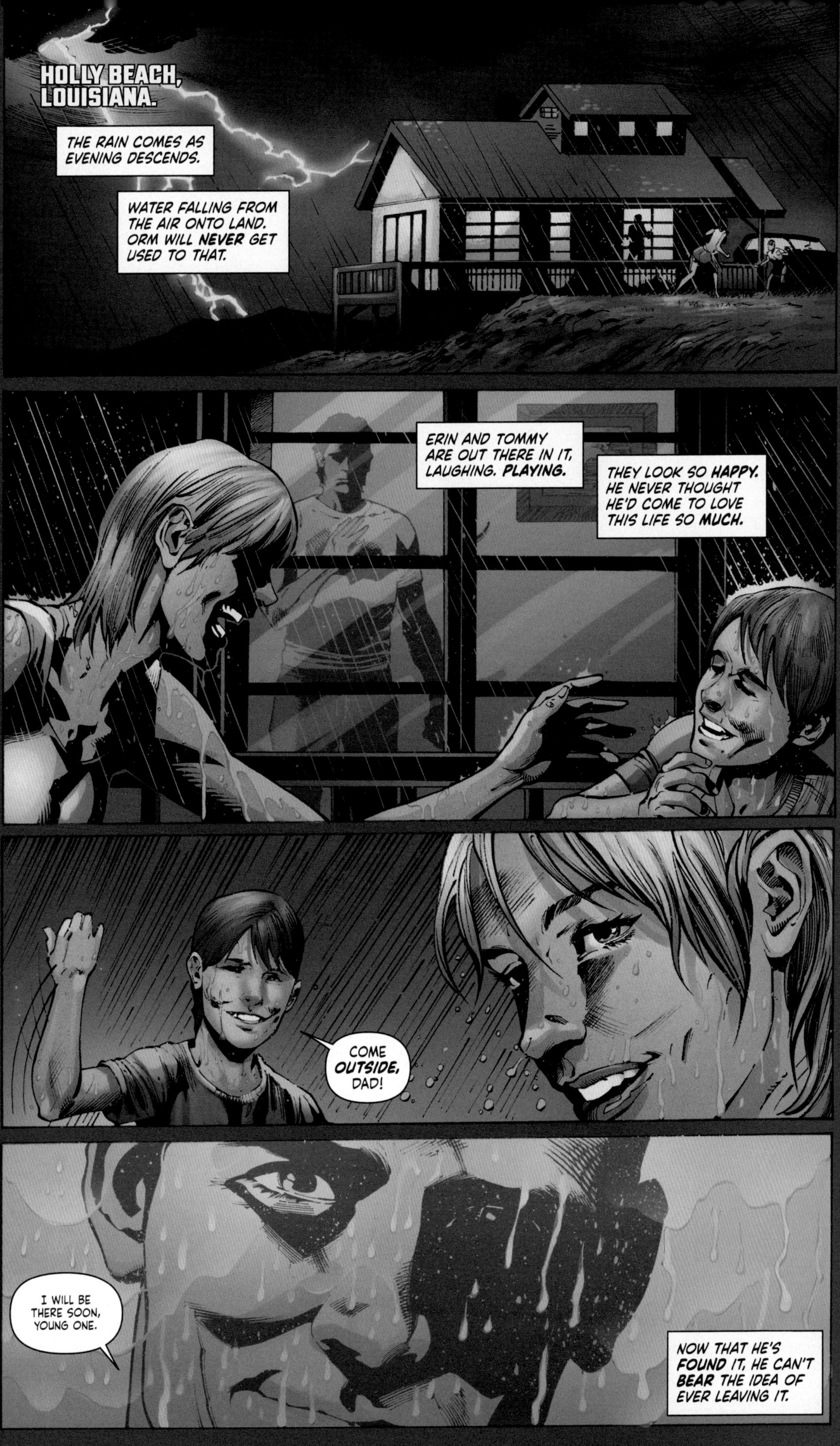

HOLLY BEACH, LOUISIANA.
THE RAIN COMES AS EVENING DESCENDS.
WATER FALLING FROM THE AIR ONTO LAND. ORM WILL NEVER GET USED TO THAT.
ERIN AND TOMMY ARE OUT THERE IN IT, LAUGHING. PLAYING.
THEY LOOK SO HAPPY. HE NEVER THOUGHT HE'D COME TO LOVE THIS LIFE SO MUCH.
COME OUTSIDE, DAD!
I WILL BE THERE SOON, YOUNG ONE.
NOW THAT HE'S FOUND IT, HE CAN'T BEAR THE IDEA OF EVER LEAVING IT.

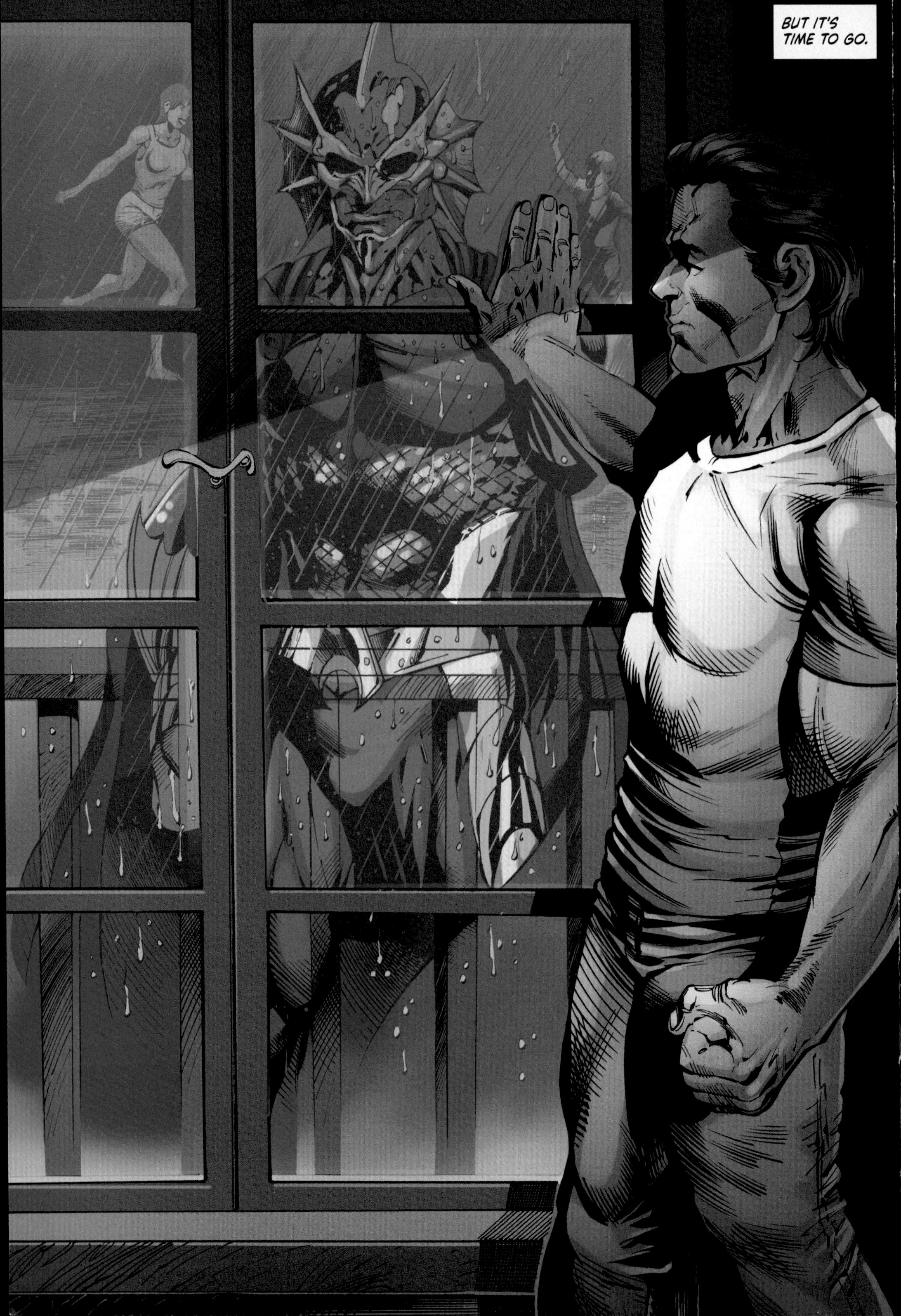
BUT IT'S TIME TO GO.

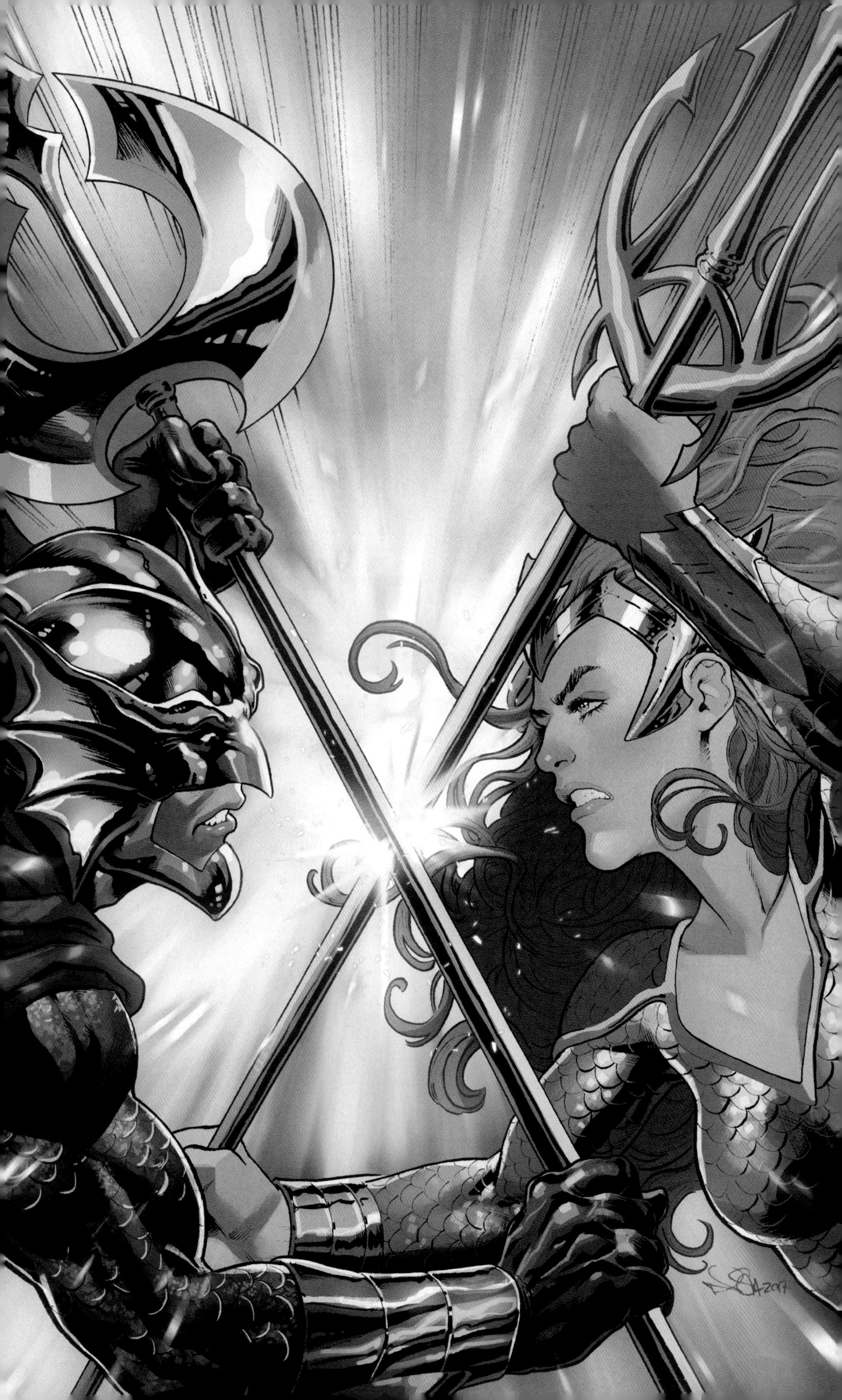

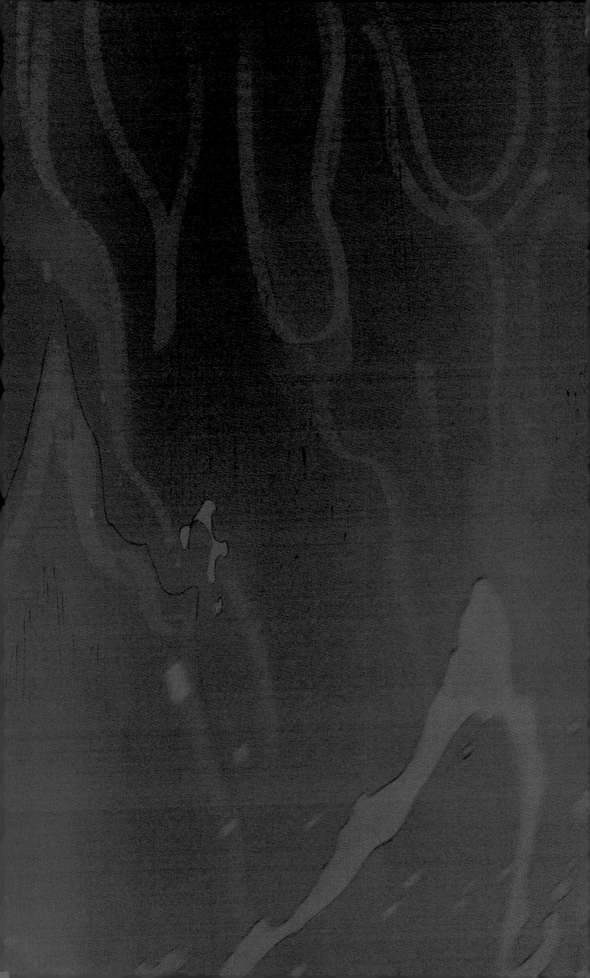

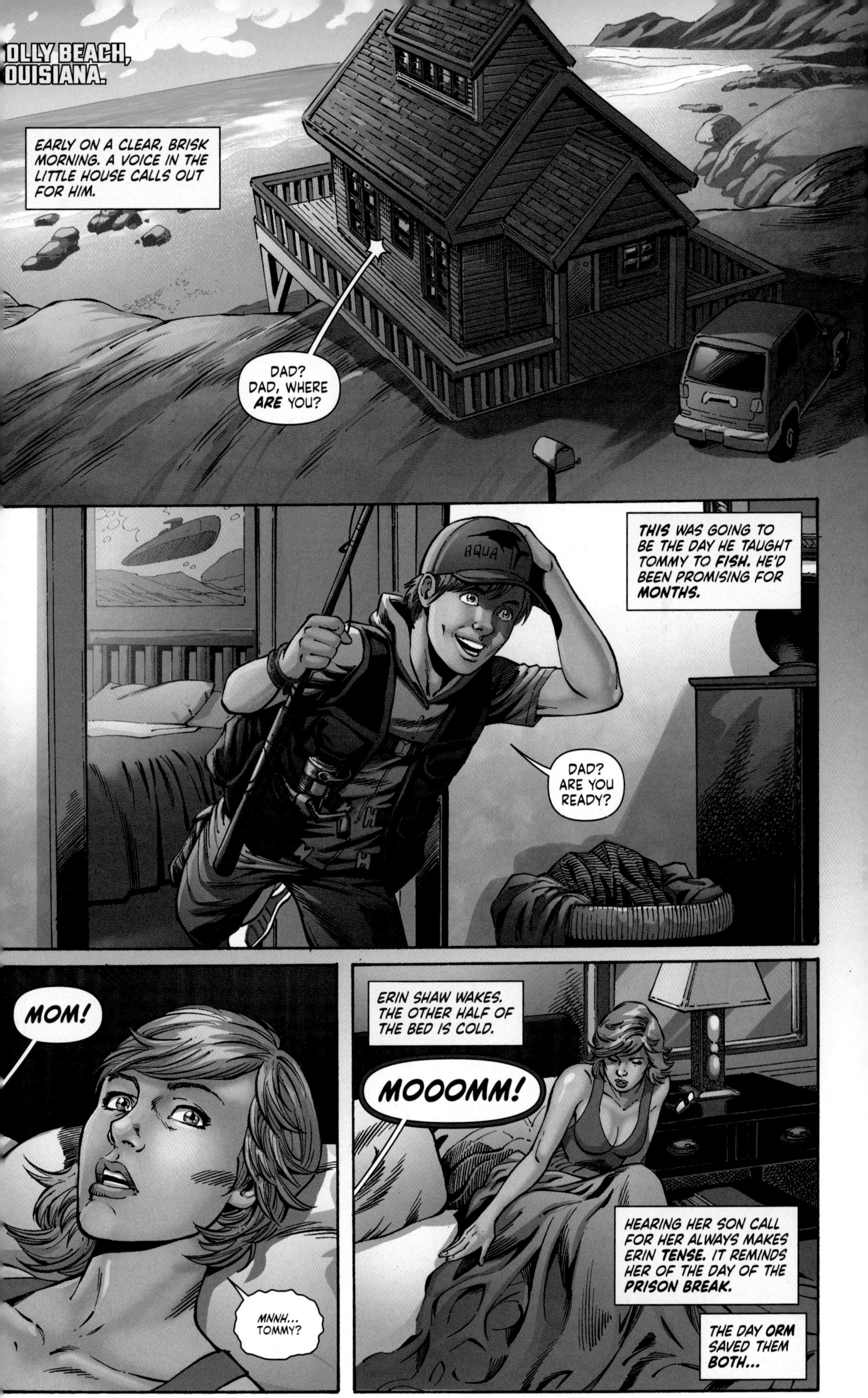

OLLY BEACH, OUISIANA.
EARLY ON A CLEAR, BRISK MORNING. A VOICE IN THE LITTLE HOUSE CALLS OUT FOR HIM.
DAD? DAD, WHERE ARE YOU?
AQUA
THIS WAS GOING TO BE THE DAY HE TAUGHT TOMMY TO FISH. HE'D BEEN PROMISING FOR MONTHS.
DAD? ARE YOU READY?
MOM!
MNNH... TOMMY?
ERIN SHAW WAKES. THE OTHER HALF OF THE BED IS COLD.
MOOOMM!
HEARING HER SON CALL FOR HER ALWAYS MAKES ERIN TENSE. IT REMINDS HER OF THE DAY OF THE PRISON BREAK.
THE DAY ORM SAVED THEM BOTH...

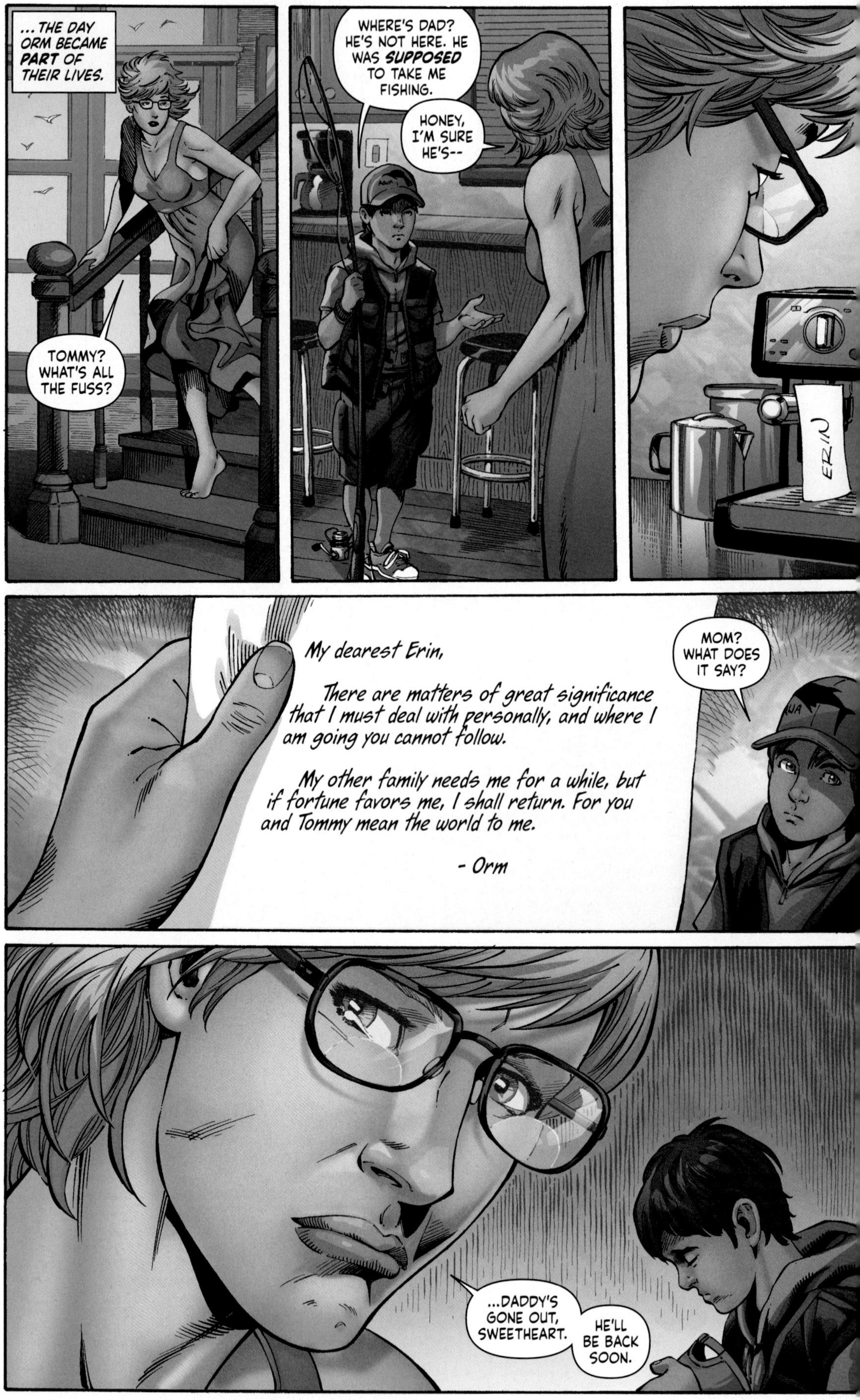
...THE DAY ORM BECAME PART OF THEIR LIVES.
TOMMY? WHAT'S ALL THE FUSS?
WHERE'S DAD? HE'S NOT HERE. HE WAS SUPPOSED TO TAKE ME FISHING.
HONEY, I'M SURE HE'S--
ERIN
My dearest Erin,
There are matters of great significance that I must deal with personally, and where I am going you cannot follow.
My other family needs me for a while, but if fortune favors me, I shall return. For you and Tommy mean the world to me.
- Orm
MOM? WHAT DOES IT SAY?
...DADDY'S GONE OUT, SWEETHEART.
HE'LL BE BACK SOON.

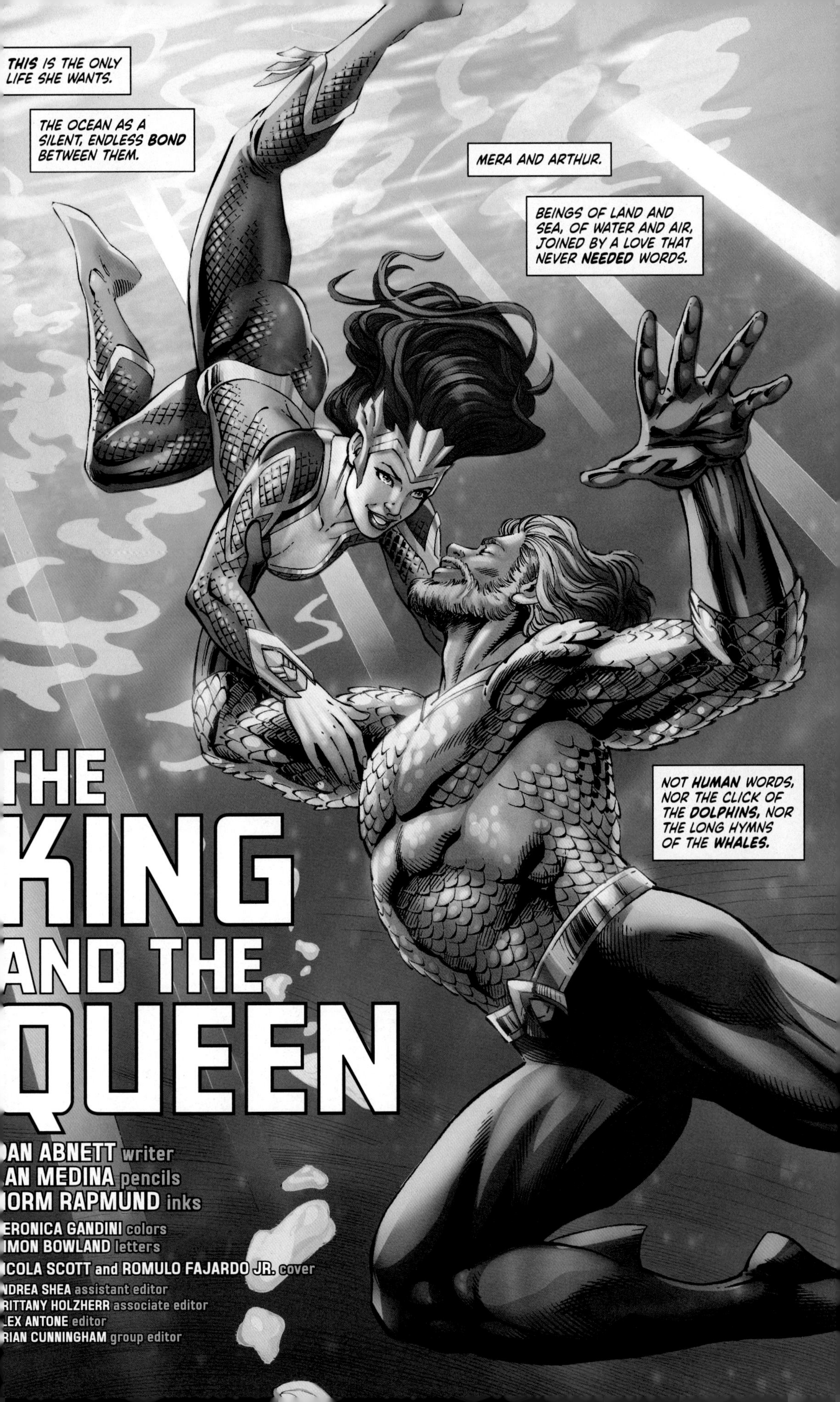
THIS IS THE ONLY LIFE SHE WANTS.
THE OCEAN AS A SILENT, ENDLESS BOND BETWEEN THEM.
MERA AND ARTHUR.
BEINGS OF LAND AND SEA, OF WATER AND AIR, JOINED BY A LOVE THAT NEVER NEEDED WORDS.
NOT HUMAN WORDS, NOR THE CLICK OF THE DOLPHINS, NOR THE LONG HYMNS OF THE WHALES.
THE KING AND THE QUEEN
AN ABNETT writer
AN MEDINA pencils
ORM RAPMUND inks
ERONICA GANDINI colors
IMON BOWLAND letters
ICOLA SCOTT and ROMULO FAJARDO JR. cover
NDREA SHEA assistant editor
RITTANY HOLZHERR associate editor
LEX ANTONE editor
RIAN CUNNINGHAM group editor

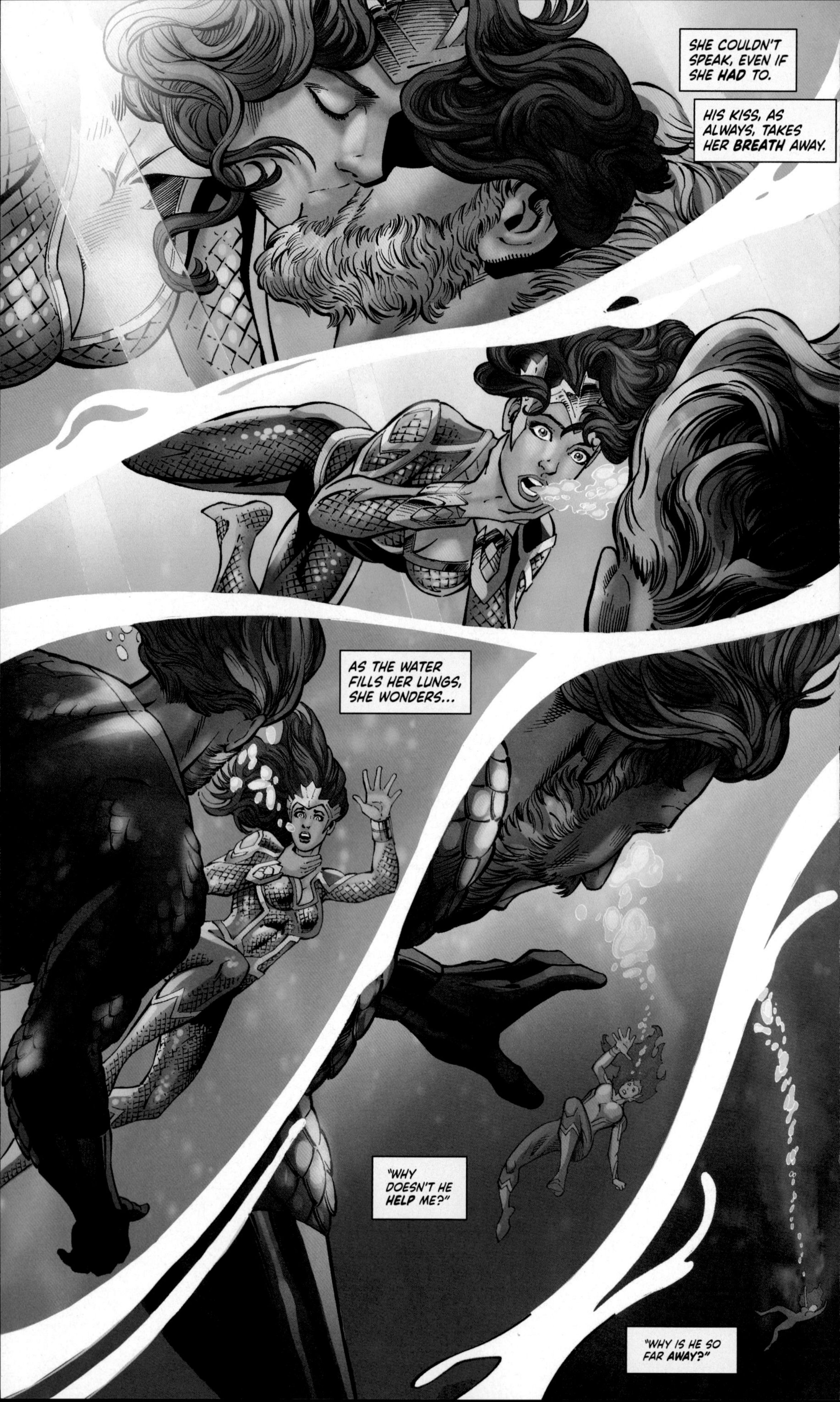
SHE COULDN'T SPEAK, EVEN IF SHE **HAD** TO.
HIS KISS, AS ALWAYS, TAKES HER **BREATH** AWAY.
AS THE WATER FILLS HER LUNGS, SHE WONDERS...
"WHY DOESN'T HE **HELP** ME?"
"WHY IS HE SO FAR **AWAY**?"

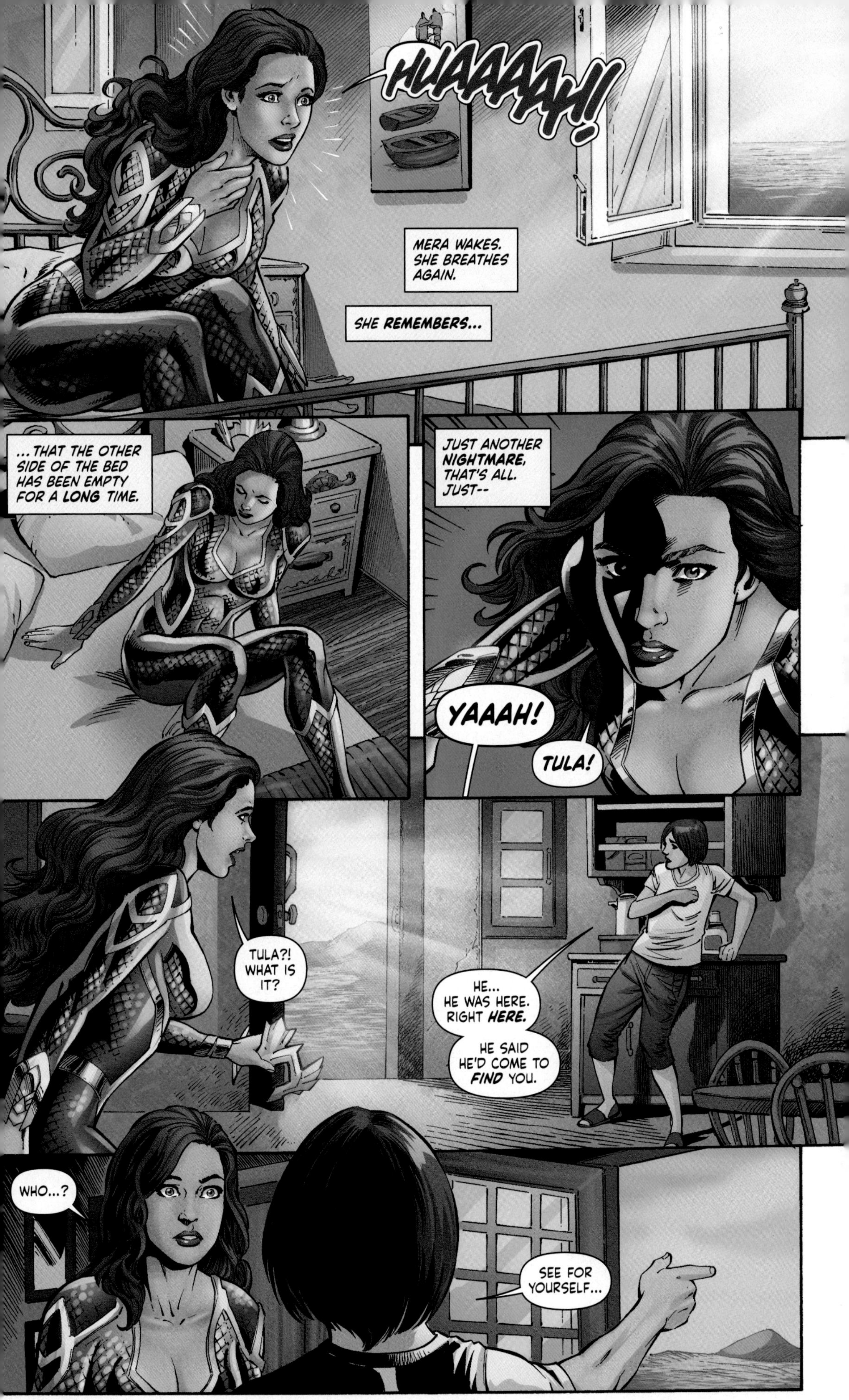
HUAAAAAH!!
MERA WAKES. SHE BREATHES AGAIN.
SHE REMEMBERS...
...THAT THE OTHER SIDE OF THE BED HAS BEEN EMPTY FOR A LONG TIME.
JUST ANOTHER NIGHTMARE, THAT'S ALL. JUST--
YAAAH!
TULA!
TULA?! WHAT IS IT?
HE... HE WAS HERE. RIGHT HERE.
HE SAID HE'D COME TO FIND YOU.
WHO...?
SEE FOR YOURSELF...

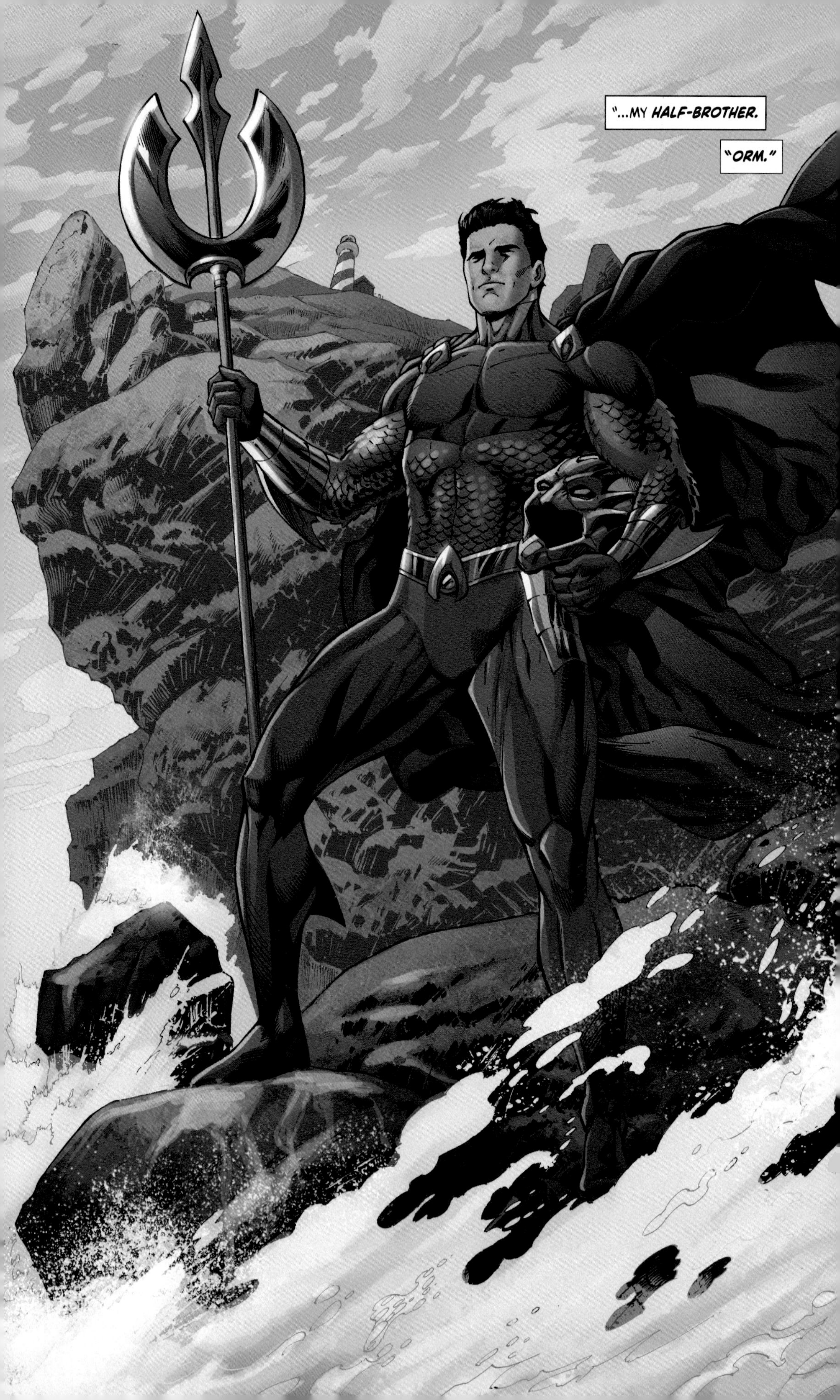
"...MY HALF-BROTHER.
"ORM."

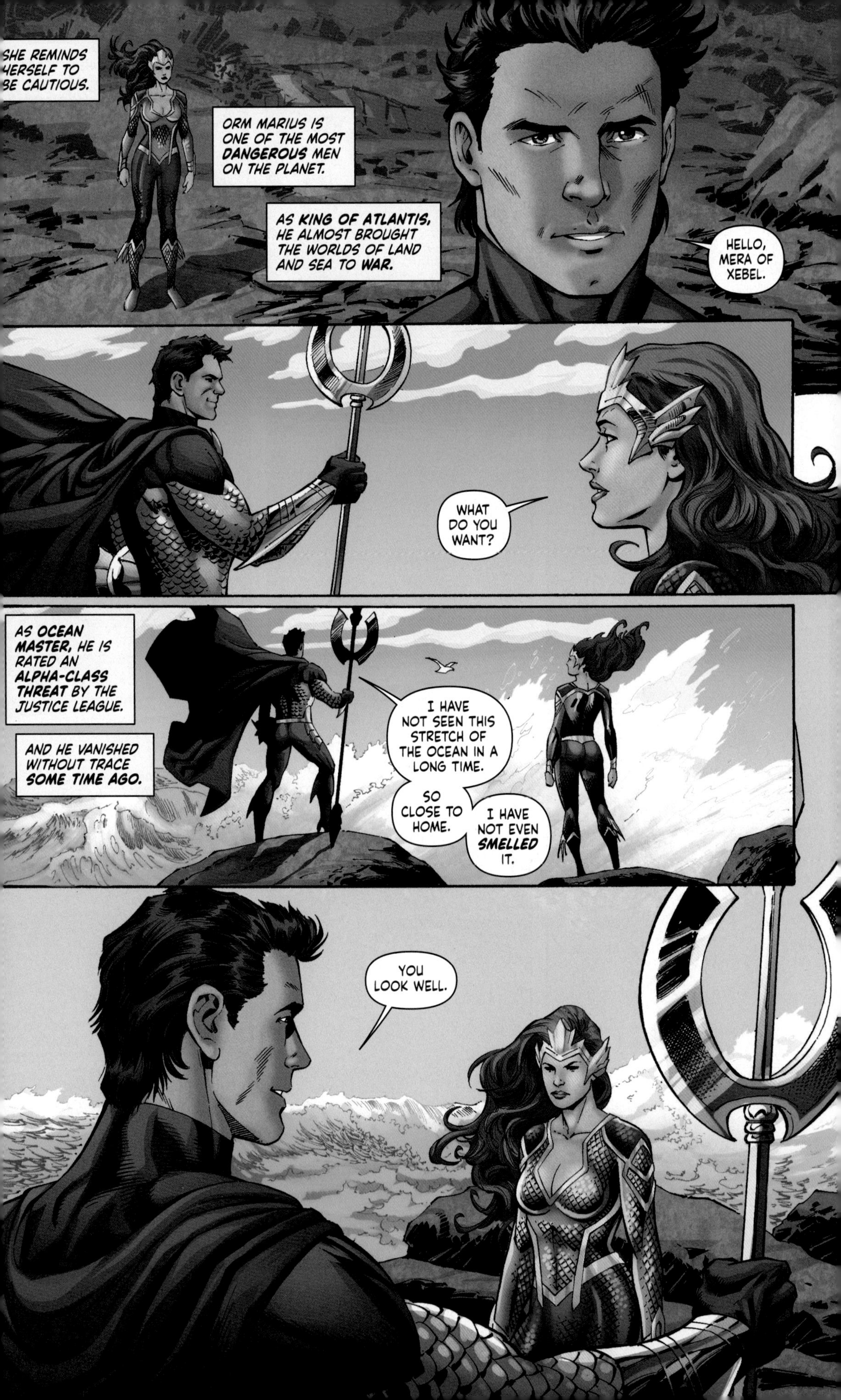
SHE REMINDS HERSELF TO BE CAUTIOUS.
ORM MARIUS IS ONE OF THE MOST DANGEROUS MEN ON THE PLANET.
AS KING OF ATLANTIS, HE ALMOST BROUGHT THE WORLDS OF LAND AND SEA TO WAR.
HELLO, MERA OF XEBEL.
WHAT DO YOU WANT?
AS OCEAN MASTER, HE IS RATED AN ALPHA-CLASS THREAT BY THE JUSTICE LEAGUE.
AND HE VANISHED WITHOUT TRACE SOME TIME AGO.
I HAVE NOT SEEN THIS STRETCH OF THE OCEAN IN A LONG TIME.
SO CLOSE TO HOME.
I HAVE NOT EVEN SMELLED IT.
YOU LOOK WELL.

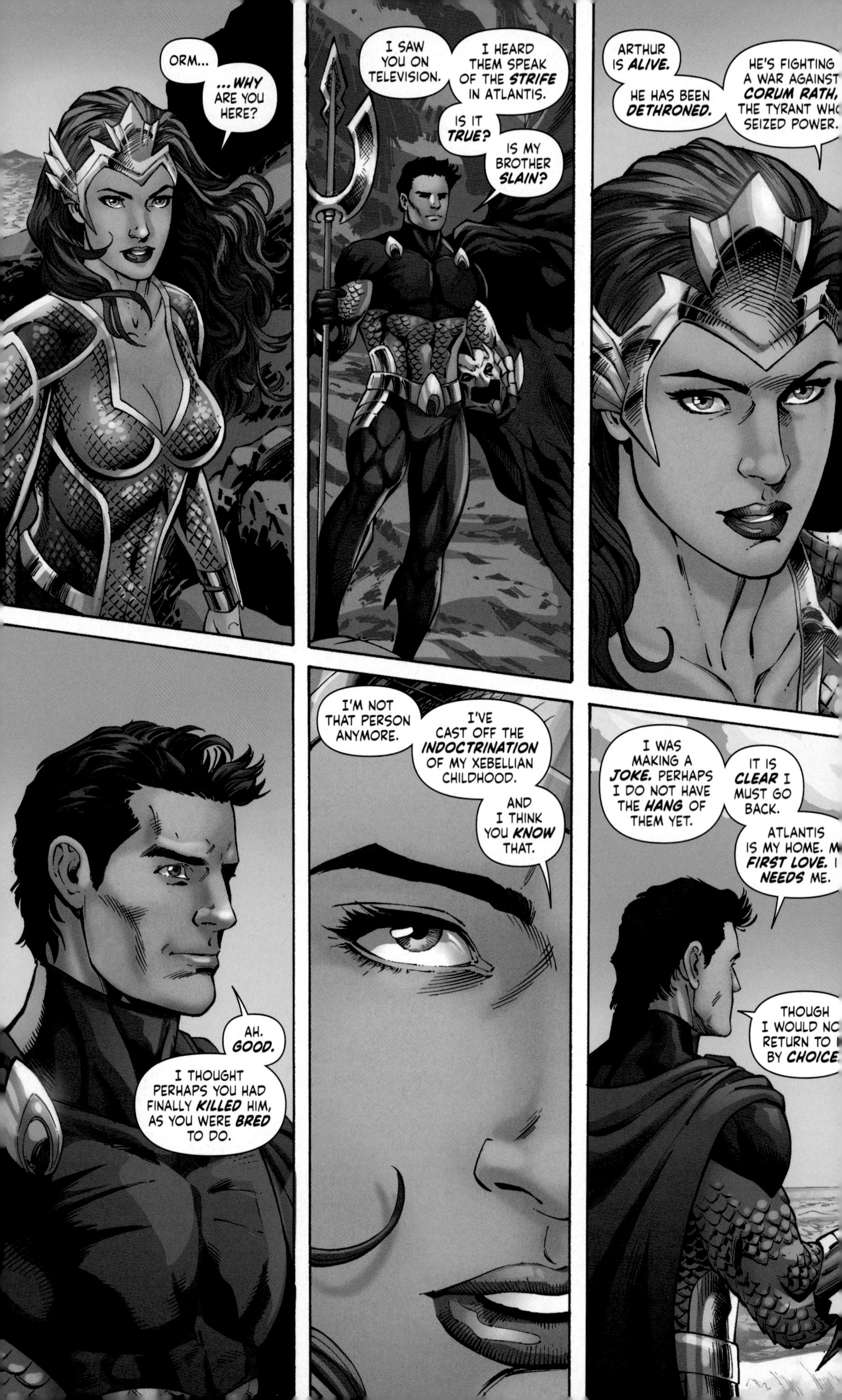
ORM...
...WHY ARE YOU HERE?
I SAW YOU ON TELEVISION.
I HEARD THEM SPEAK OF THE STRIFE IN ATLANTIS.
IS IT TRUE?
IS MY BROTHER SLAIN?
ARTHUR IS ALIVE.
HE HAS BEEN DETHRONED.
HE'S FIGHTING A WAR AGAINST CORUM RATH, THE TYRANT WHO SEIZED POWER.
AH. GOOD.
I THOUGHT PERHAPS YOU HAD FINALLY KILLED HIM, AS YOU WERE BRED TO DO.
I'M NOT THAT PERSON ANYMORE.
I'VE CAST OFF THE INDOCTRINATION OF MY XEBELLIAN CHILDHOOD.
AND I THINK YOU KNOW THAT.
I WAS MAKING A JOKE. PERHAPS I DO NOT HAVE THE HANG OF THEM YET.
IT IS CLEAR I MUST GO BACK.
ATLANTIS IS MY HOME. MY FIRST LOVE. IT NEEDS ME.
THOUGH I WOULD NOT RETURN TO IT BY CHOICE.

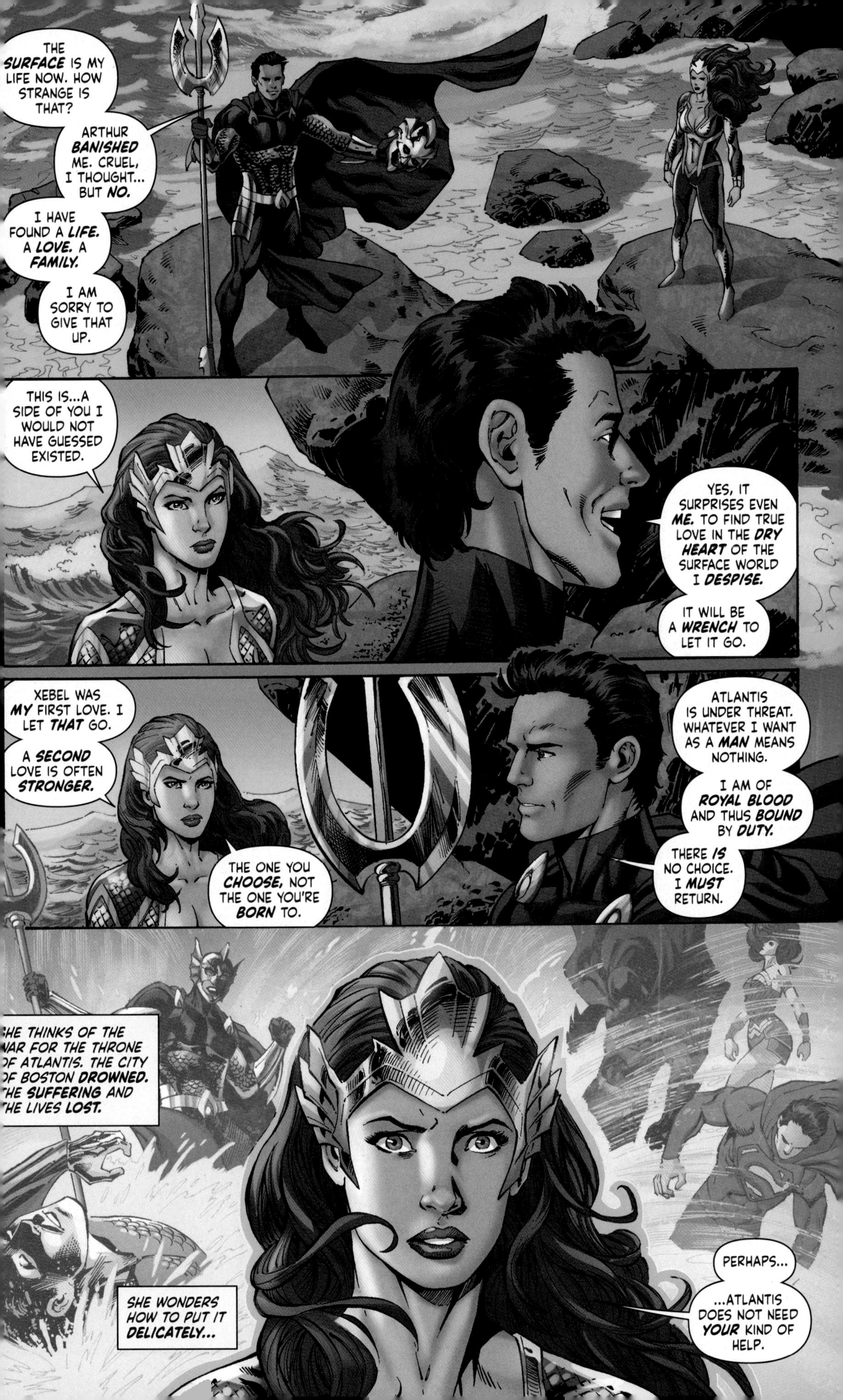
THE SURFACE IS MY LIFE NOW. HOW STRANGE IS THAT?
ARTHUR BANISHED ME. CRUEL, I THOUGHT... BUT NO.
I HAVE FOUND A LIFE. A LOVE. A FAMILY.
I AM SORRY TO GIVE THAT UP.
THIS IS...A SIDE OF YOU I WOULD NOT HAVE GUESSED EXISTED.
YES, IT SURPRISES EVEN ME. TO FIND TRUE LOVE IN THE DRY HEART OF THE SURFACE WORLD I DESPISE.
IT WILL BE A WRENCH TO LET IT GO.
XEBEL WAS MY FIRST LOVE. I LET THAT GO.
A SECOND LOVE IS OFTEN STRONGER.
THE ONE YOU CHOOSE, NOT THE ONE YOU'RE BORN TO.
ATLANTIS IS UNDER THREAT. WHATEVER I WANT AS A MAN MEANS NOTHING.
I AM OF ROYAL BLOOD AND THUS BOUND BY DUTY.
THERE IS NO CHOICE. I MUST RETURN.
HE THINKS OF THE WAR FOR THE THRONE OF ATLANTIS. THE CITY OF BOSTON DROWNED. THE SUFFERING AND THE LIVES LOST.
SHE WONDERS HOW TO PUT IT DELICATELY...
PERHAPS...
...ATLANTIS DOES NOT NEED YOUR KIND OF HELP.

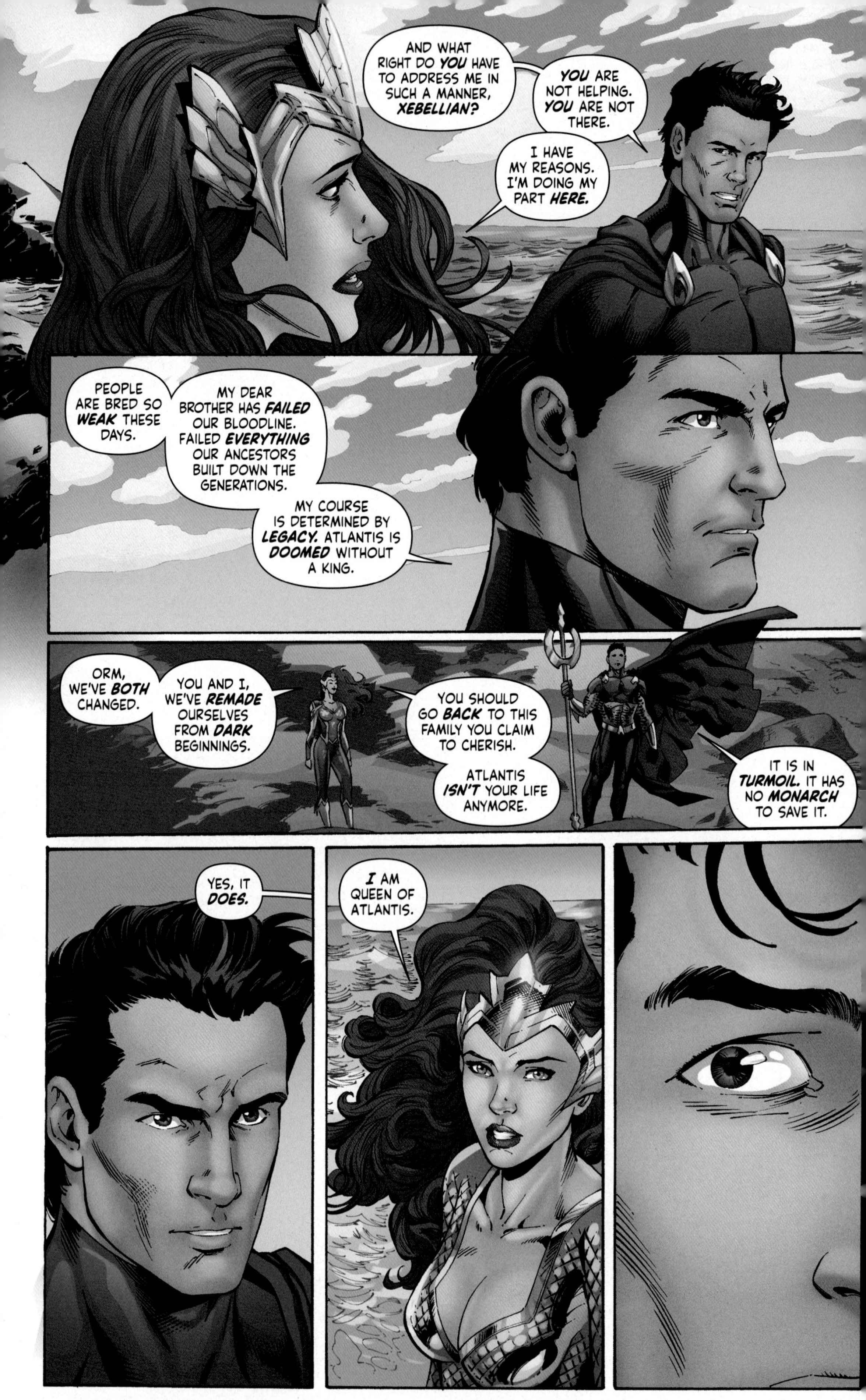

AND WHAT RIGHT DO YOU HAVE TO ADDRESS ME IN SUCH A MANNER, XEBELLIAN?
YOU ARE NOT HELPING. YOU ARE NOT THERE.
I HAVE MY REASONS. I'M DOING MY PART HERE.
PEOPLE ARE BRED SO WEAK THESE DAYS.
MY DEAR BROTHER HAS FAILED OUR BLOODLINE. FAILED EVERYTHING OUR ANCESTORS BUILT DOWN THE GENERATIONS.
MY COURSE IS DETERMINED BY LEGACY. ATLANTIS IS DOOMED WITHOUT A KING.
ORM, WE'VE BOTH CHANGED.
YOU AND I, WE'VE REMADE OURSELVES FROM DARK BEGINNINGS.
YOU SHOULD GO BACK TO THIS FAMILY YOU CLAIM TO CHERISH.
ATLANTIS ISN'T YOUR LIFE ANYMORE.
IT IS IN TURMOIL. IT HAS NO MONARCH TO SAVE IT.
YES, IT DOES.
I AM QUEEN OF ATLANTIS.

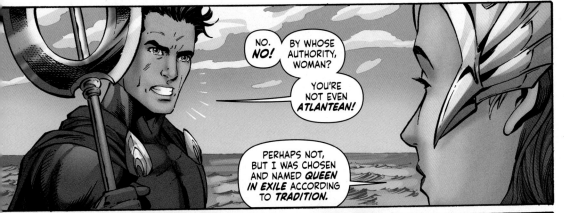

NO. **NO!** BY WHOSE AUTHORITY, WOMAN? YOU'RE NOT EVEN **ATLANTEAN!**

PERHAPS NOT, BUT I WAS CHOSEN AND NAMED **QUEEN IN EXILE** ACCORDING TO **TRADITION.**

I'LL RETURN TO ATLANTIS AND **RULE** ONCE THE WAR IS FINISHED. UNTIL THEN, I STAND VIGIL **HERE,** TO PROTECT ATLANTIS AND ITS INTERESTS FROM **EXTERNAL** THREATS.

DON'T GET DRAGGED INTO THE CHAOS OF ATLANTIS AGAIN, ORM. LAST TIME IT GOT YOU EXILED.

YOU'VE **MADE** SOMETHING OF THAT. GO **BACK** TO YOUR HAPPY LIFE. **LIVE** IT.

IF I COULD **TRADE PLACES** WITH YOU, I **WOULD.**

HNH! YOU HAVE **NO** AUTHORITY OVER ME.

I CAME TO AMNESTY BAY AS A **COURTESY** TO MY BROTHER BEFORE BEGINNING MY CAMPAIGN.

I SEE NOW THAT WAS A **MISTAKE...**

...AND I WILL DO WHAT I **HAVE** TO DO **ALONE.**

ORM--

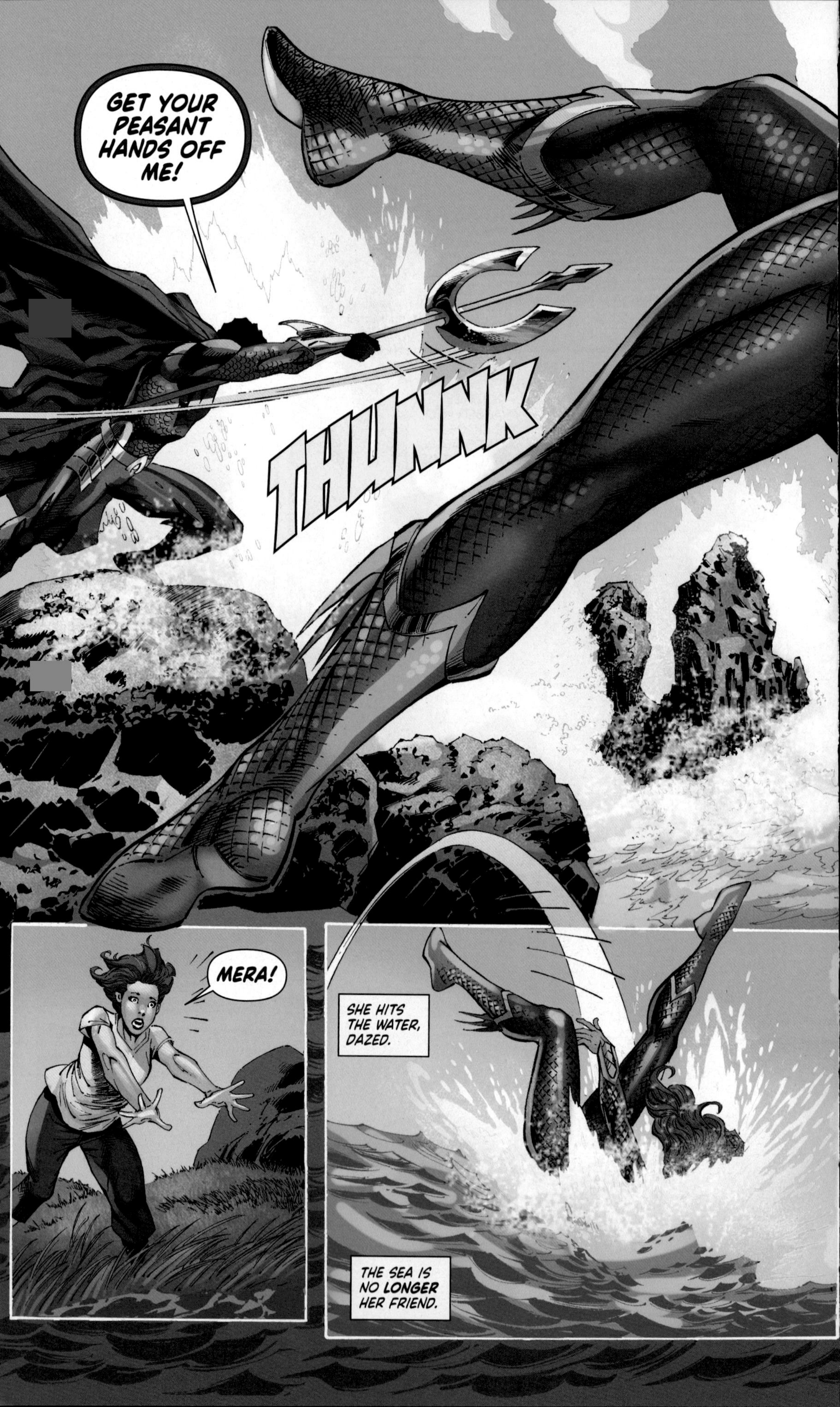
GET YOUR PEASANT HANDS OFF ME!
THUNNK
MERA!
SHE HITS THE WATER, DAZED.
THE SEA IS NO LONGER HER FRIEND.

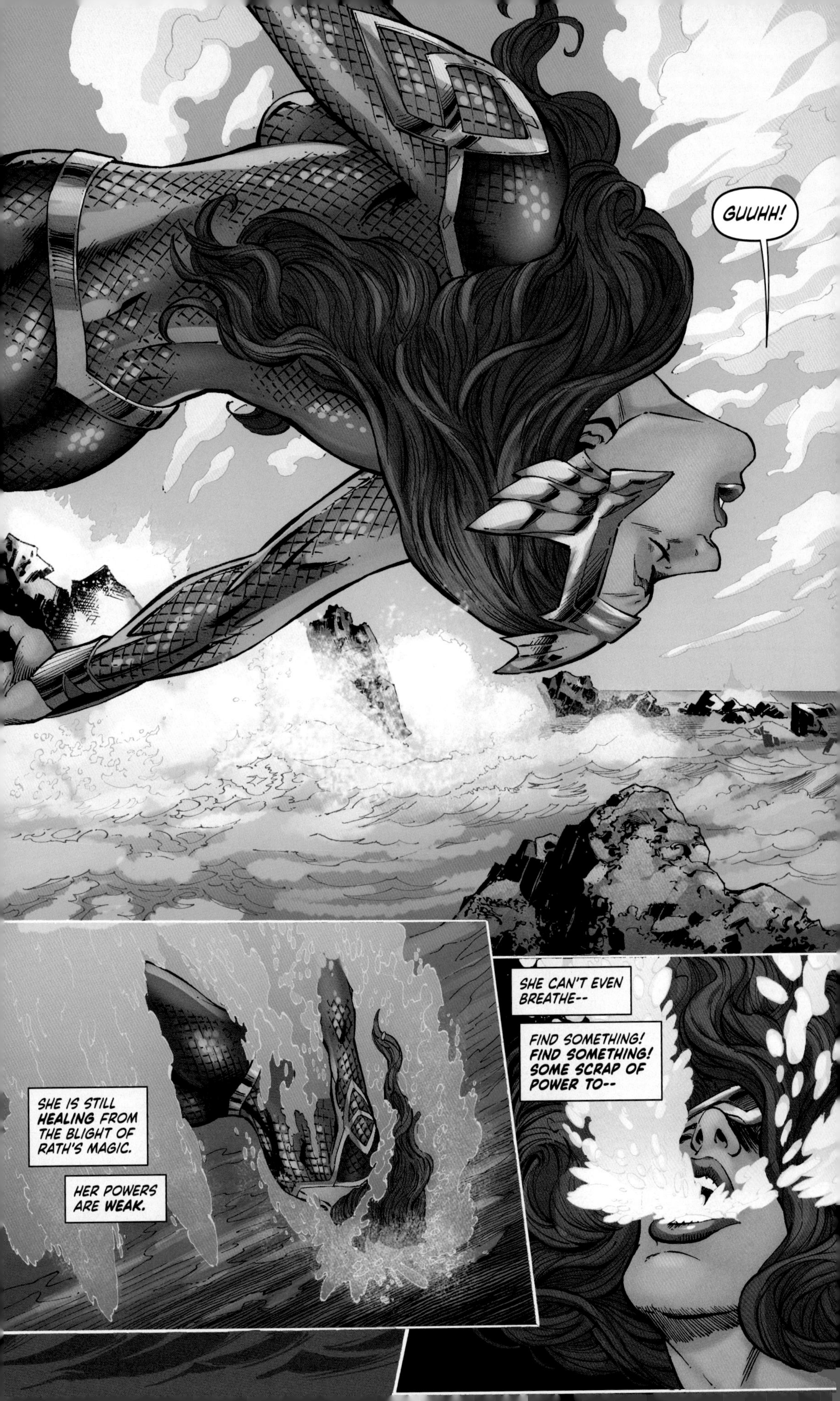
GUUHH!
SHE IS STILL HEALING FROM THE BLIGHT OF RATH'S MAGIC.
HER POWERS ARE WEAK.
SHE CAN'T EVEN BREATHE--
FIND SOMETHING! FIND SOMETHING! SOME SCRAP OF POWER TO--

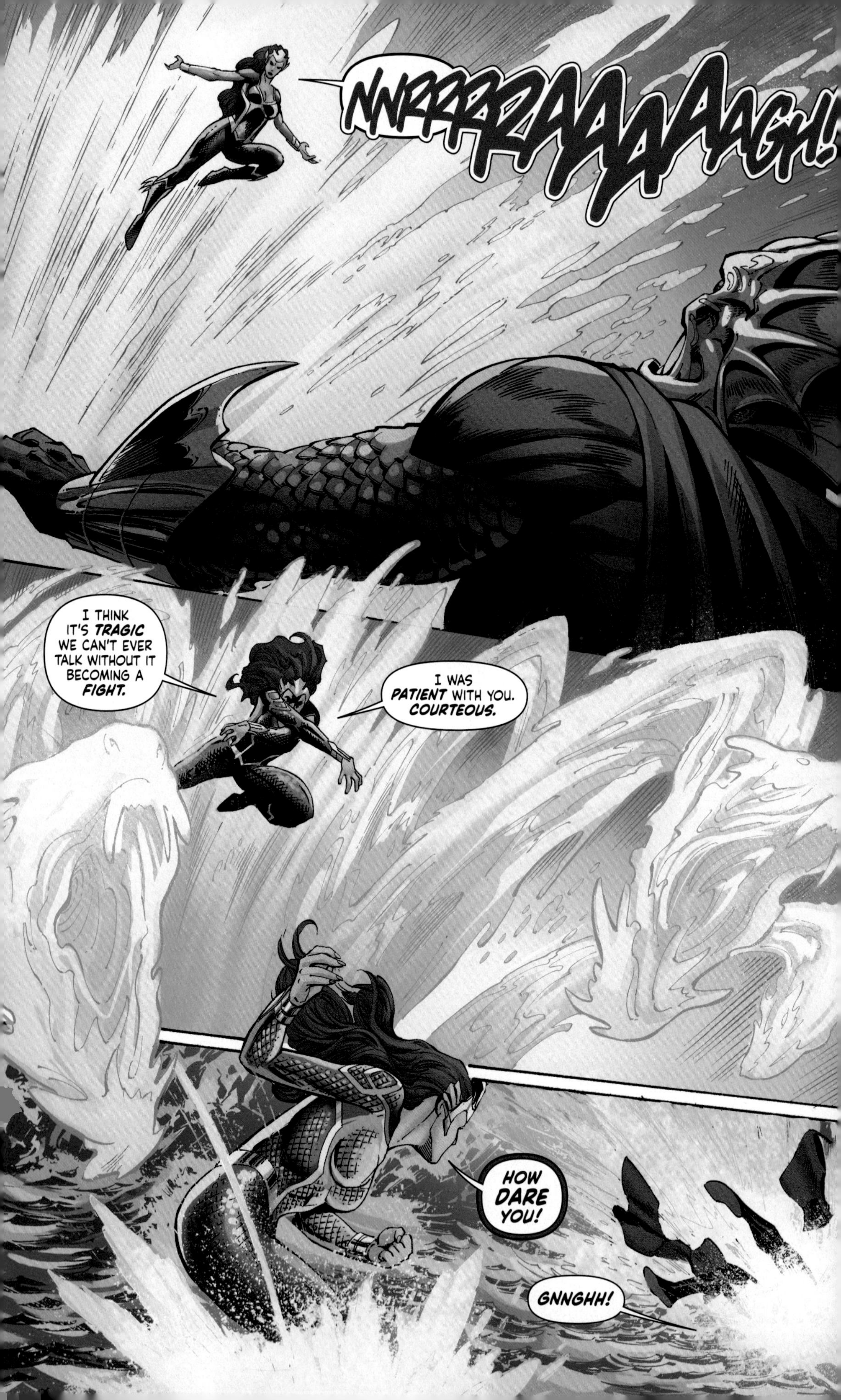
NNRRRRAAAAAAAGH!
I THINK IT'S TRAGIC WE CAN'T EVER TALK WITHOUT IT BECOMING A FIGHT.
I WAS PATIENT WITH YOU. COURTEOUS.
HOW DARE YOU!
GNNGHH!

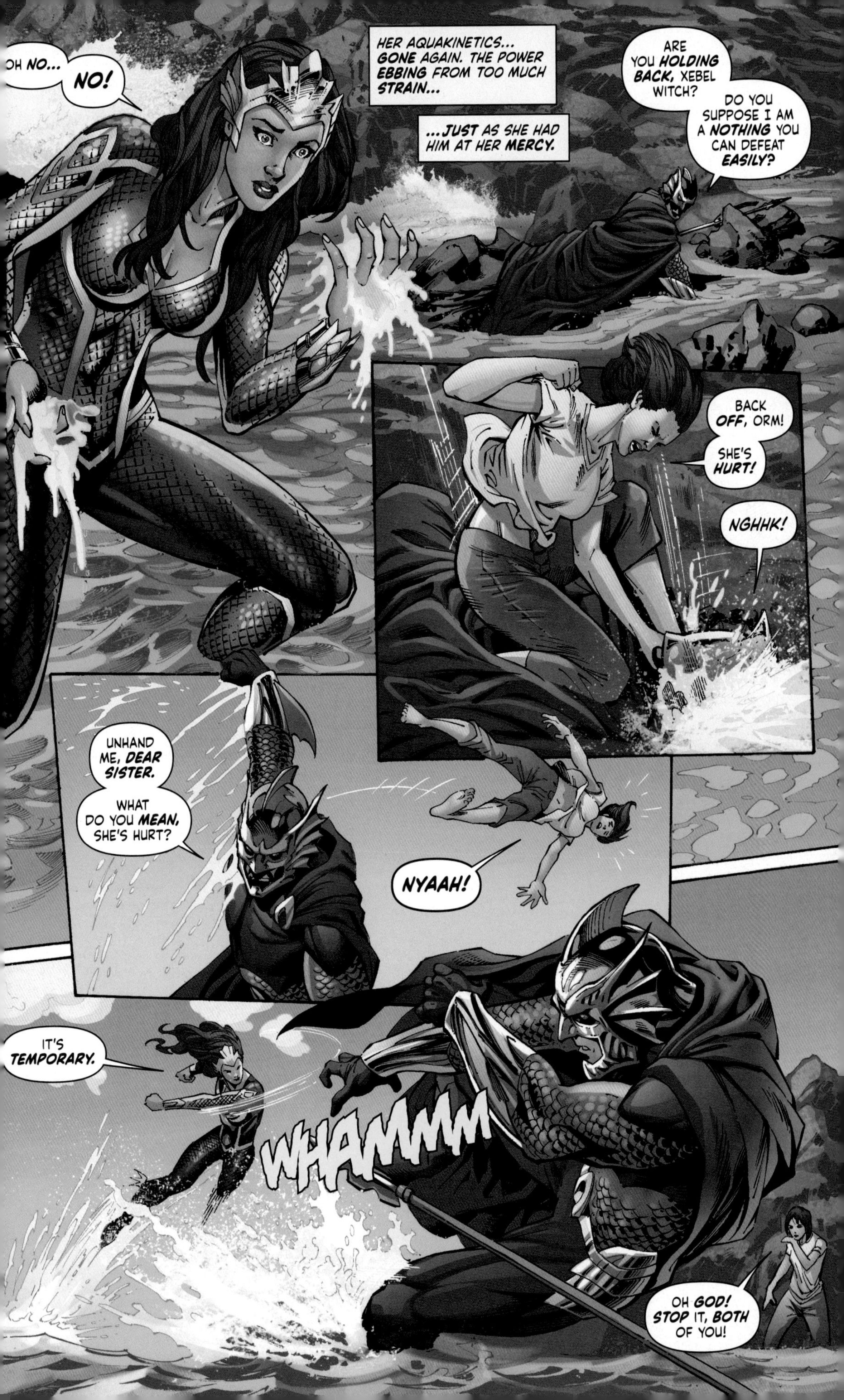
OH NO... NO!
HER AQUAKINETICS... GONE AGAIN. THE POWER EBBING FROM TOO MUCH STRAIN...
...JUST AS SHE HAD HIM AT HER MERCY.
ARE YOU HOLDING BACK, XEBEL WITCH?
DO YOU SUPPOSE I AM A NOTHING YOU CAN DEFEAT EASILY?
BACK OFF, ORM!
SHE'S HURT!
NGHHK!
UNHAND ME, DEAR SISTER.
WHAT DO YOU MEAN, SHE'S HURT?
NYAAH!
IT'S TEMPORARY.
WHAMMM
OH GOD! STOP IT, BOTH OF YOU!

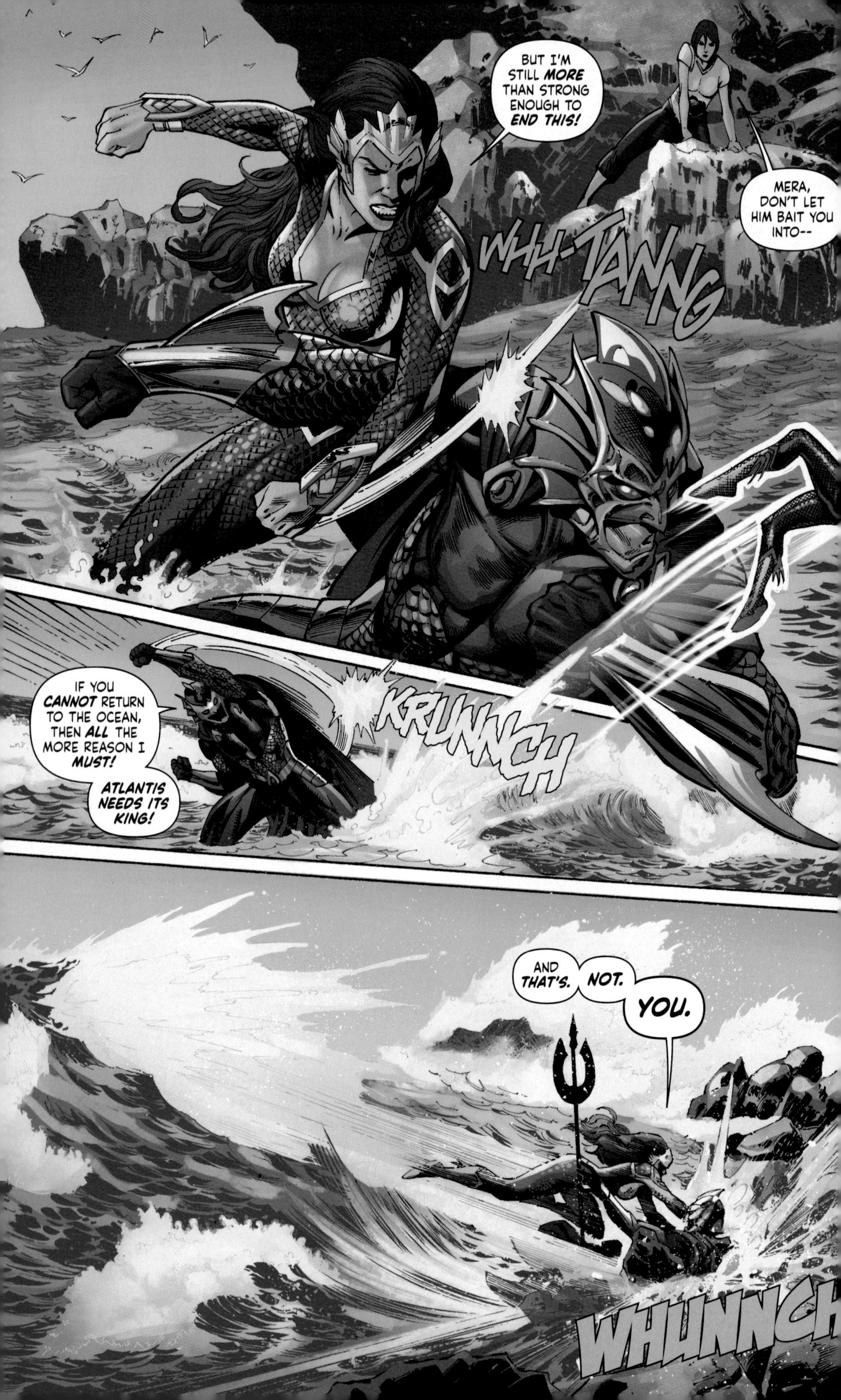

BUT I'M STILL MORE THAN STRONG ENOUGH TO END THIS!
MERA, DON'T LET HIM BAIT YOU INTO--
WHH-TANNG
KRUNNCH
IF YOU CANNOT RETURN TO THE OCEAN, THEN ALL THE MORE REASON I MUST!
ATLANTIS NEEDS ITS KING!
AND THAT'S.
NOT.
YOU.
WHUNNCH

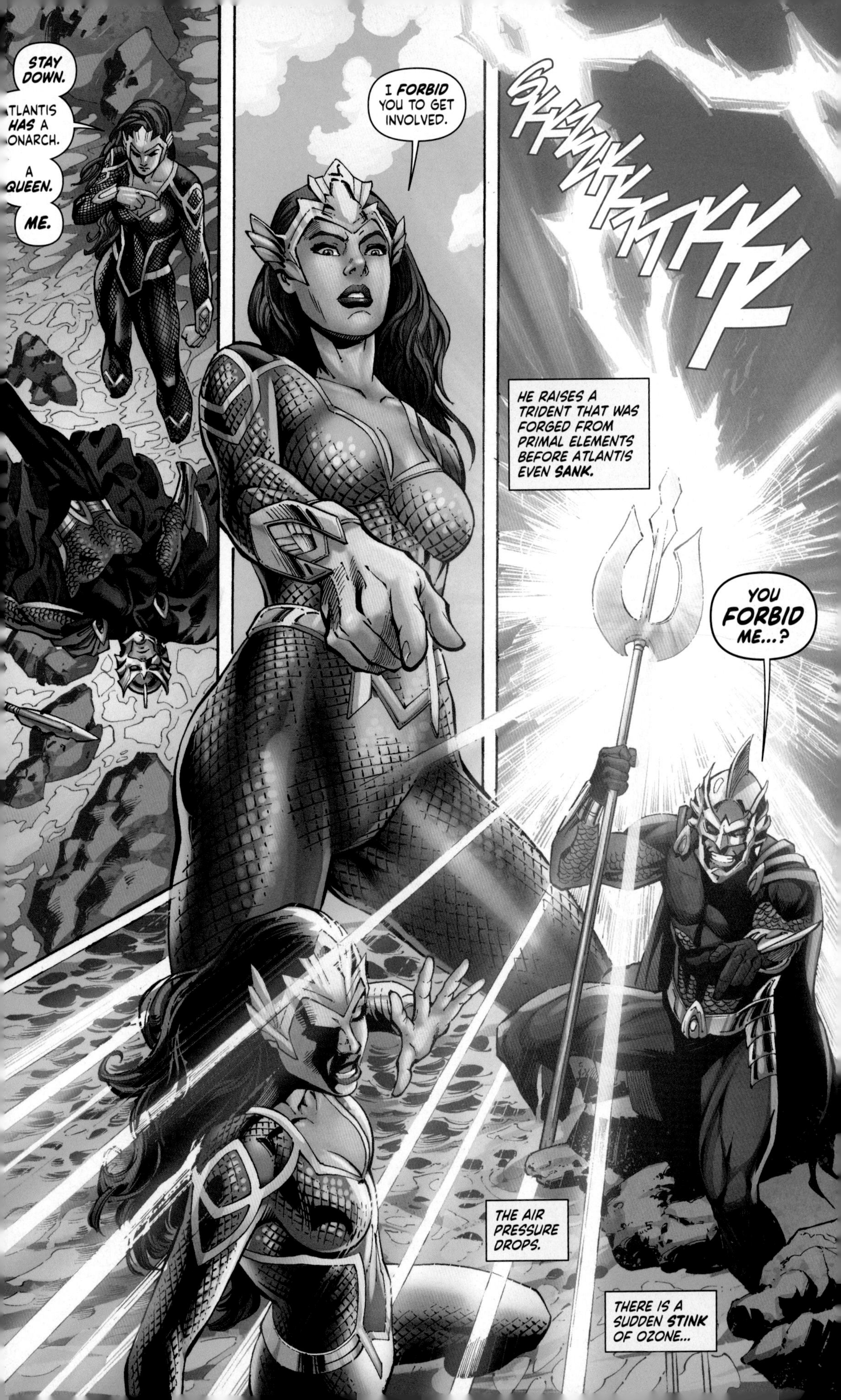

STAY DOWN.
TLANTIS HAS A ONARCH.
A QUEEN.
ME.
I FORBID YOU TO GET INVOLVED.
SKKKKKKKKKKRRK
HE RAISES A TRIDENT THAT WAS FORGED FROM PRIMAL ELEMENTS BEFORE ATLANTIS EVEN SANK.
YOU FORBID ME...?
THE AIR PRESSURE DROPS.
THERE IS A SUDDEN STINK OF OZONE...

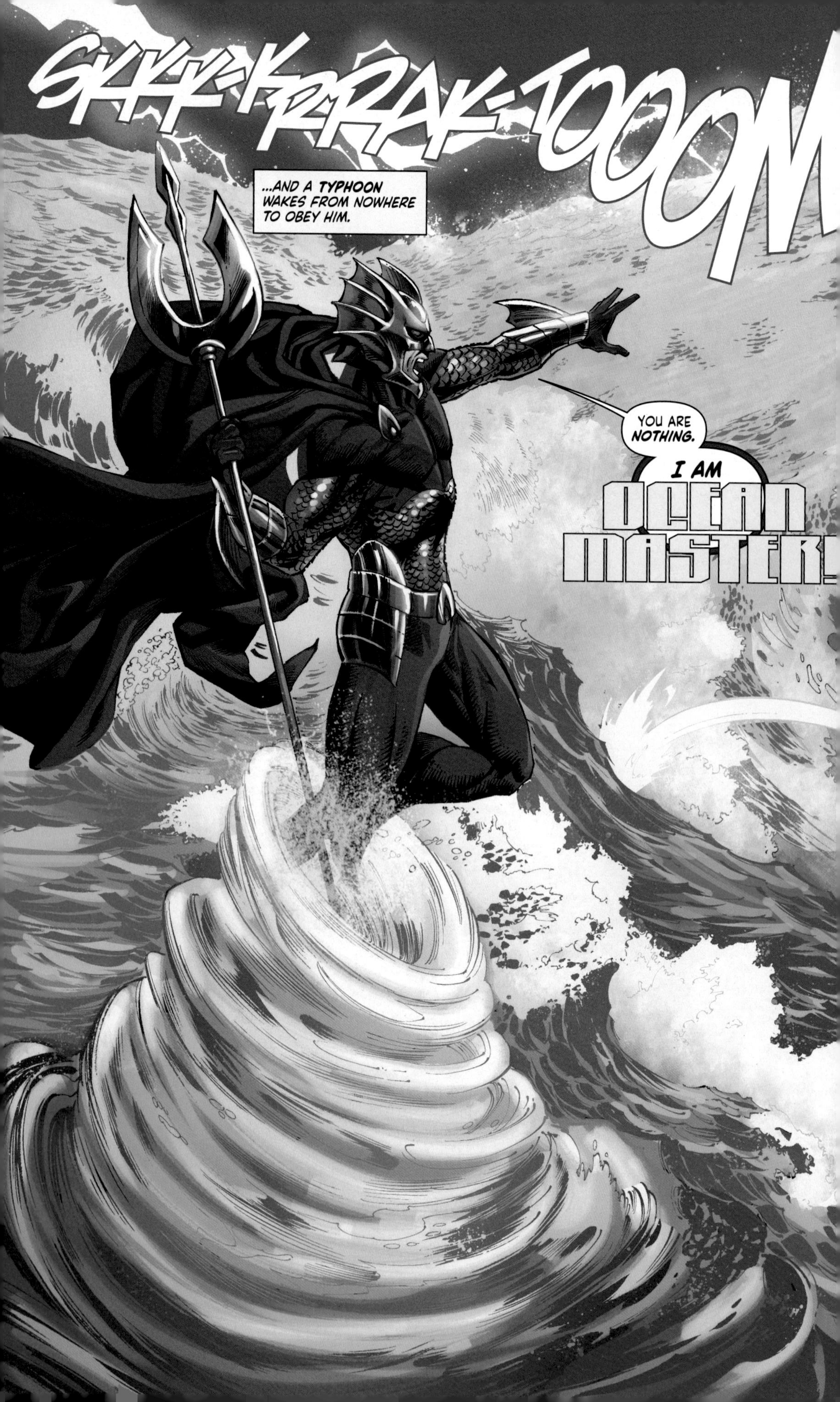

SKKK-KRRAK-TOOOM
...AND A TYPHOON WAKES FROM NOWHERE TO OBEY HIM.
YOU ARE NOTHING.
I AM OCEAN MASTER!

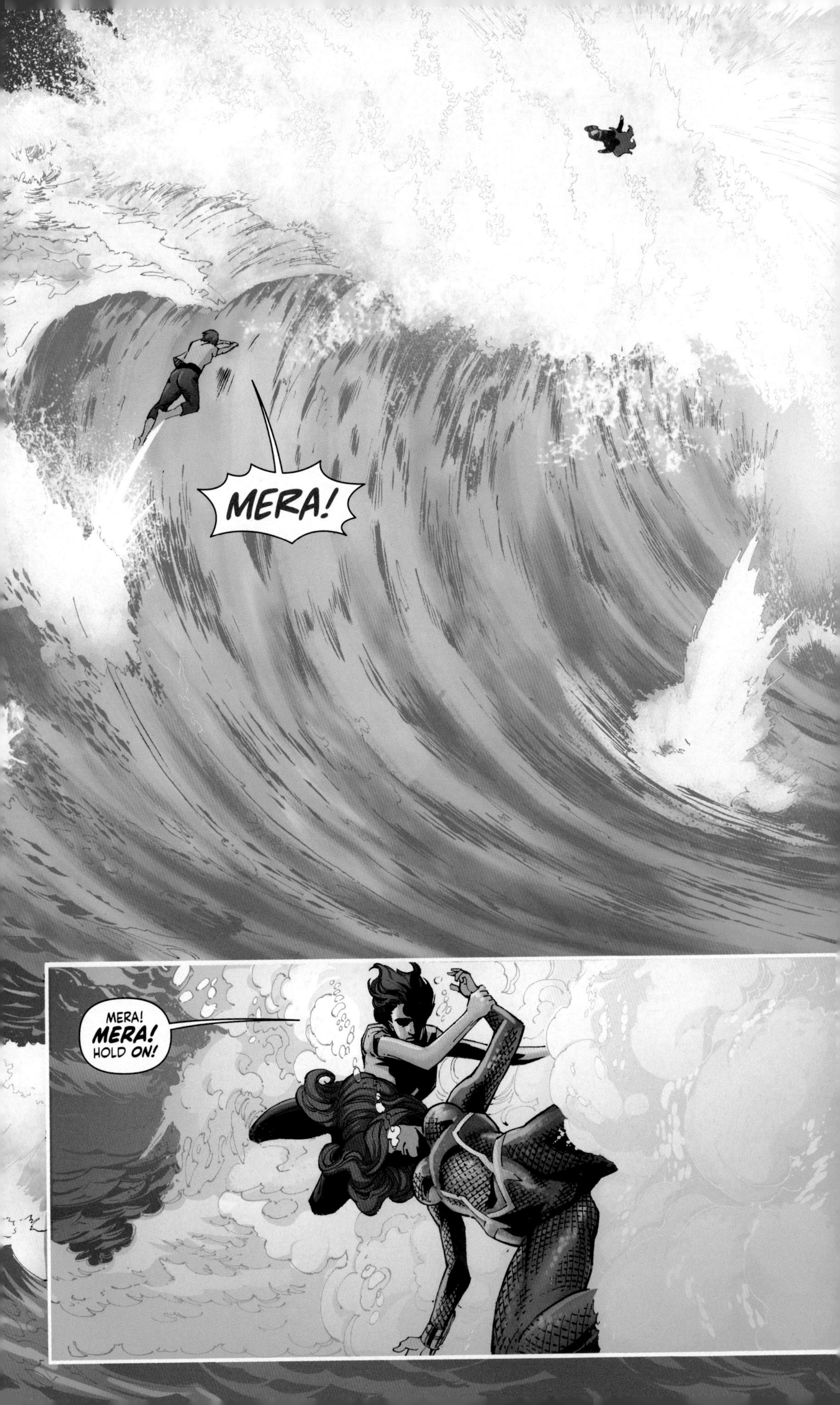
MERA!
MERA! MERA! HOLD ON!

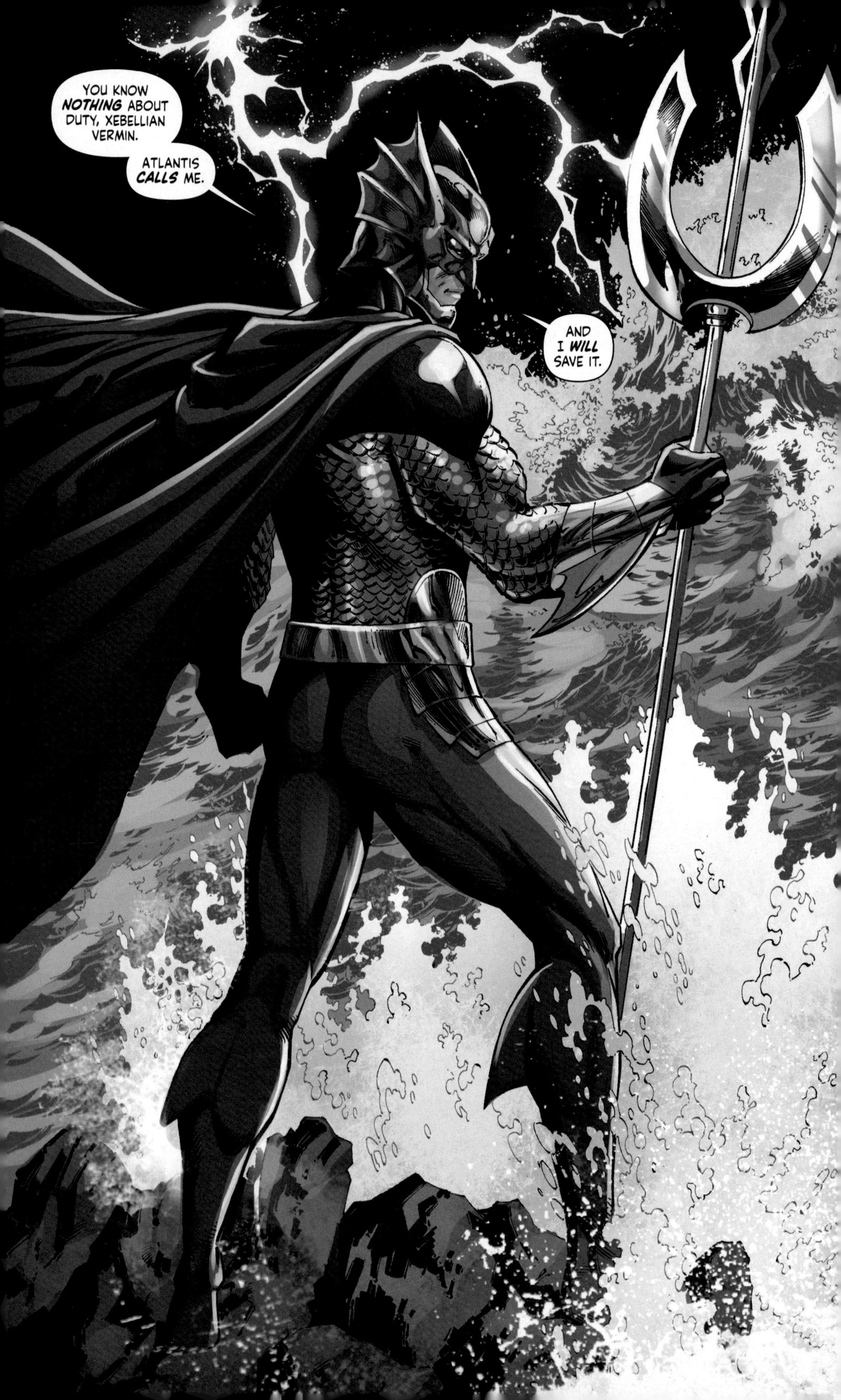

YOU KNOW **NOTHING** ABOUT DUTY, XEBELLIAN VERMIN.
ATLANTIS **CALLS** ME.
AND I **WILL** SAVE IT.

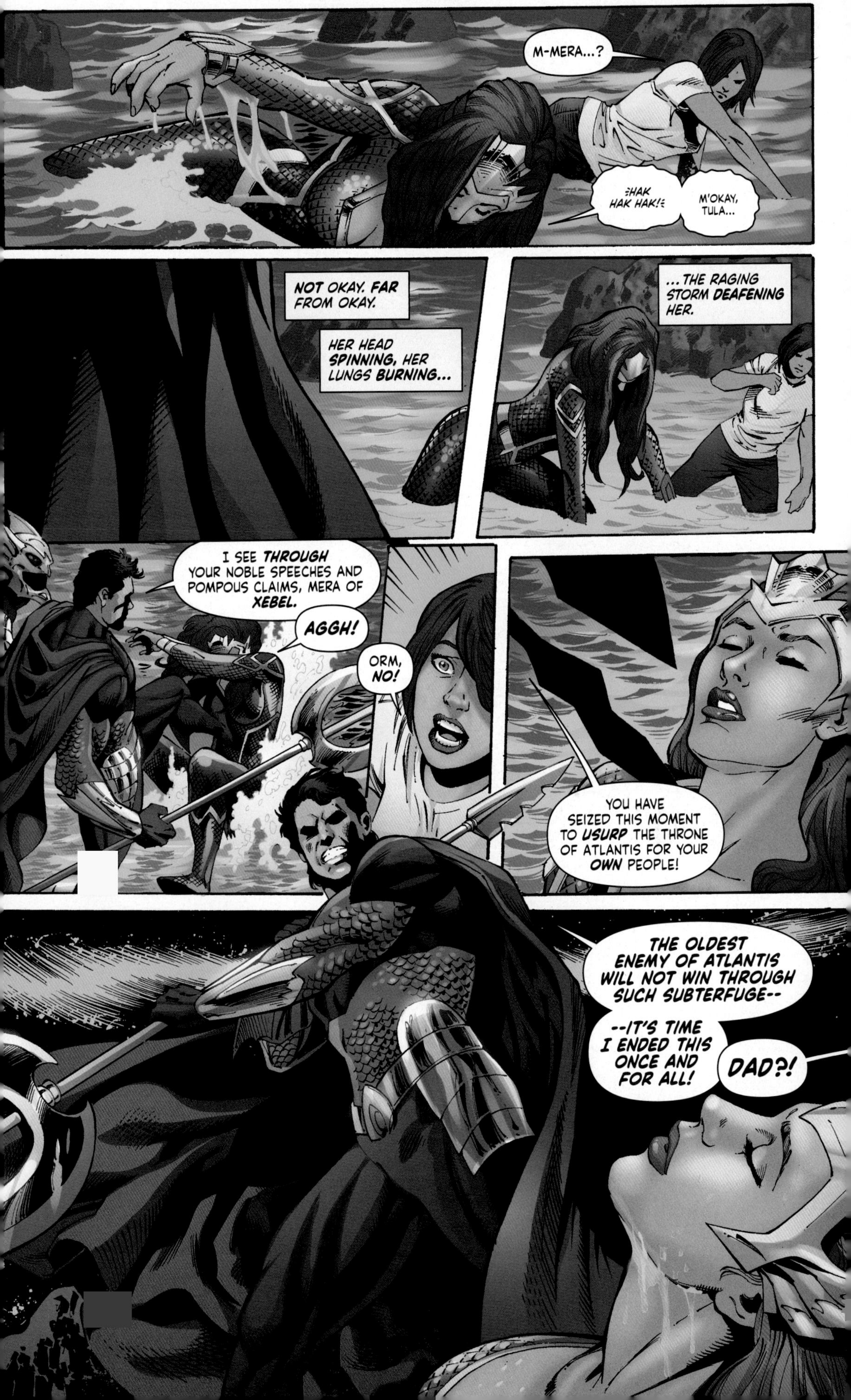
M-MERA...?
HAK HAK HAK!
M'OKAY, TULA...
NOT OKAY. FAR FROM OKAY.
HER HEAD SPINNING, HER LUNGS BURNING...
...THE RAGING STORM DEAFENING HER.
I SEE THROUGH YOUR NOBLE SPEECHES AND POMPOUS CLAIMS, MERA OF XEBEL.
AGGH!
ORM, NO!
YOU HAVE SEIZED THIS MOMENT TO USURP THE THRONE OF ATLANTIS FOR YOUR OWN PEOPLE!
THE OLDEST ENEMY OF ATLANTIS WILL NOT WIN THROUGH SUCH SUBTERFUGE--
--IT'S TIME I ENDED THIS ONCE AND FOR ALL!
DAD?!

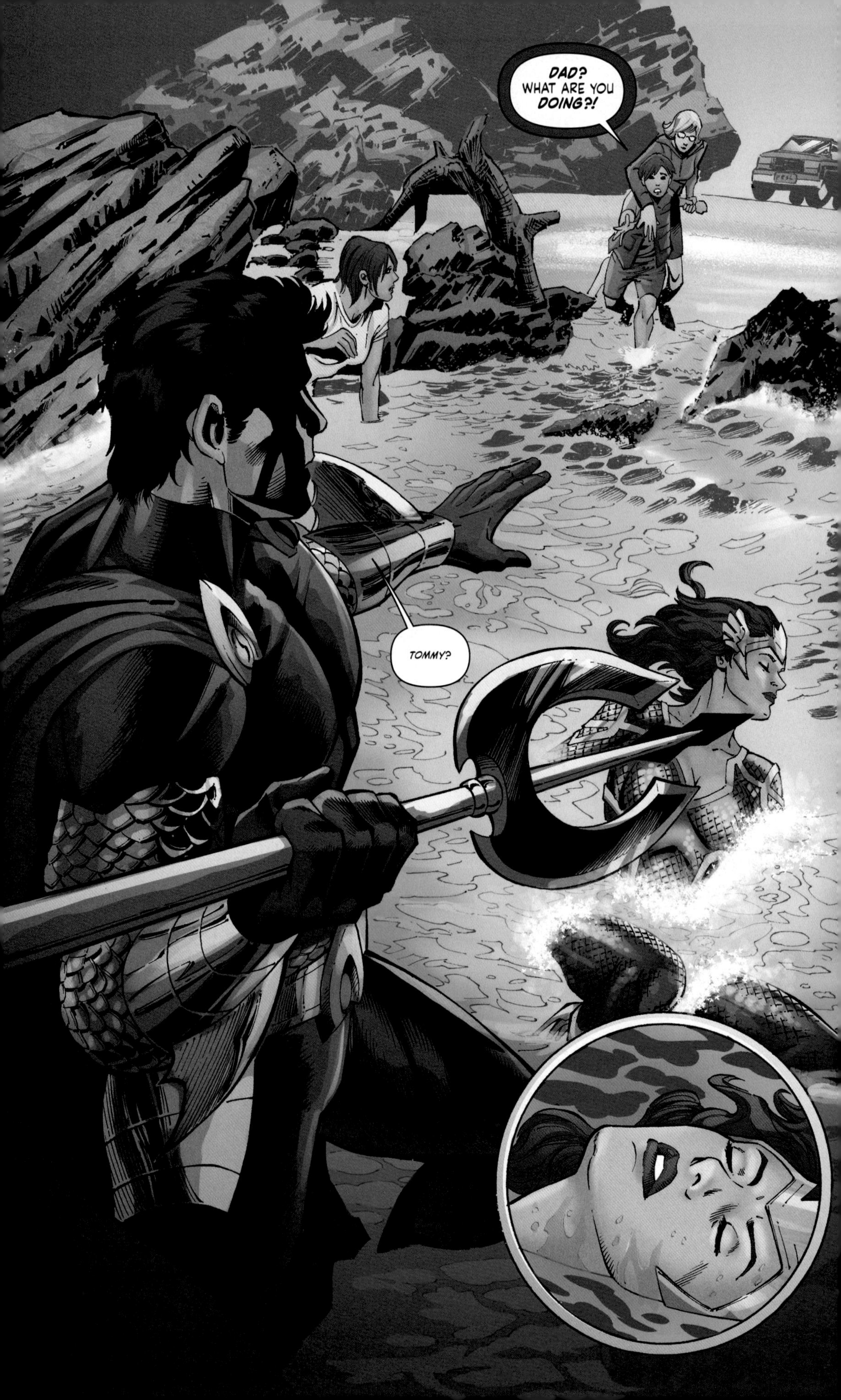
DAD? WHAT ARE YOU DOING?!
TOMMY?

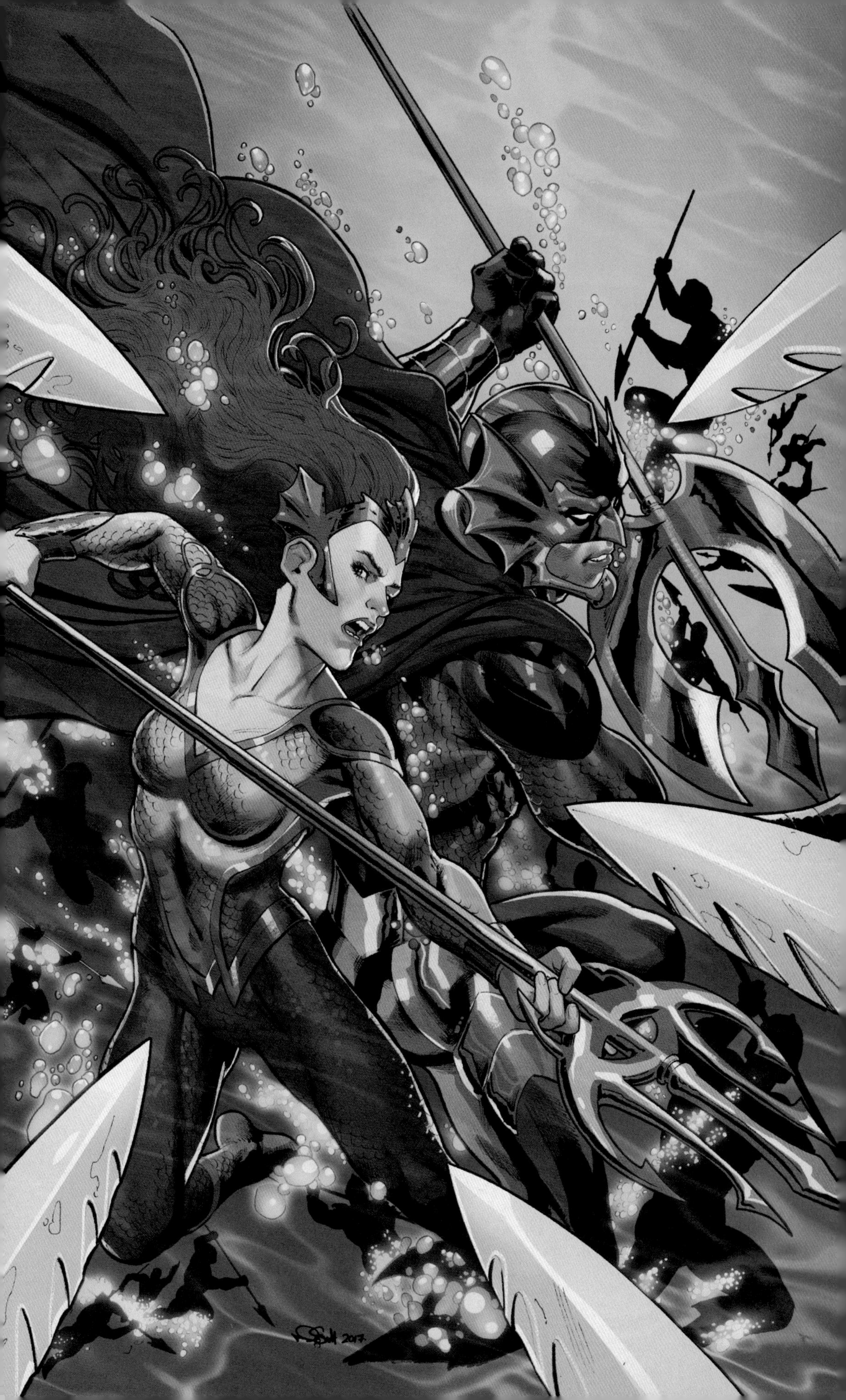

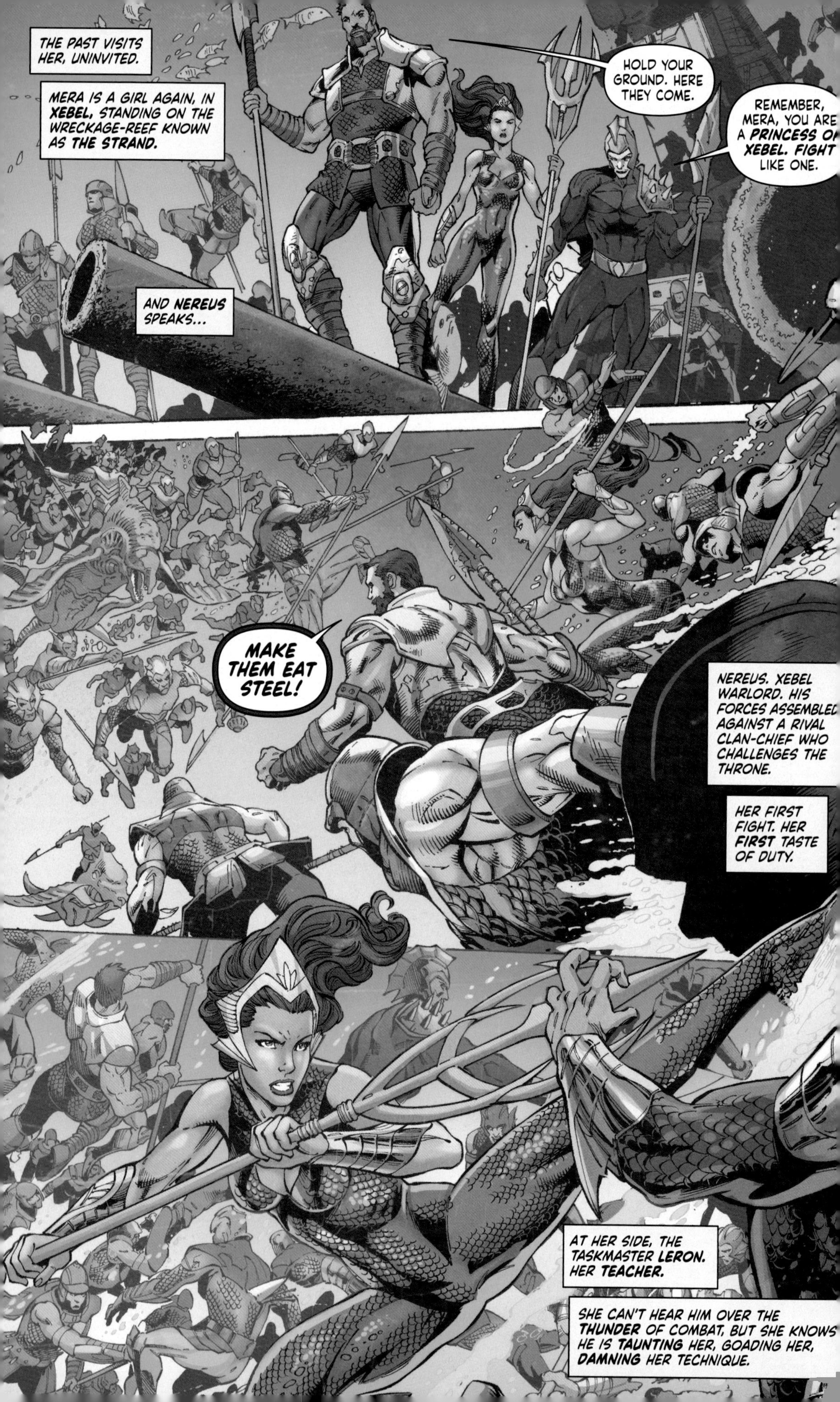

THE PAST VISITS HER, UNINVITED.
MERA IS A GIRL AGAIN, IN XEBEL, STANDING ON THE WRECKAGE-REEF KNOWN AS THE STRAND.
HOLD YOUR GROUND. HERE THEY COME.
REMEMBER, MERA, YOU ARE A PRINCESS OF XEBEL. FIGHT LIKE ONE.
AND NEREUS SPEAKS...
MAKE THEM EAT STEEL!
NEREUS. XEBEL WARLORD. HIS FORCES ASSEMBLED AGAINST A RIVAL CLAN-CHIEF WHO CHALLENGES THE THRONE.
HER FIRST FIGHT. HER FIRST TASTE OF DUTY.
AT HER SIDE, THE TASKMASTER LERON. HER TEACHER.
SHE CAN'T HEAR HIM OVER THE THUNDER OF COMBAT, BUT SHE KNOWS HE IS TAUNTING HER, GOADING HER, DAMNING HER TECHNIQUE.

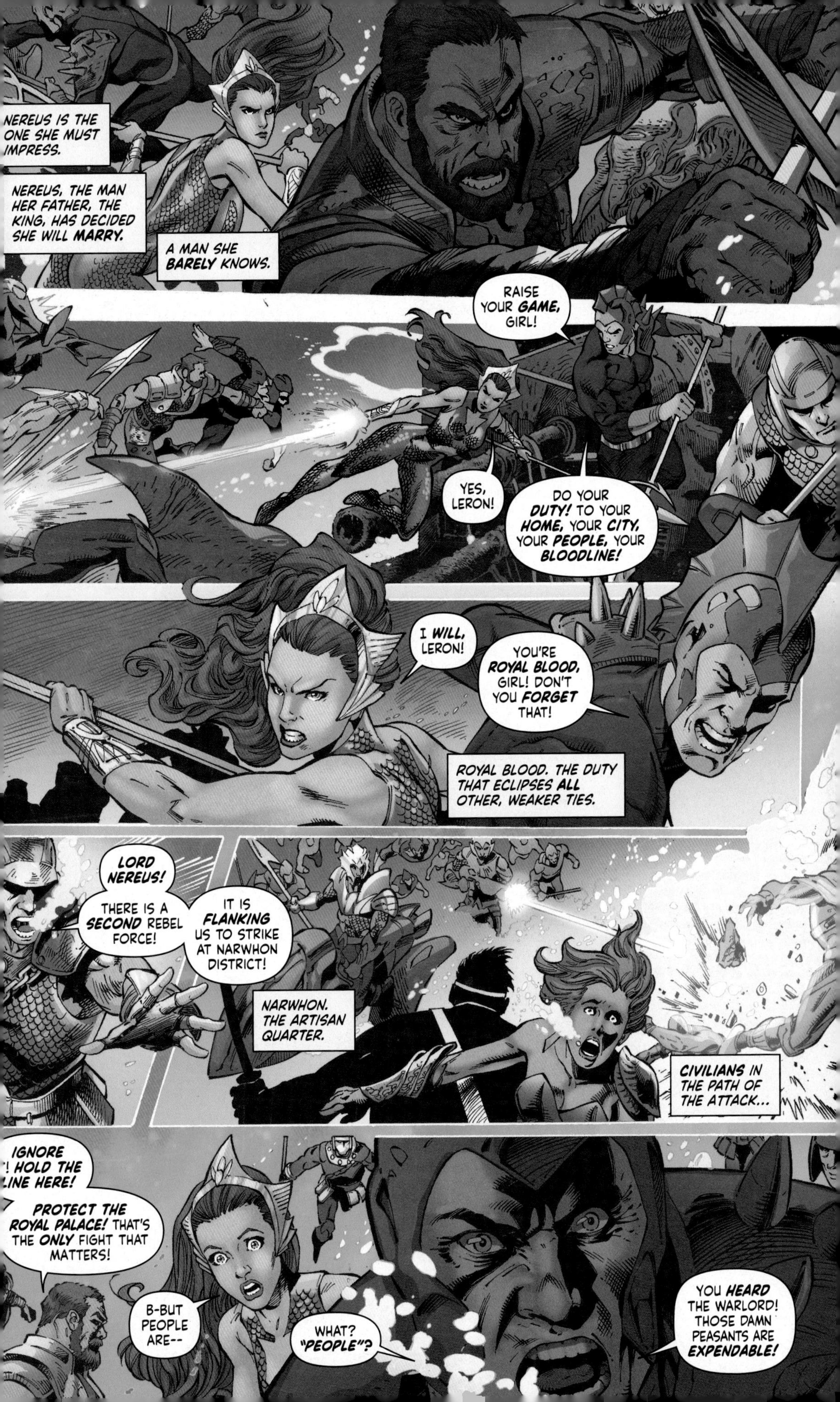
NEREUS IS THE ONE SHE MUST IMPRESS.
NEREUS, THE MAN HER FATHER, THE KING, HAS DECIDED SHE WILL MARRY.
A MAN SHE BARELY KNOWS.
RAISE YOUR GAME, GIRL!
YES, LERON!
DO YOUR DUTY! TO YOUR HOME, YOUR CITY, YOUR PEOPLE, YOUR BLOODLINE!
I WILL, LERON!
YOU'RE ROYAL BLOOD, GIRL! DON'T YOU FORGET THAT!
ROYAL BLOOD. THE DUTY THAT ECLIPSES ALL OTHER, WEAKER TIES.
LORD NEREUS!
THERE IS A SECOND REBEL FORCE!
IT IS FLANKING US TO STRIKE AT NARWHON DISTRICT!
NARWHON. THE ARTISAN QUARTER.
CIVILIANS IN THE PATH OF THE ATTACK...
IGNORE ! HOLD THE LINE HERE!
PROTECT THE ROYAL PALACE! THAT'S THE ONLY FIGHT THAT MATTERS!
B-BUT PEOPLE ARE--
WHAT? "PEOPLE"?
YOU HEARD THE WARLORD! THOSE DAMN PEASANTS ARE EXPENDABLE!

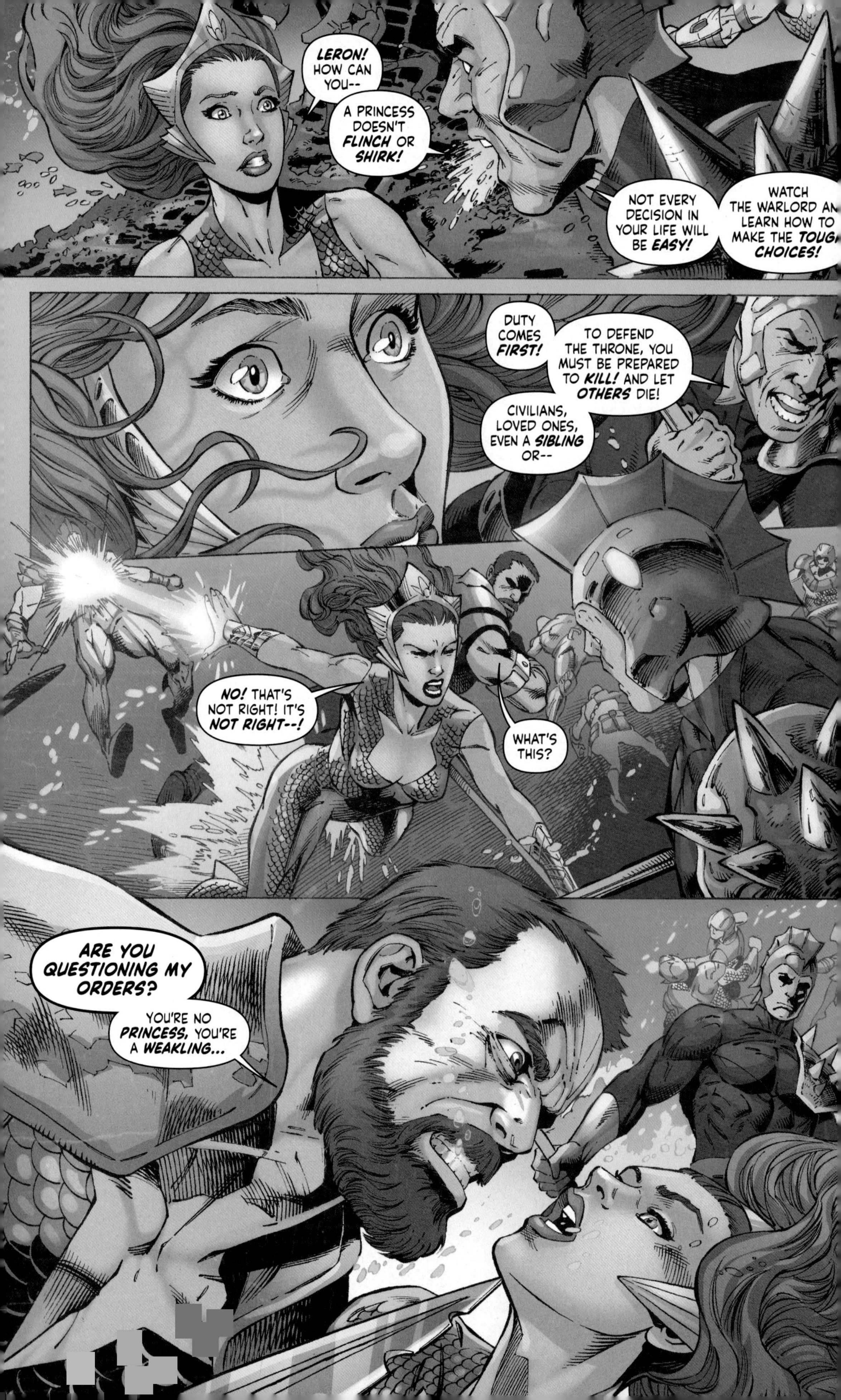
LERON! HOW CAN YOU--
A PRINCESS DOESN'T FLINCH OR SHIRK!
NOT EVERY DECISION IN YOUR LIFE WILL BE EASY!
WATCH THE WARLORD AN LEARN HOW TO MAKE THE TOUG CHOICES!
DUTY COMES FIRST!
TO DEFEND THE THRONE, YOU MUST BE PREPARED TO KILL! AND LET OTHERS DIE!
CIVILIANS, LOVED ONES, EVEN A SIBLING OR--
NO! THAT'S NOT RIGHT! IT'S NOT RIGHT--!
WHAT'S THIS?
ARE YOU QUESTIONING MY ORDERS?
YOU'RE NO PRINCESS, YOU'RE A WEAKLING...

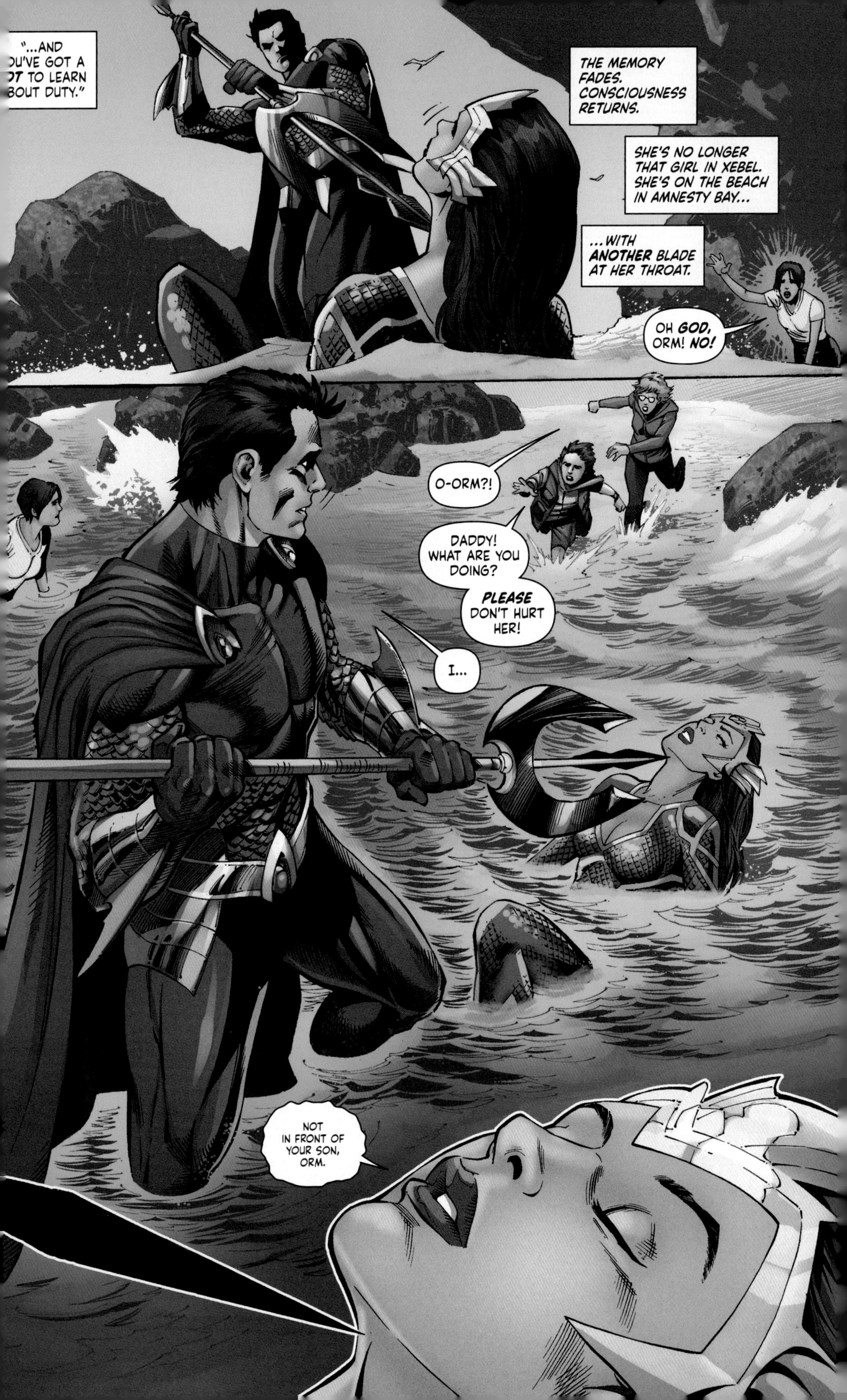
"...AND OU'VE GOT A OT TO LEARN BOUT DUTY."
THE MEMORY FADES. CONSCIOUSNESS RETURNS.
SHE'S NO LONGER THAT GIRL IN XEBEL. SHE'S ON THE BEACH IN AMNESTY BAY...
...WITH ANOTHER BLADE AT HER THROAT.
OH GOD, ORM! NO!
O-ORM?!
DADDY! WHAT ARE YOU DOING?
PLEASE DON'T HURT HER!
I...
NOT IN FRONT OF YOUR SON, ORM.

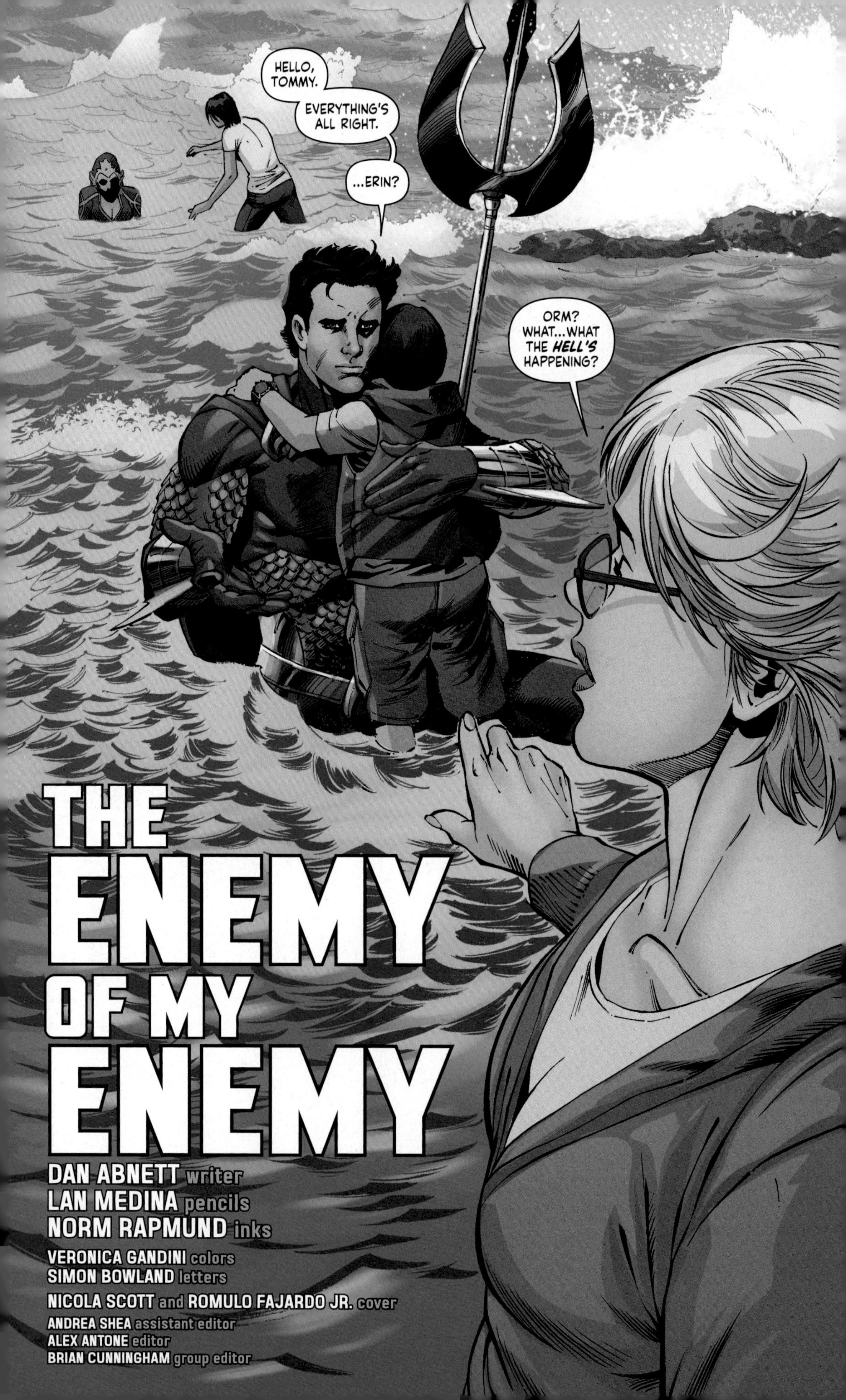
HELLO, TOMMY.
EVERYTHING'S ALL RIGHT.
...ERIN?
ORM? WHAT...WHAT THE *HELL'S* HAPPENING?
THE ENEMY OF MY ENEMY
DAN ABNETT writer
LAN MEDINA pencils
NORM RAPMUND inks
VERONICA GANDINI colors
SIMON BOWLAND letters
NICOLA SCOTT and ROMULO FAJARDO JR. cover
ANDREA SHEA assistant editor
ALEX ANTONE editor
BRIAN CUNNINGHAM group editor

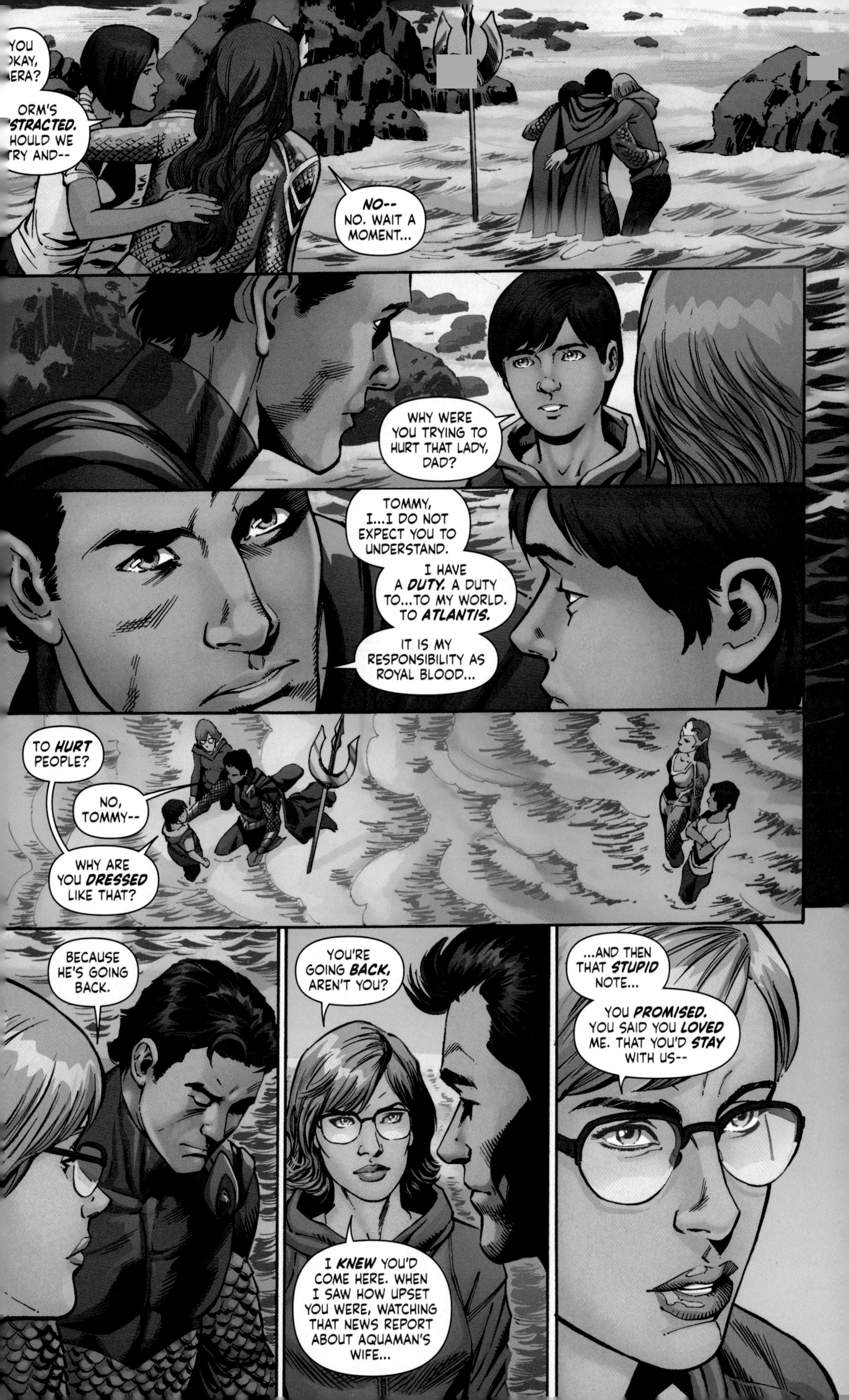
YOU OKAY, ERA?
ORM'S STRACTED. HOULD WE TRY AND--
NO-- NO. WAIT A MOMENT...
WHY WERE YOU TRYING TO HURT THAT LADY, DAD?
TOMMY, I...I DO NOT EXPECT YOU TO UNDERSTAND.
I HAVE A DUTY. A DUTY TO...TO MY WORLD. TO ATLANTIS.
IT IS MY RESPONSIBILITY AS ROYAL BLOOD...
TO HURT PEOPLE?
NO, TOMMY--
WHY ARE YOU DRESSED LIKE THAT?
BECAUSE HE'S GOING BACK.
YOU'RE GOING BACK, AREN'T YOU?
I KNEW YOU'D COME HERE. WHEN I SAW HOW UPSET YOU WERE, WATCHING THAT NEWS REPORT ABOUT AQUAMAN'S WIFE...
...AND THEN THAT STUPID NOTE...
YOU PROMISED. YOU SAID YOU LOVED ME. THAT YOU'D STAY WITH US--

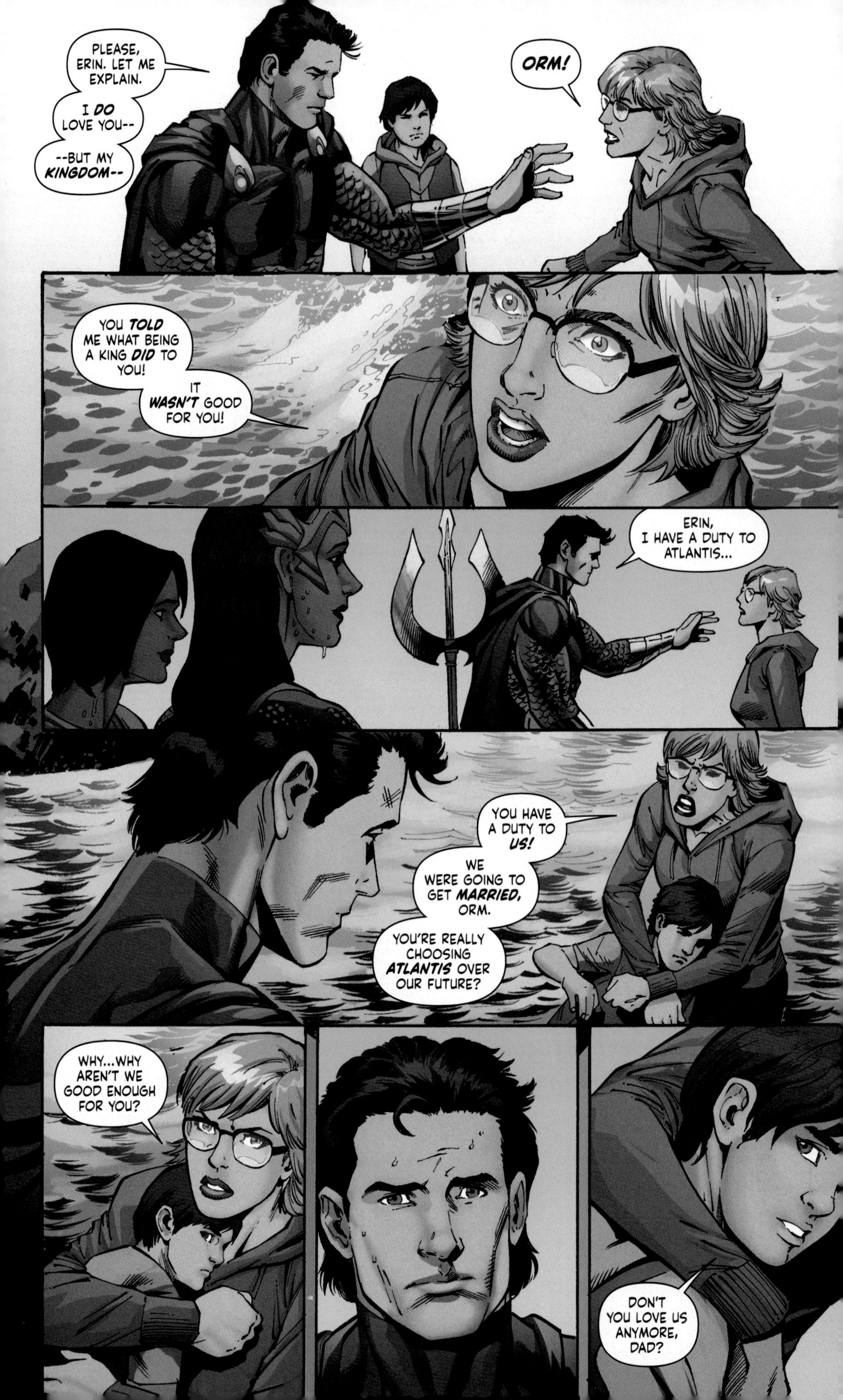
PLEASE, ERIN. LET ME EXPLAIN.
I DO LOVE YOU--
--BUT MY KINGDOM--
ORM!
YOU TOLD ME WHAT BEING A KING DID TO YOU!
IT WASN'T GOOD FOR YOU!
ERIN, I HAVE A DUTY TO ATLANTIS...
YOU HAVE A DUTY TO US!
WE WERE GOING TO GET MARRIED, ORM.
YOU'RE REALLY CHOOSING ATLANTIS OVER OUR FUTURE?
WHY...WHY AREN'T WE GOOD ENOUGH FOR YOU?
DON'T YOU LOVE US ANYMORE, DAD?

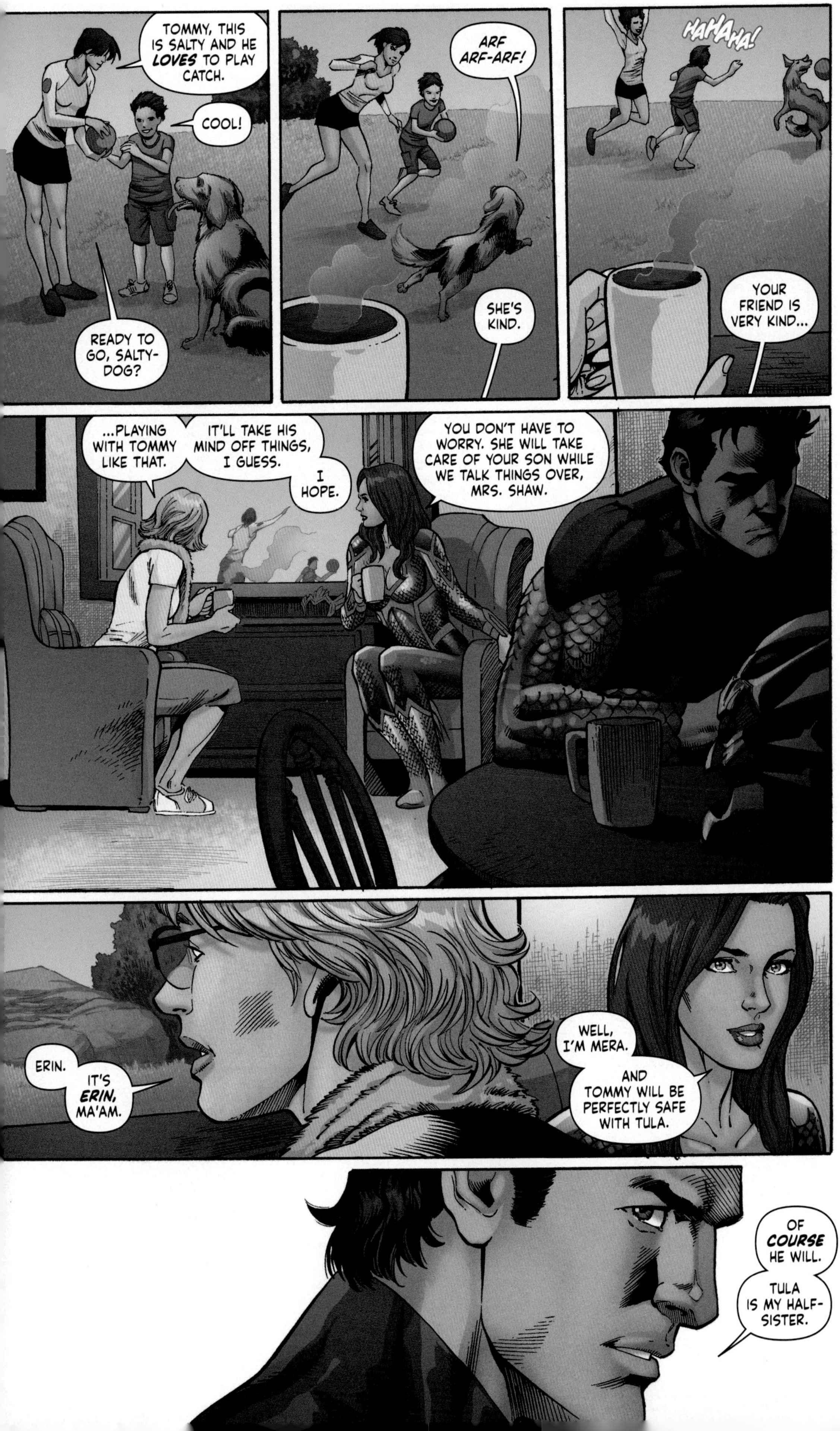
TOMMY, THIS IS SALTY AND HE **LOVES** TO PLAY CATCH.
COOL!
READY TO GO, SALTY-DOG?
ARF ARF-ARF!
SHE'S KIND.
HAHAHA!
YOUR FRIEND IS VERY KIND...
...PLAYING WITH TOMMY LIKE THAT.
IT'LL TAKE HIS MIND OFF THINGS, I GUESS.
I HOPE.
YOU DON'T HAVE TO WORRY. SHE WILL TAKE CARE OF YOUR SON WHILE WE TALK THINGS OVER, MRS. SHAW.
ERIN.
IT'S ***ERIN,*** MA'AM.
WELL, I'M MERA.
AND TOMMY WILL BE PERFECTLY SAFE WITH TULA.
OF ***COURSE*** HE WILL.
TULA IS MY HALF-SISTER.

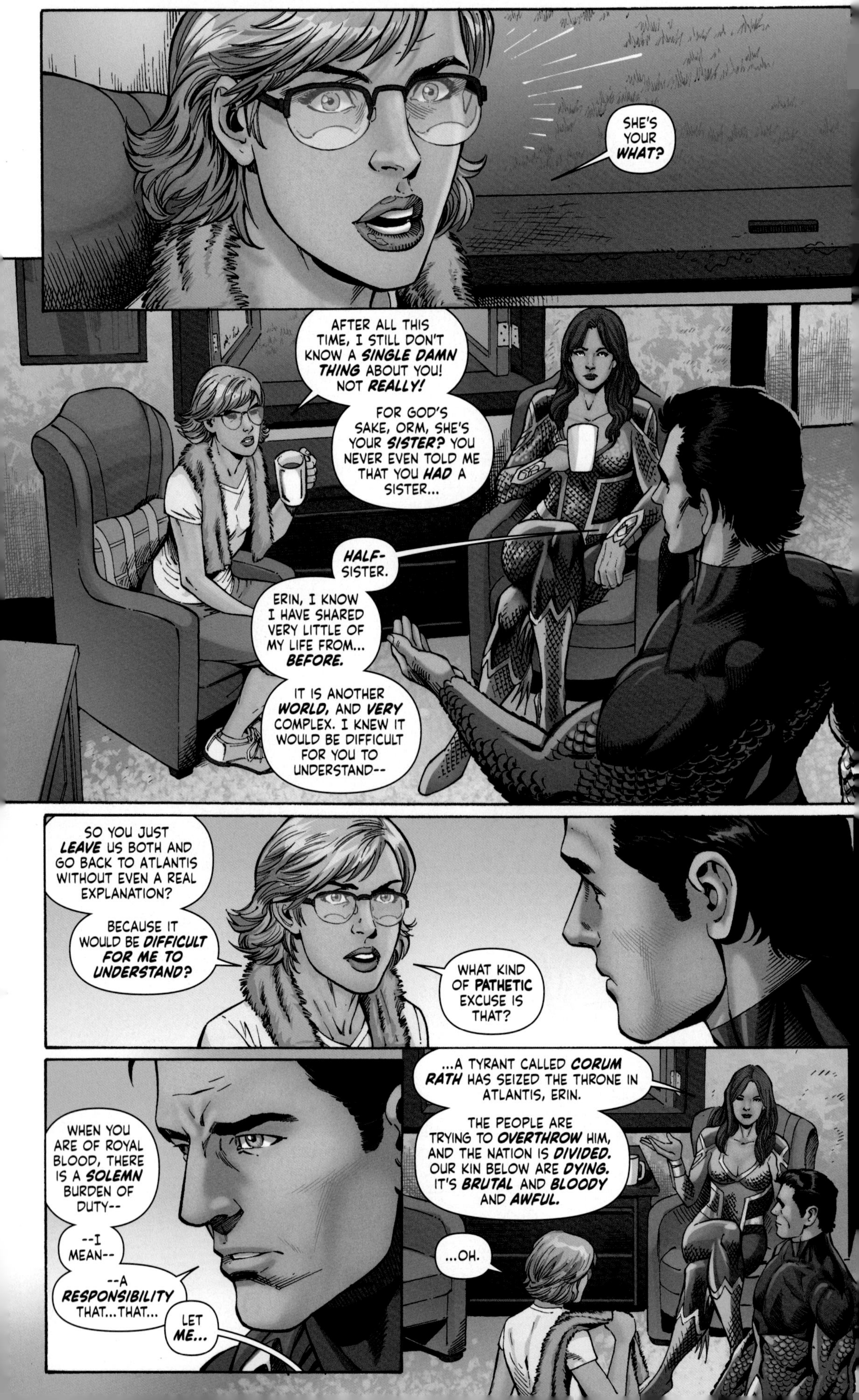
SHE'S YOUR WHAT?
AFTER ALL THIS TIME, I STILL DON'T KNOW A SINGLE DAMN THING ABOUT YOU! NOT REALLY!
FOR GOD'S SAKE, ORM, SHE'S YOUR SISTER? YOU NEVER EVEN TOLD ME THAT YOU HAD A SISTER...
HALF-SISTER.
ERIN, I KNOW I HAVE SHARED VERY LITTLE OF MY LIFE FROM... BEFORE.
IT IS ANOTHER WORLD, AND VERY COMPLEX. I KNEW IT WOULD BE DIFFICULT FOR YOU TO UNDERSTAND--
SO YOU JUST LEAVE US BOTH AND GO BACK TO ATLANTIS WITHOUT EVEN A REAL EXPLANATION?
BECAUSE IT WOULD BE DIFFICULT FOR ME TO UNDERSTAND?
WHAT KIND OF PATHETIC EXCUSE IS THAT?
WHEN YOU ARE OF ROYAL BLOOD, THERE IS A SOLEMN BURDEN OF DUTY--
--I MEAN--
--A RESPONSIBILITY THAT...THAT...
LET ME...
...A TYRANT CALLED CORUM RATH HAS SEIZED THE THRONE IN ATLANTIS, ERIN.
THE PEOPLE ARE TRYING TO OVERTHROW HIM, AND THE NATION IS DIVIDED. OUR KIN BELOW ARE DYING. IT'S BRUTAL AND BLOODY AND AWFUL.
...OH.

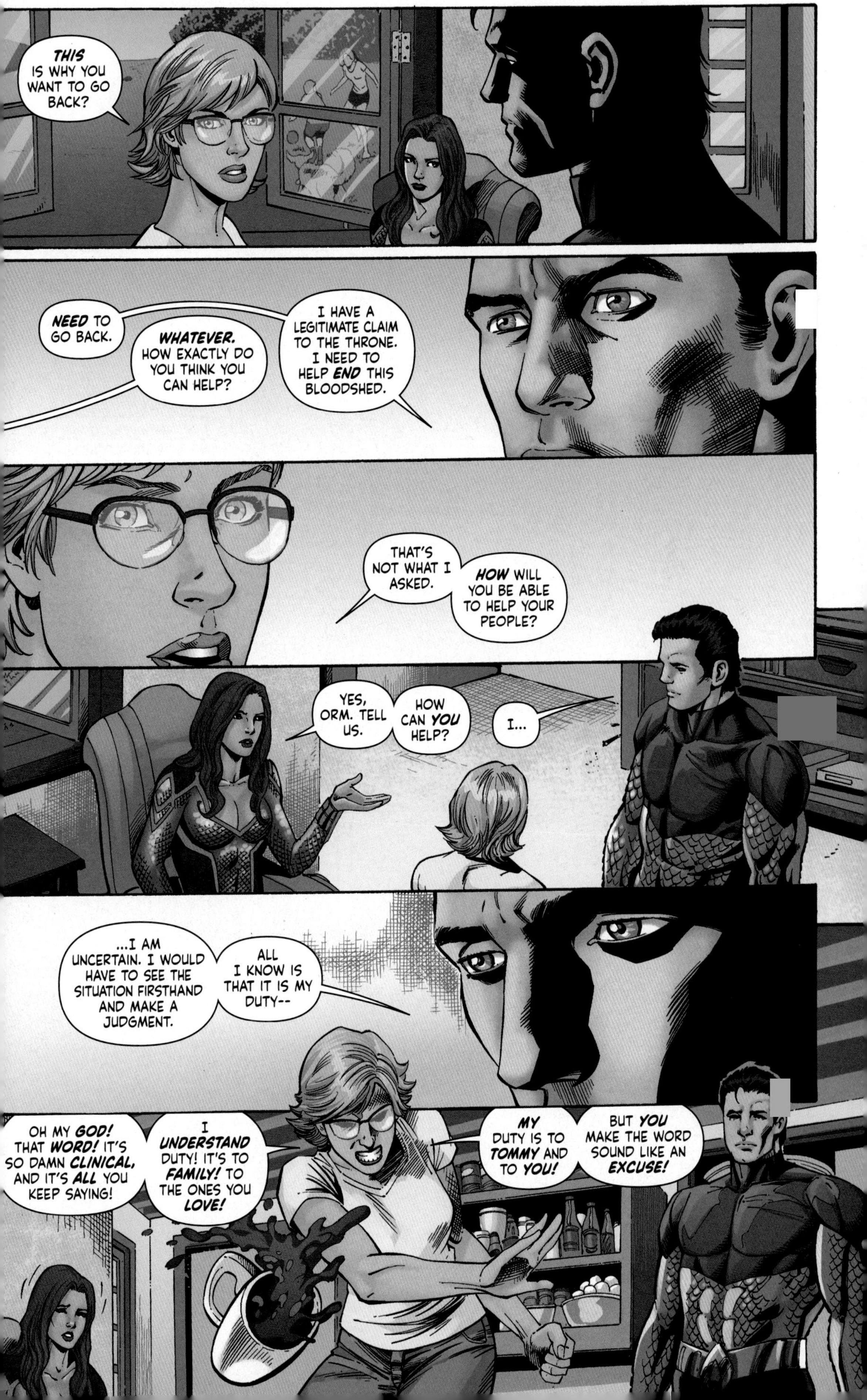
THIS IS WHY YOU WANT TO GO BACK?
I HAVE A LEGITIMATE CLAIM TO THE THRONE. I NEED TO HELP END THIS BLOODSHED.
NEED TO GO BACK.
WHATEVER. HOW EXACTLY DO YOU THINK YOU CAN HELP?
THAT'S NOT WHAT I ASKED.
HOW WILL YOU BE ABLE TO HELP YOUR PEOPLE?
YES, ORM. TELL US.
HOW CAN YOU HELP?
I...
...I AM UNCERTAIN. I WOULD HAVE TO SEE THE SITUATION FIRSTHAND AND MAKE A JUDGMENT.
ALL I KNOW IS THAT IT IS MY DUTY--
OH MY GOD! THAT WORD! IT'S SO DAMN CLINICAL, AND IT'S ALL YOU KEEP SAYING!
I UNDERSTAND DUTY! IT'S TO FAMILY! TO THE ONES YOU LOVE!
MY DUTY IS TO TOMMY AND TO YOU!
BUT YOU MAKE THE WORD SOUND LIKE AN EXCUSE!

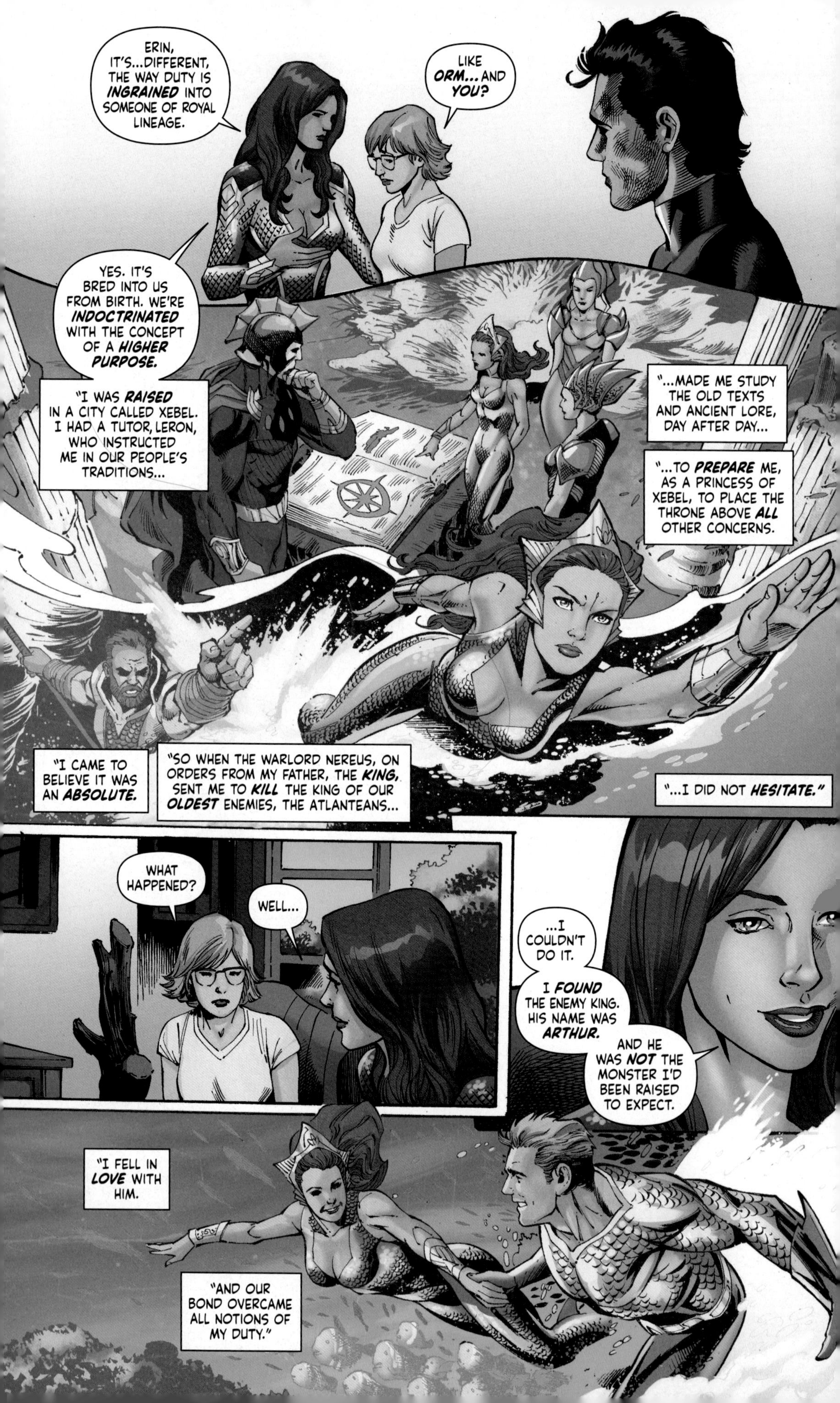
ERIN, IT'S...DIFFERENT, THE WAY DUTY IS *INGRAINED* INTO SOMEONE OF ROYAL LINEAGE.
LIKE *ORM...* AND *YOU?*
YES. IT'S BRED INTO US FROM BIRTH. WE'RE *INDOCTRINATED* WITH THE CONCEPT OF A *HIGHER PURPOSE.*
"I WAS *RAISED* IN A CITY CALLED XEBEL. I HAD A TUTOR, LERON, WHO INSTRUCTED ME IN OUR PEOPLE'S TRADITIONS...
"...MADE ME STUDY THE OLD TEXTS AND ANCIENT LORE, DAY AFTER DAY...
"...TO *PREPARE* ME, AS A PRINCESS OF XEBEL, TO PLACE THE THRONE ABOVE *ALL* OTHER CONCERNS.
"I CAME TO BELIEVE IT WAS AN *ABSOLUTE.*
"SO WHEN THE WARLORD NEREUS, ON ORDERS FROM MY FATHER, THE *KING,* SENT ME TO *KILL* THE KING OF OUR *OLDEST* ENEMIES, THE ATLANTEANS...
"...I DID NOT *HESITATE.*"
WHAT HAPPENED?
WELL...
...I COULDN'T DO IT.
I *FOUND* THE ENEMY KING. HIS NAME WAS *ARTHUR.*
AND HE WAS *NOT* THE MONSTER I'D BEEN RAISED TO EXPECT.
"I FELL IN *LOVE* WITH HIM.
"AND OUR BOND OVERCAME ALL NOTIONS OF MY DUTY."

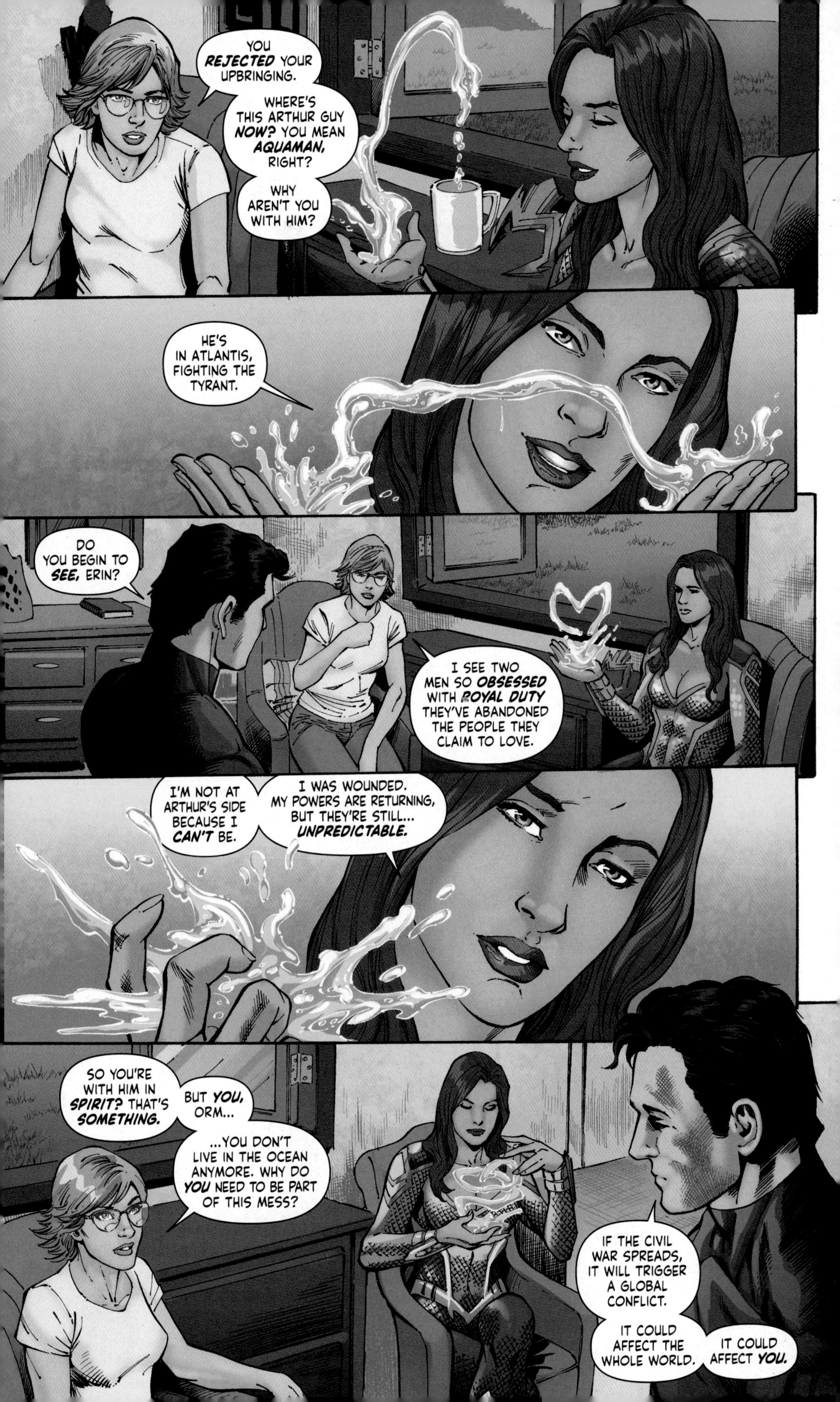

YOU **REJECTED** YOUR UPBRINGING.
WHERE'S THIS ARTHUR GUY **NOW?** YOU MEAN **AQUAMAN,** RIGHT?
WHY AREN'T YOU WITH HIM?
HE'S IN ATLANTIS, FIGHTING THE TYRANT.
DO YOU BEGIN TO **SEE,** ERIN?
I SEE TWO MEN SO **OBSESSED** WITH **ROYAL DUTY** THEY'VE ABANDONED THE PEOPLE THEY CLAIM TO LOVE.
I'M NOT AT ARTHUR'S SIDE BECAUSE I **CAN'T** BE.
I WAS WOUNDED. MY POWERS ARE RETURNING, BUT THEY'RE STILL... **UNPREDICTABLE.**
SO YOU'RE WITH HIM IN **SPIRIT?** THAT'S **SOMETHING.**
BUT **YOU,** ORM...
...YOU DON'T LIVE IN THE OCEAN ANYMORE. WHY DO **YOU** NEED TO BE PART OF THIS MESS?
IF THE CIVIL WAR SPREADS, IT WILL TRIGGER A GLOBAL CONFLICT.
IT COULD AFFECT THE WHOLE WORLD.
IT COULD AFFECT **YOU.**

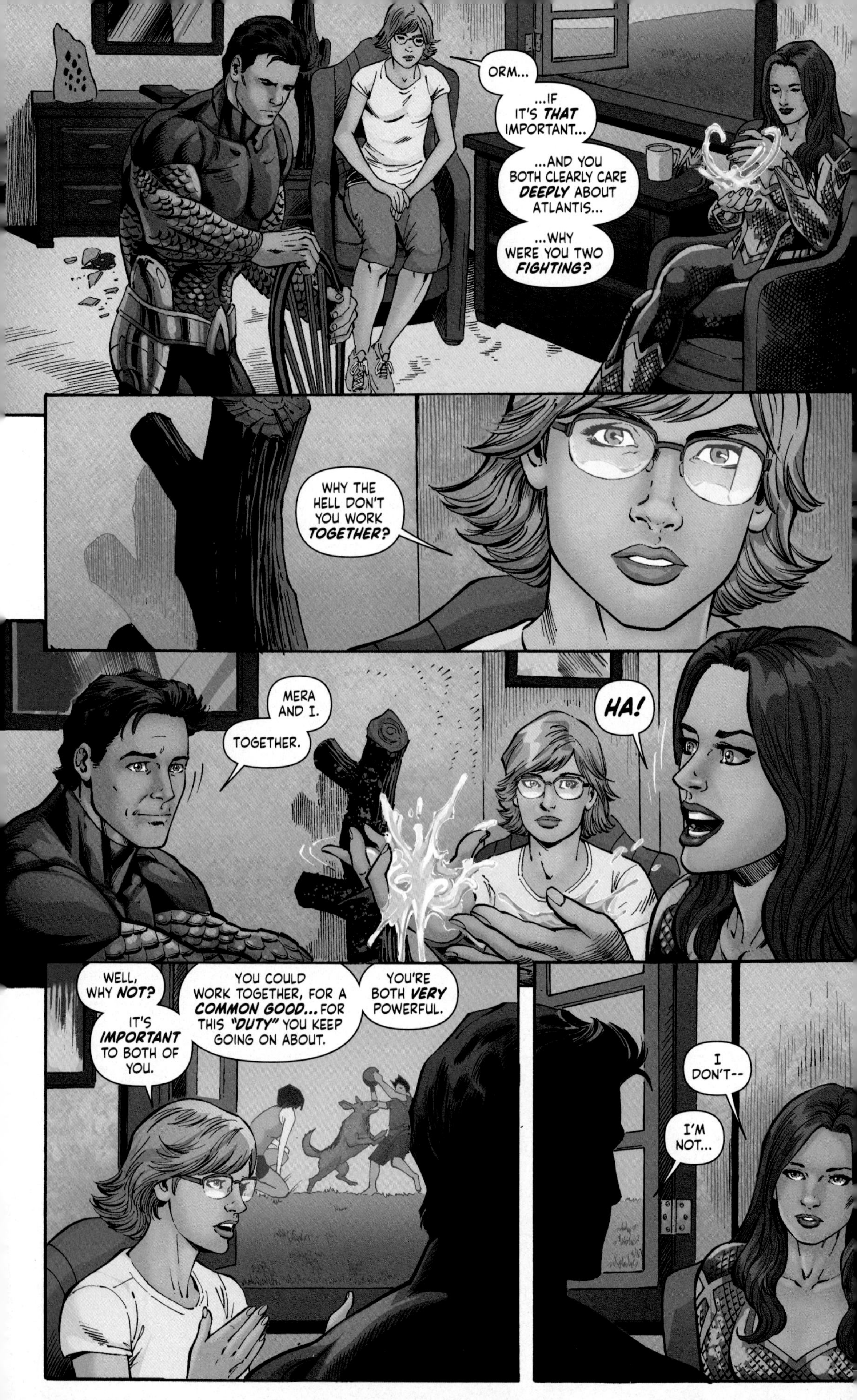
ORM...
...IF IT'S THAT IMPORTANT...
...AND YOU BOTH CLEARLY CARE DEEPLY ABOUT ATLANTIS...
...WHY WERE YOU TWO FIGHTING?
WHY THE HELL DON'T YOU WORK TOGETHER?
MERA AND I.
TOGETHER.
HA!
WELL, WHY NOT?
IT'S IMPORTANT TO BOTH OF YOU.
YOU COULD WORK TOGETHER, FOR A COMMON GOOD... FOR THIS "DUTY" YOU KEEP GOING ON ABOUT.
YOU'RE BOTH VERY POWERFUL.
I DON'T--
I'M NOT...

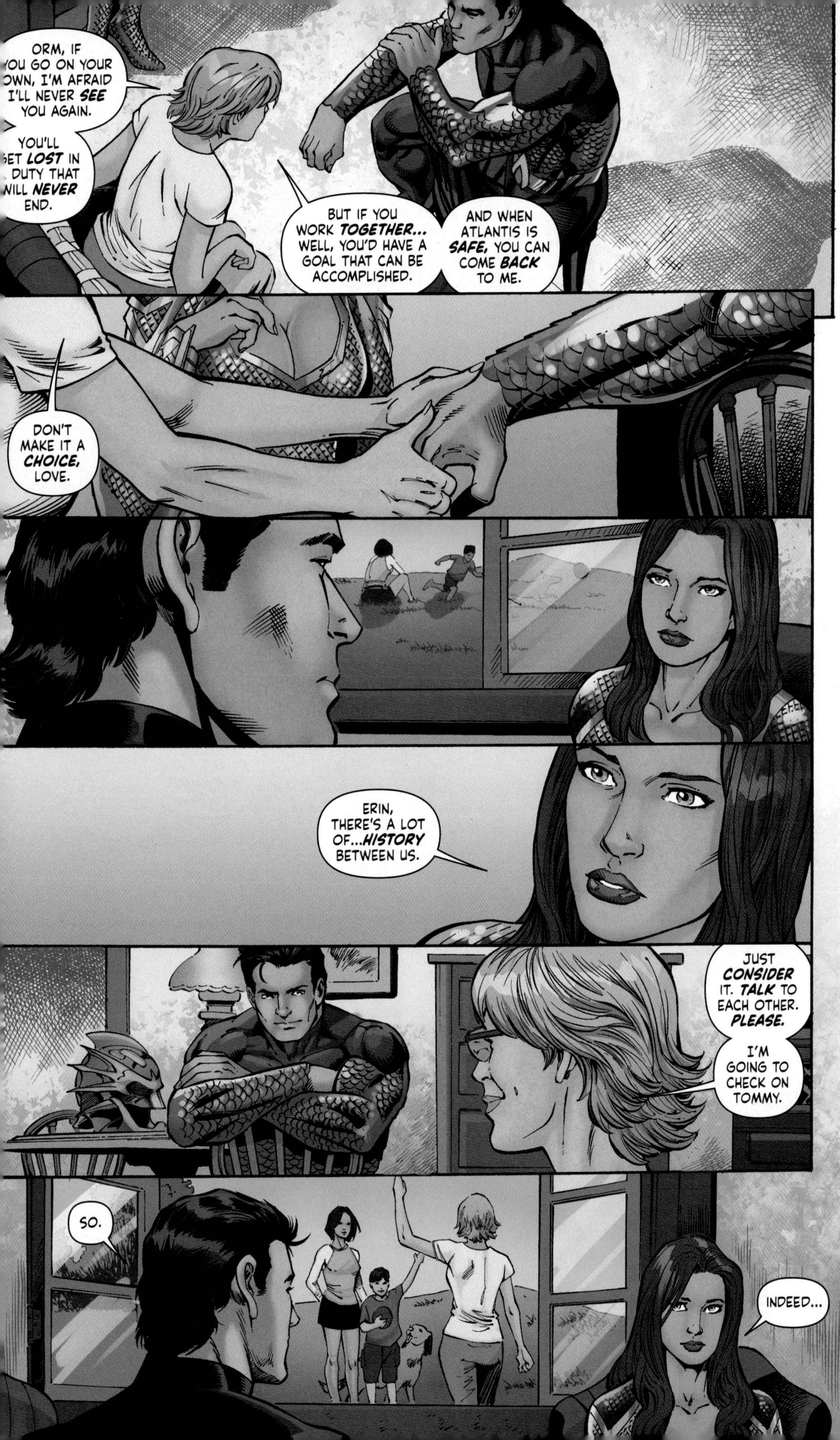
ORM, IF OU GO ON YOUR WN, I'M AFRAID I'LL NEVER SEE YOU AGAIN.
YOU'LL ET LOST IN DUTY THAT WILL NEVER END.
BUT IF YOU WORK TOGETHER... WELL, YOU'D HAVE A GOAL THAT CAN BE ACCOMPLISHED.
AND WHEN ATLANTIS IS SAFE, YOU CAN COME BACK TO ME.
DON'T MAKE IT A CHOICE, LOVE.
ERIN, THERE'S A LOT OF...HISTORY BETWEEN US.
JUST CONSIDER IT. TALK TO EACH OTHER. PLEASE.
I'M GOING TO CHECK ON TOMMY.
SO.
INDEED...

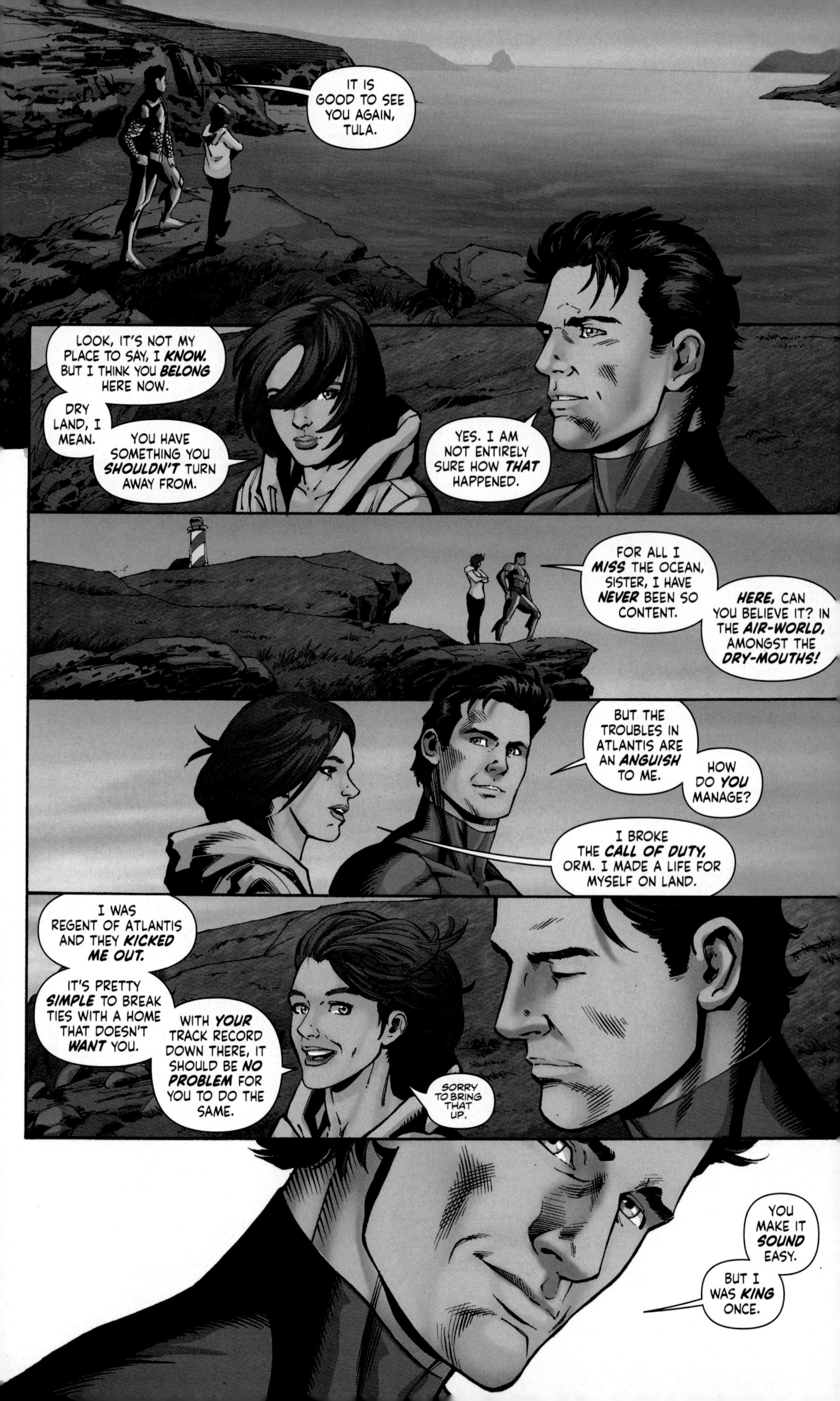

IT IS GOOD TO SEE YOU AGAIN, TULA.
LOOK, IT'S NOT MY PLACE TO SAY, I KNOW. BUT I THINK YOU BELONG HERE NOW.
DRY LAND, I MEAN.
YOU HAVE SOMETHING YOU SHOULDN'T TURN AWAY FROM.
YES. I AM NOT ENTIRELY SURE HOW THAT HAPPENED.
FOR ALL I MISS THE OCEAN, SISTER, I HAVE NEVER BEEN SO CONTENT.
HERE, CAN YOU BELIEVE IT? IN THE AIR-WORLD, AMONGST THE DRY-MOUTHS!
BUT THE TROUBLES IN ATLANTIS ARE AN ANGUISH TO ME.
HOW DO YOU MANAGE?
I BROKE THE CALL OF DUTY, ORM. I MADE A LIFE FOR MYSELF ON LAND.
I WAS REGENT OF ATLANTIS AND THEY KICKED ME OUT.
IT'S PRETTY SIMPLE TO BREAK TIES WITH A HOME THAT DOESN'T WANT YOU.
WITH YOUR TRACK RECORD DOWN THERE, IT SHOULD BE NO PROBLEM FOR YOU TO DO THE SAME.
SORRY TO BRING THAT UP.
YOU MAKE IT SOUND EASY.
BUT I WAS KING ONCE.

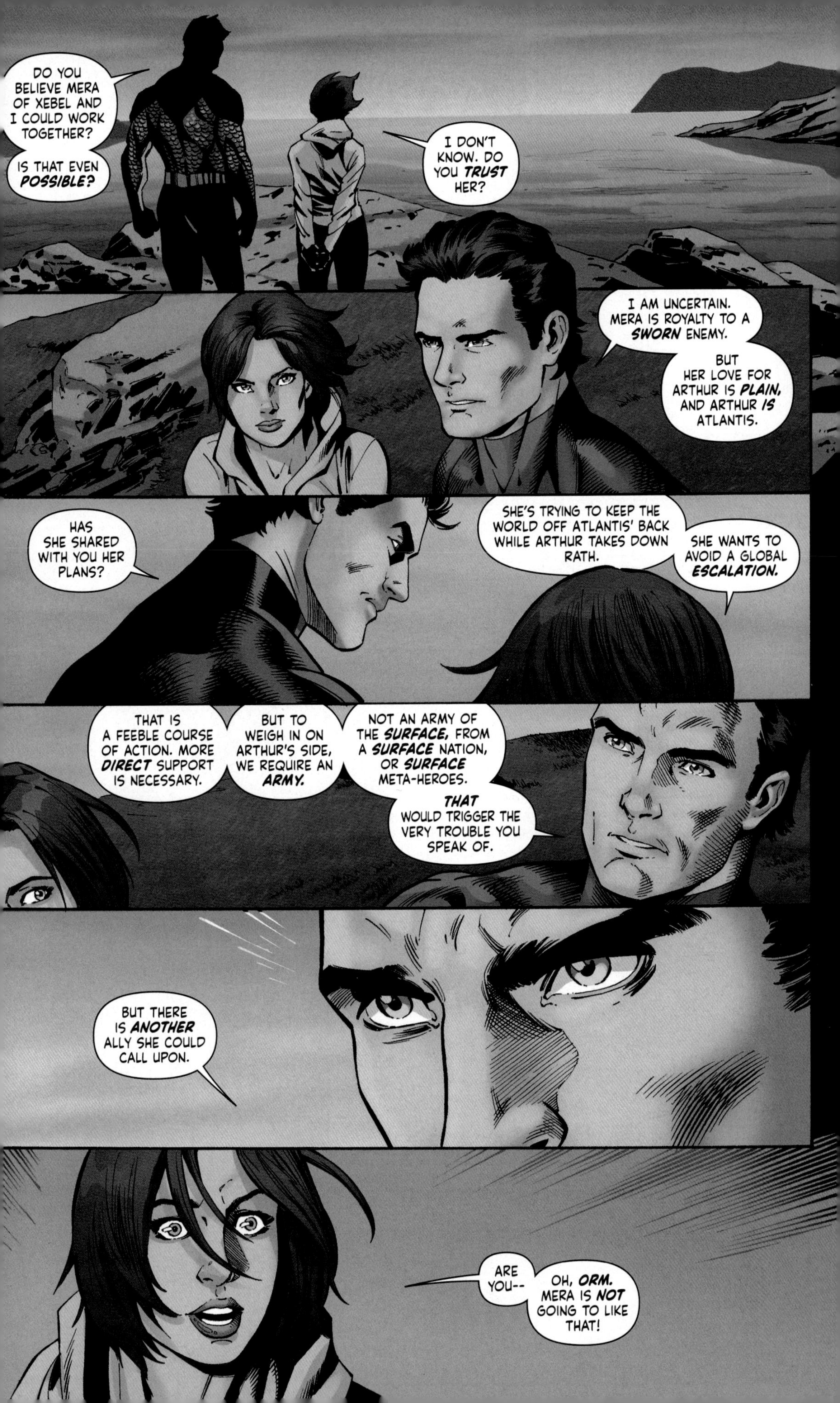
DO YOU BELIEVE MERA OF XEBEL AND I COULD WORK TOGETHER?
IS THAT EVEN ***POSSIBLE?***
I DON'T KNOW. DO YOU ***TRUST*** HER?
I AM UNCERTAIN. MERA IS ROYALTY TO A ***SWORN*** ENEMY.
BUT HER LOVE FOR ARTHUR IS ***PLAIN,*** AND ARTHUR ***IS*** ATLANTIS.
HAS SHE SHARED WITH YOU HER PLANS?
SHE'S TRYING TO KEEP THE WORLD OFF ATLANTIS' BACK WHILE ARTHUR TAKES DOWN RATH.
SHE WANTS TO AVOID A GLOBAL ***ESCALATION.***
THAT IS A FEEBLE COURSE OF ACTION. MORE ***DIRECT*** SUPPORT IS NECESSARY.
BUT TO WEIGH IN ON ARTHUR'S SIDE, WE REQUIRE AN ***ARMY.***
NOT AN ARMY OF THE ***SURFACE,*** FROM A ***SURFACE*** NATION, OR ***SURFACE*** META-HEROES.
THAT WOULD TRIGGER THE VERY TROUBLE YOU SPEAK OF.
BUT THERE IS ***ANOTHER*** ALLY SHE COULD CALL UPON.
ARE YOU--
OH, ***ORM.*** MERA IS ***NOT*** GOING TO LIKE THAT!

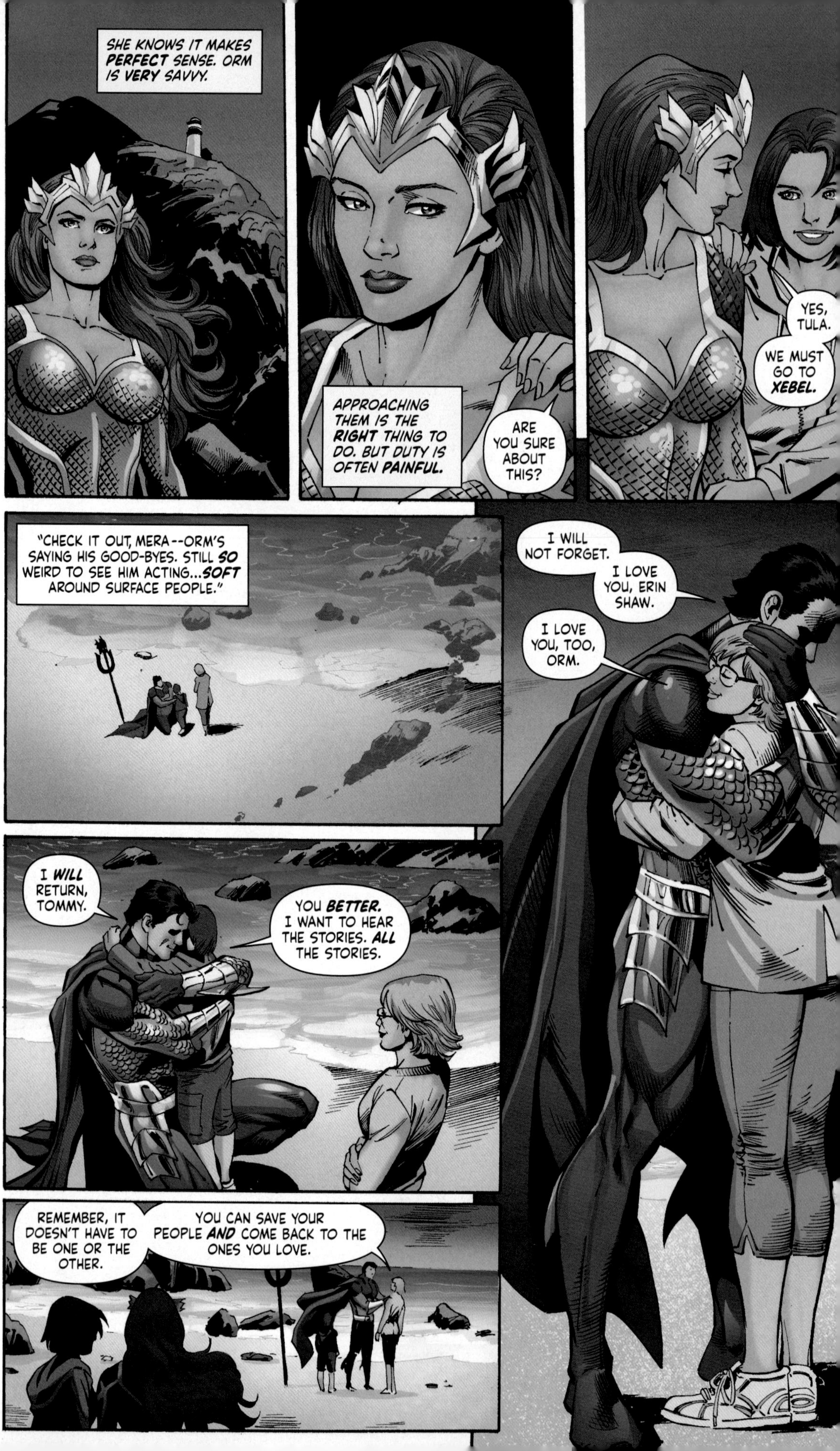

SHE KNOWS IT MAKES PERFECT SENSE. ORM IS VERY SAVVY.
APPROACHING THEM IS THE RIGHT THING TO DO. BUT DUTY IS OFTEN PAINFUL.
ARE YOU SURE ABOUT THIS?
YES, TULA.
WE MUST GO TO XEBEL.
"CHECK IT OUT, MERA--ORM'S SAYING HIS GOOD-BYES. STILL SO WEIRD TO SEE HIM ACTING...SOFT AROUND SURFACE PEOPLE."
I WILL RETURN, TOMMY.
YOU BETTER. I WANT TO HEAR THE STORIES. ALL THE STORIES.
REMEMBER, IT DOESN'T HAVE TO BE ONE OR THE OTHER.
YOU CAN SAVE YOUR PEOPLE AND COME BACK TO THE ONES YOU LOVE.
I WILL NOT FORGET.
I LOVE YOU, ERIN SHAW.
I LOVE YOU, TOO, ORM.

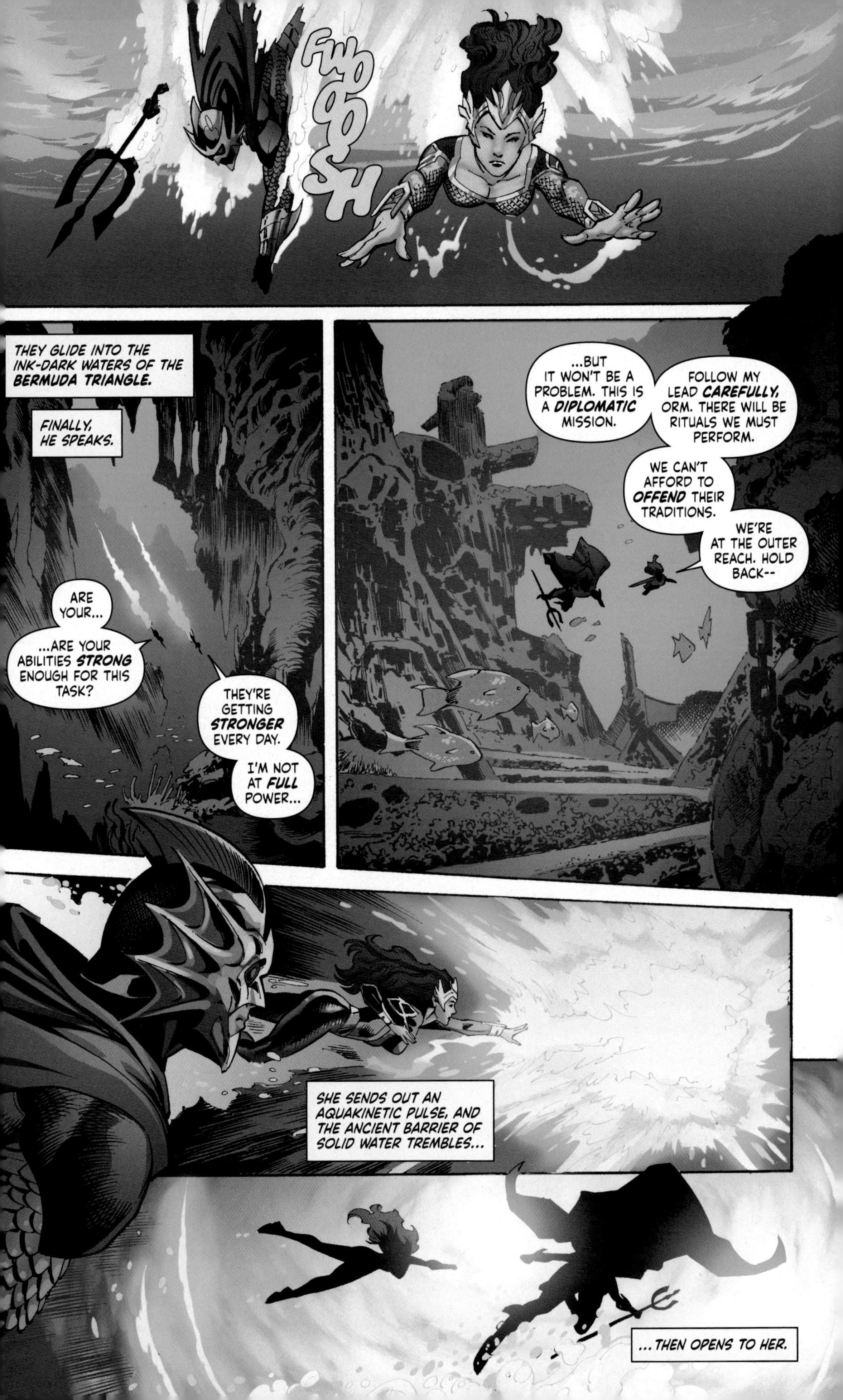
FWOOOSH
THEY GLIDE INTO THE INK-DARK WATERS OF THE BERMUDA TRIANGLE.
FINALLY, HE SPEAKS.
ARE YOUR...
...ARE YOUR ABILITIES STRONG ENOUGH FOR THIS TASK?
THEY'RE GETTING STRONGER EVERY DAY.
I'M NOT AT FULL POWER...
...BUT IT WON'T BE A PROBLEM. THIS IS A DIPLOMATIC MISSION.
FOLLOW MY LEAD CAREFULLY, ORM. THERE WILL BE RITUALS WE MUST PERFORM.
WE CAN'T AFFORD TO OFFEND THEIR TRADITIONS.
WE'RE AT THE OUTER REACH. HOLD BACK--
SHE SENDS OUT AN AQUAKINETIC PULSE, AND THE ANCIENT BARRIER OF SOLID WATER TREMBLES...
...THEN OPENS TO HER.

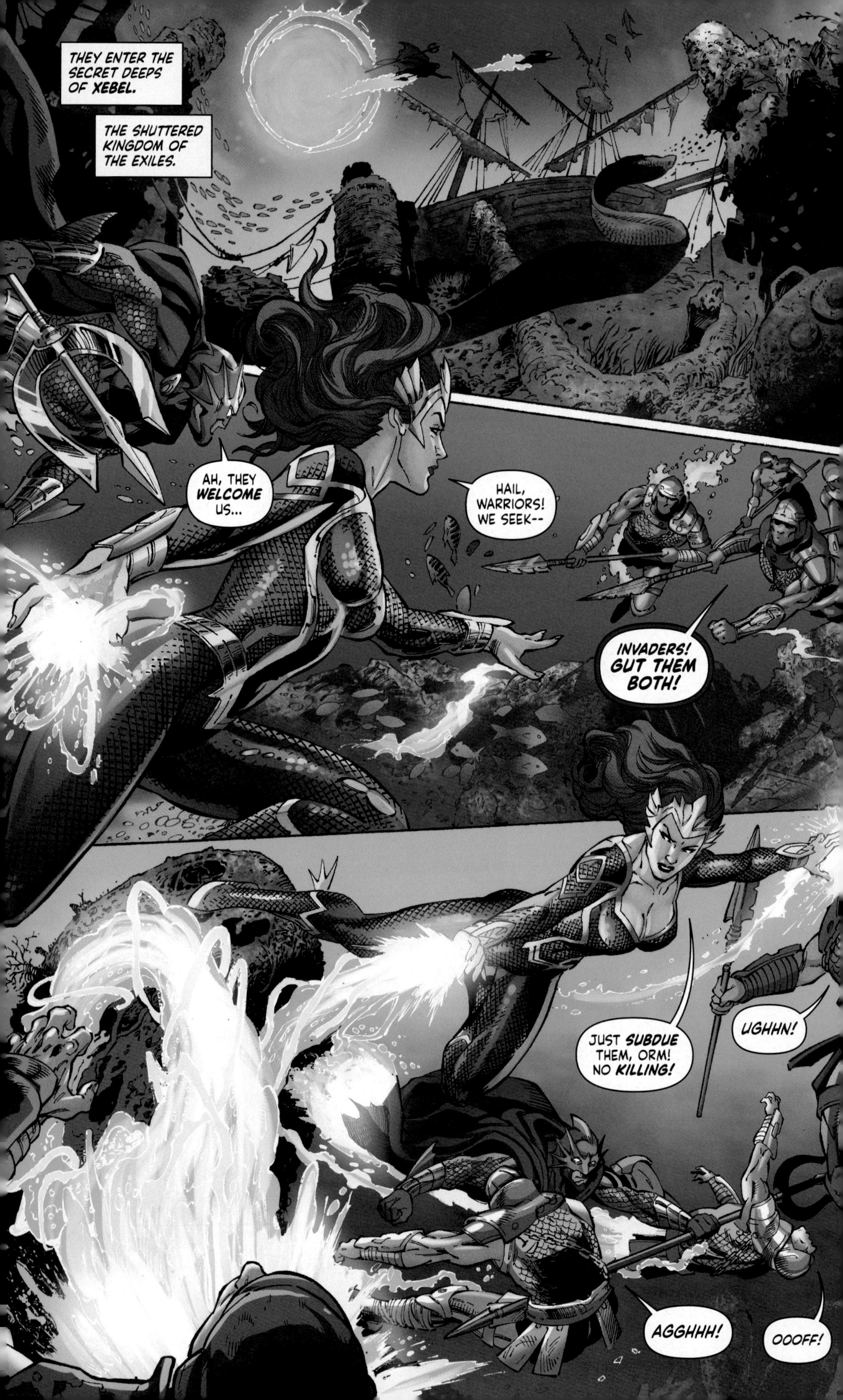
THEY ENTER THE SECRET DEEPS OF XEBEL.
THE SHUTTERED KINGDOM OF THE EXILES.
AH, THEY WELCOME US...
HAIL, WARRIORS! WE SEEK--
INVADERS! GUT THEM BOTH!
JUST SUBDUE THEM, ORM! NO KILLING!
UGHHN!
AGGHHH!
OOOFF!

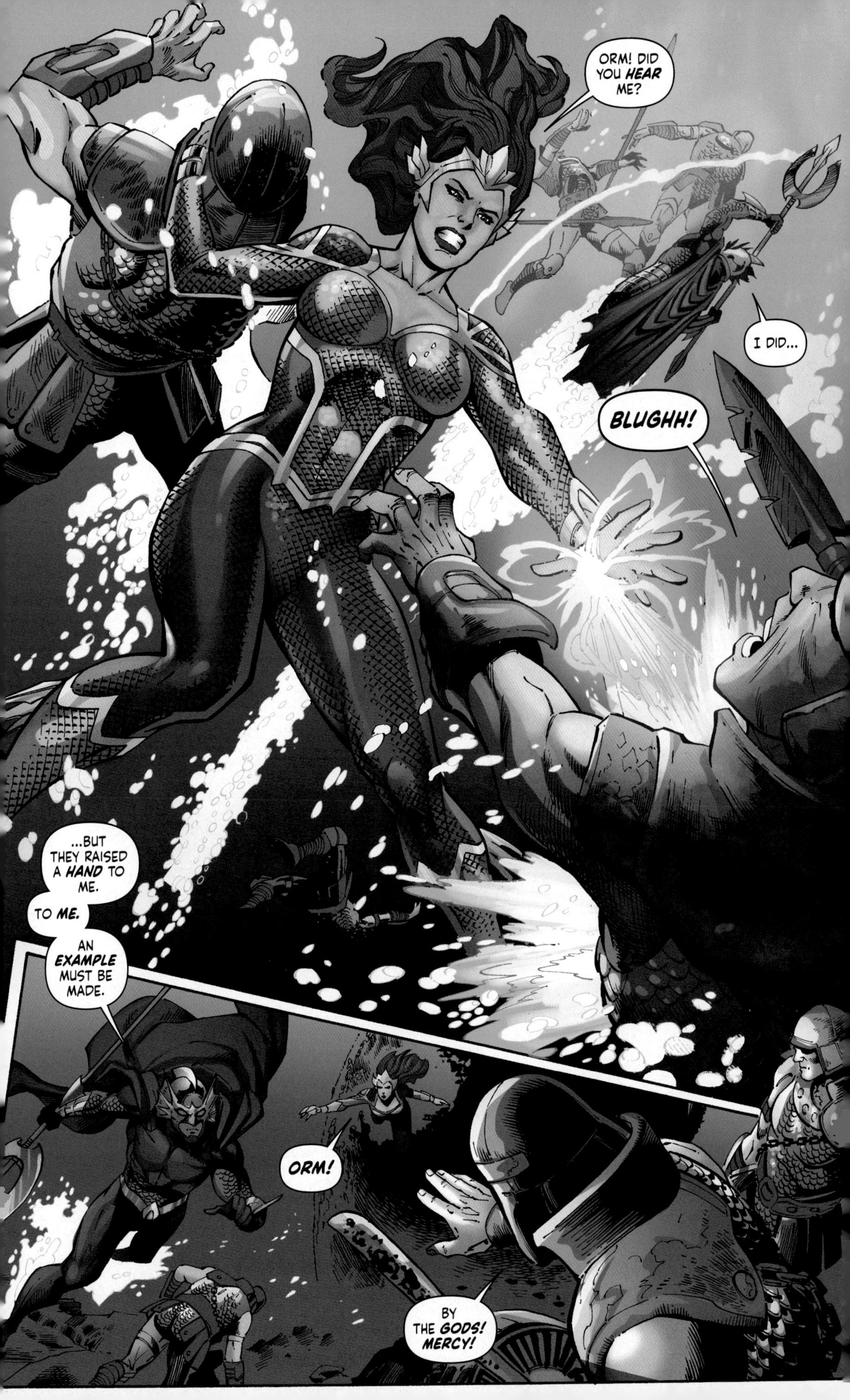
ORM! DID YOU **HEAR** ME?
I DID...
BLUGHH!
...BUT THEY RAISED A **HAND** TO ME.
TO **ME.**
AN **EXAMPLE** MUST BE MADE.
ORM!
BY THE **GODS! MERCY!**

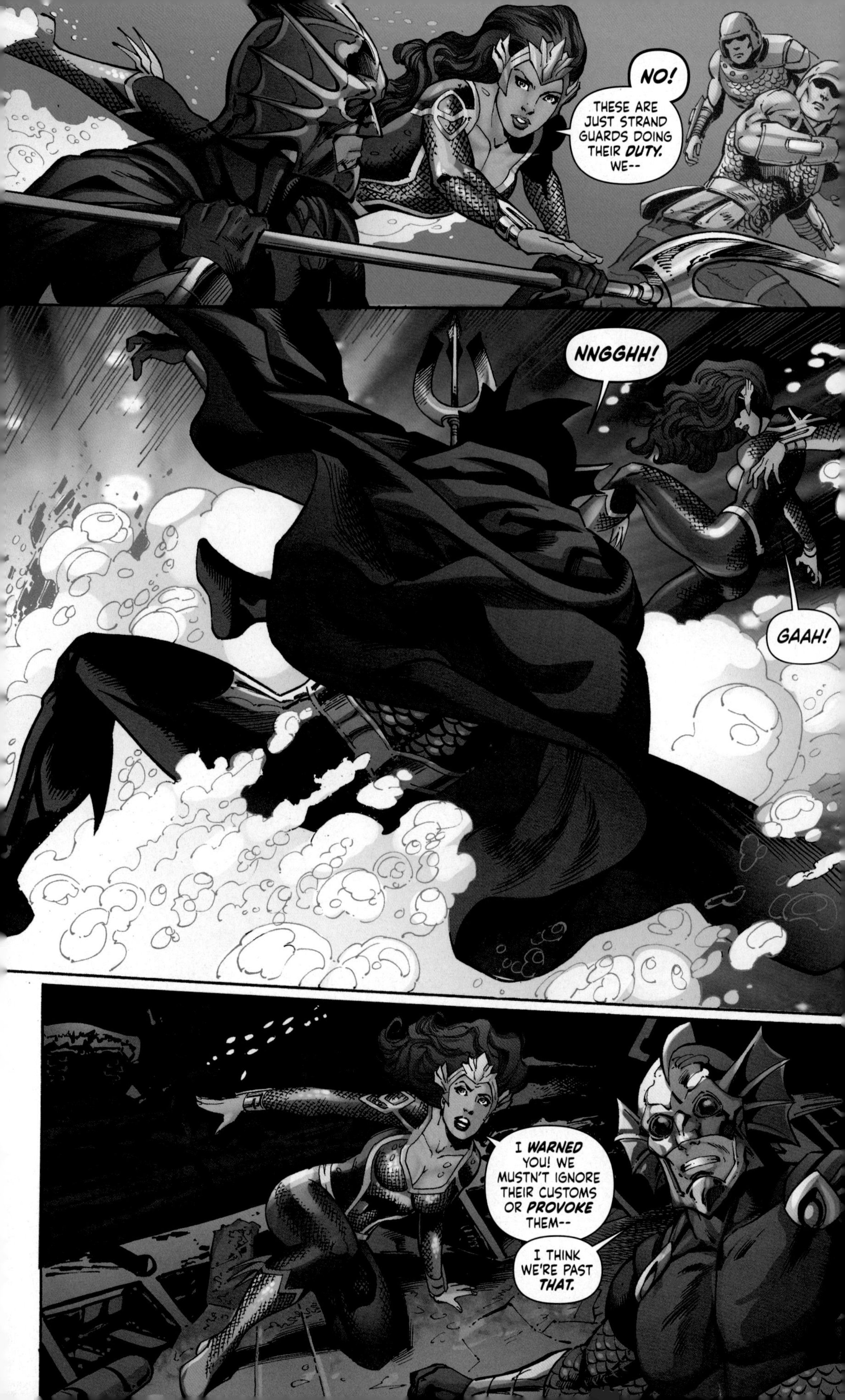
NO!
THESE ARE JUST STRAND GUARDS DOING THEIR DUTY. WE--
NNGGHH!
GAAH!
I WARNED YOU! WE MUSTN'T IGNORE THEIR CUSTOMS OR PROVOKE THEM--
I THINK WE'RE PAST THAT.

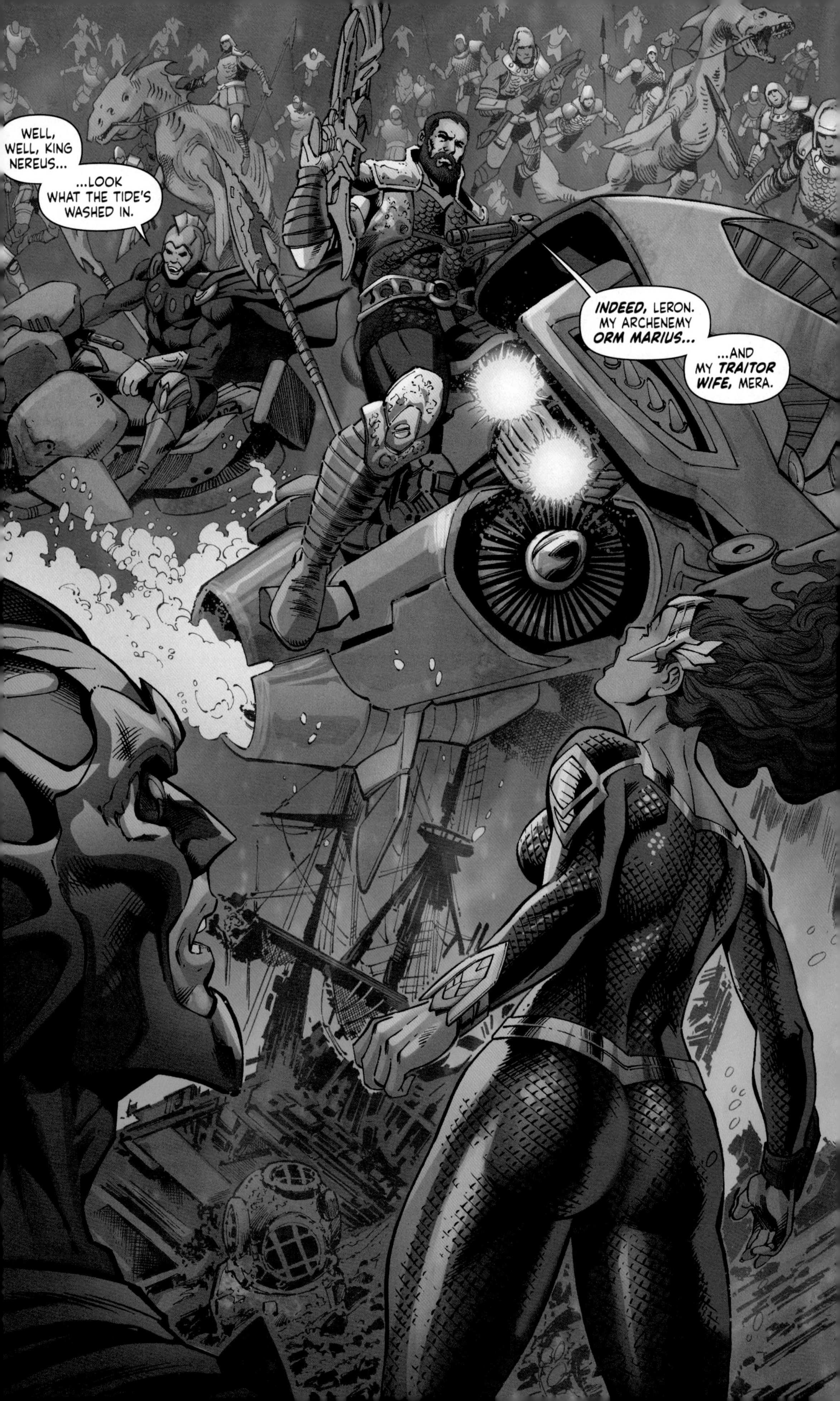
WELL, WELL, KING NEREUS...
...LOOK WHAT THE TIDE'S WASHED IN.
INDEED, LERON. MY ARCHENEMY ORM MARIUS...
...AND MY TRAITOR WIFE, MERA.

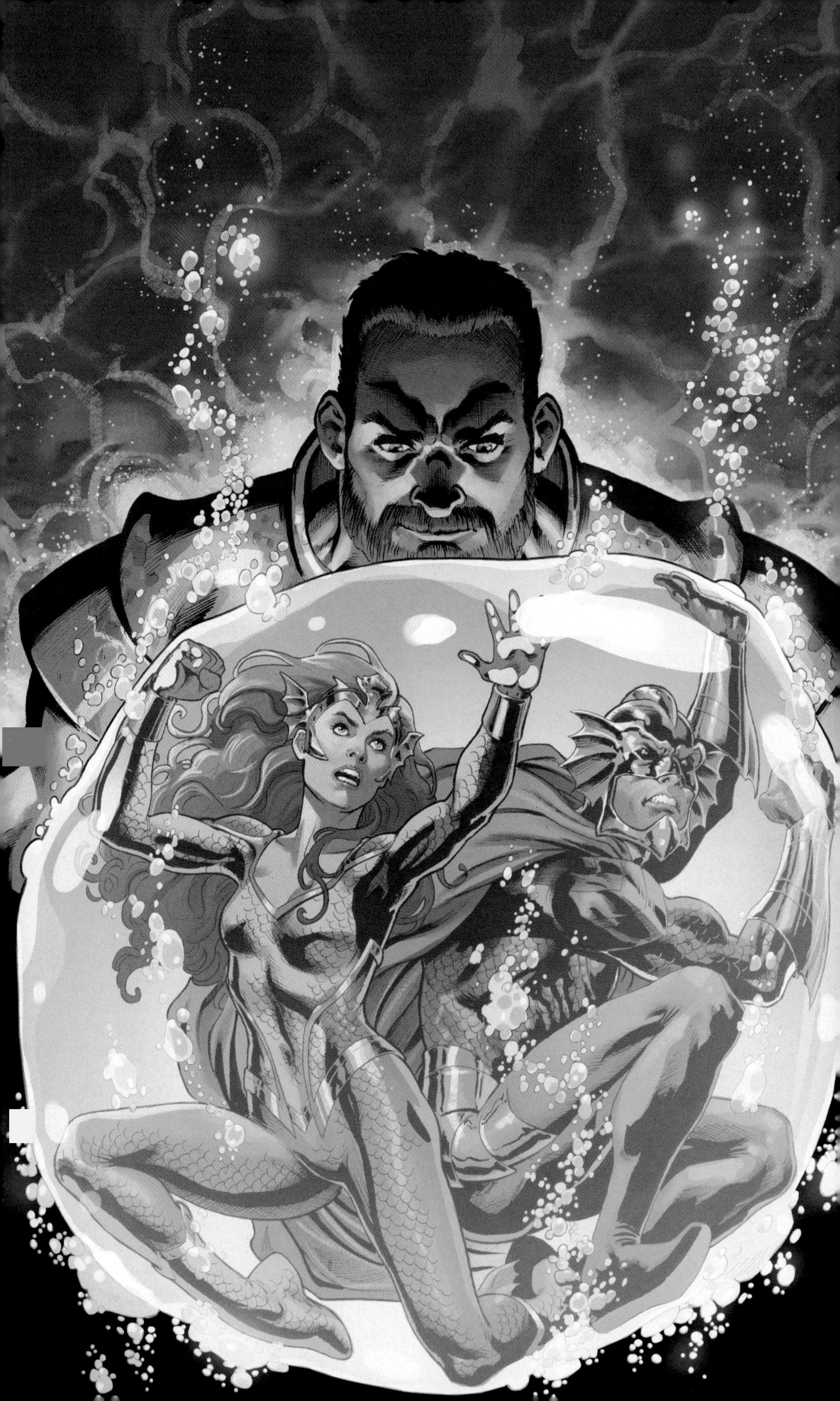

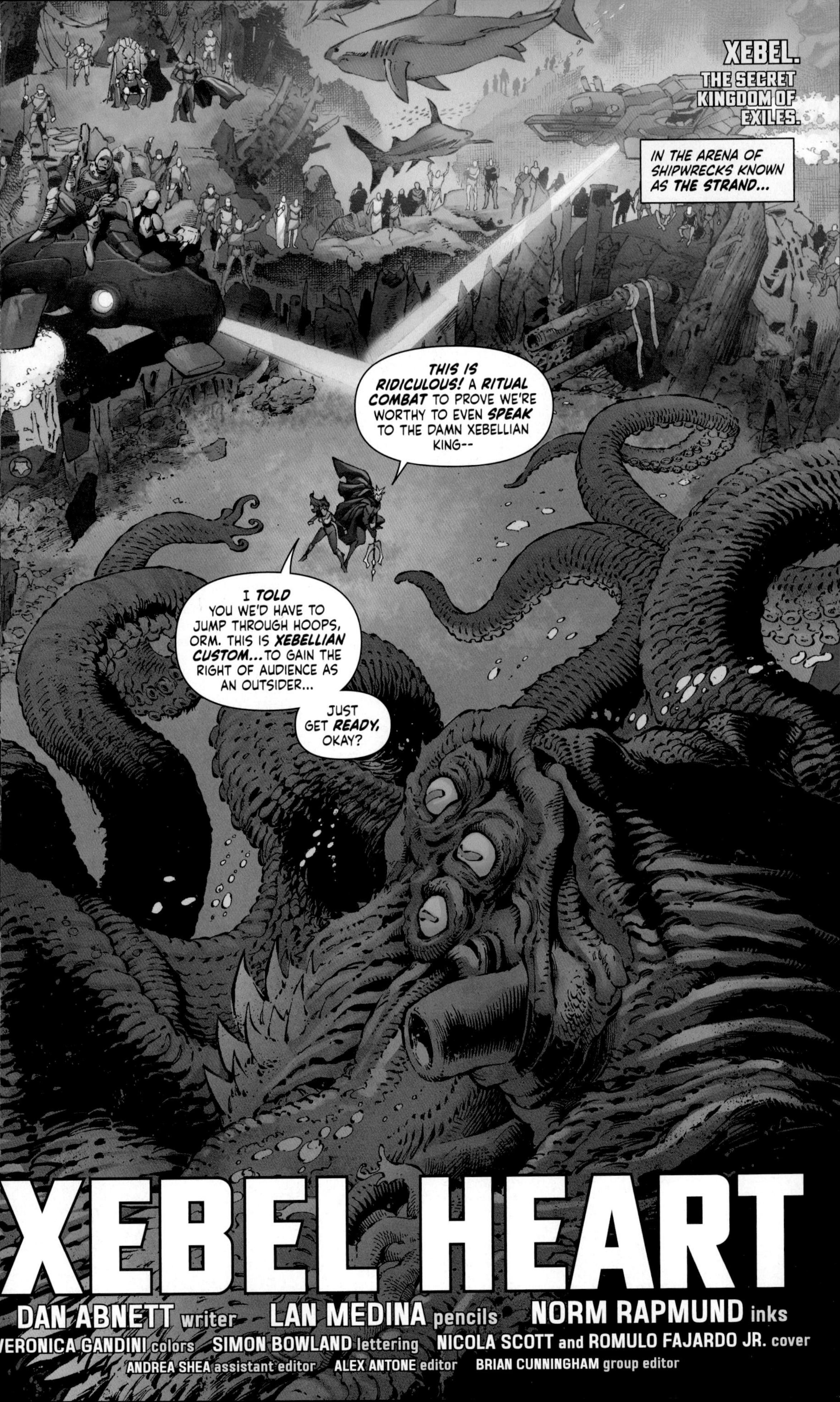
XEBEL. THE SECRET KINGDOM OF EXILES.
IN THE ARENA OF SHIPWRECKS KNOWN AS THE STRAND...
THIS IS RIDICULOUS! A RITUAL COMBAT TO PROVE WE'RE WORTHY TO EVEN SPEAK TO THE DAMN XEBELLIAN KING--
I TOLD YOU WE'D HAVE TO JUMP THROUGH HOOPS, ORM. THIS IS XEBELLIAN CUSTOM...TO GAIN THE RIGHT OF AUDIENCE AS AN OUTSIDER...
JUST GET READY, OKAY?

XEBEL HEART

DAN ABNETT writer LAN MEDINA pencils NORM RAPMUND inks
VERONICA GANDINI colors SIMON BOWLAND lettering NICOLA SCOTT and ROMULO FAJARDO JR. cover
ANDREA SHEA assistant editor ALEX ANTONE editor BRIAN CUNNINGHAM group editor

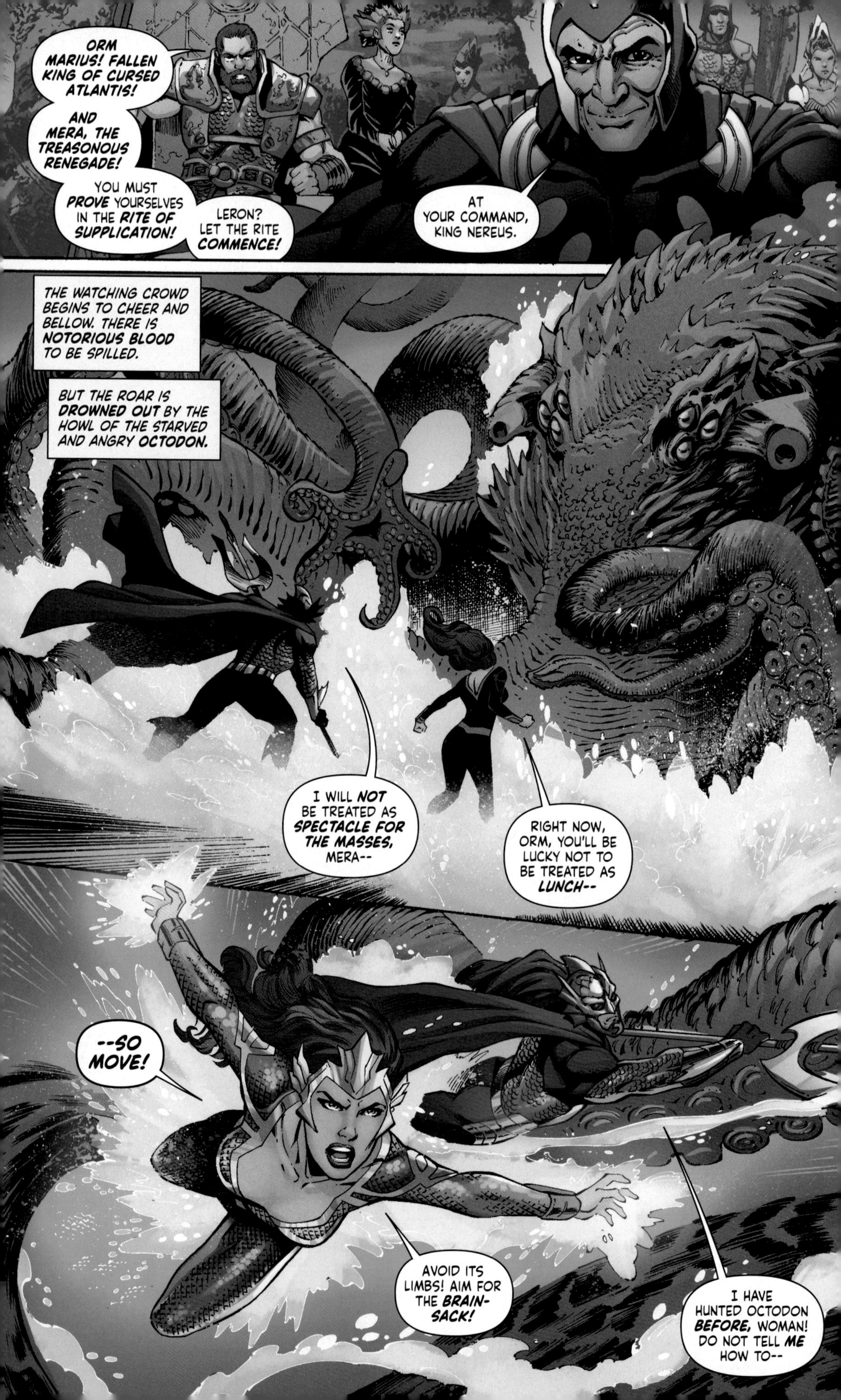
ORM MARIUS! FALLEN KING OF CURSED ATLANTIS!
AND MERA, THE TREASONOUS RENEGADE!
YOU MUST PROVE YOURSELVES IN THE RITE OF SUPPLICATION!
LERON? LET THE RITE COMMENCE!
AT YOUR COMMAND, KING NEREUS.
THE WATCHING CROWD BEGINS TO CHEER AND BELLOW. THERE IS NOTORIOUS BLOOD TO BE SPILLED.
BUT THE ROAR IS DROWNED OUT BY THE HOWL OF THE STARVED AND ANGRY OCTODON.
I WILL NOT BE TREATED AS SPECTACLE FOR THE MASSES, MERA--
RIGHT NOW, ORM, YOU'LL BE LUCKY NOT TO BE TREATED AS LUNCH--
--SO MOVE!
AVOID ITS LIMBS! AIM FOR THE BRAIN-SACK!
I HAVE HUNTED OCTODON BEFORE, WOMAN! DO NOT TELL ME HOW TO--

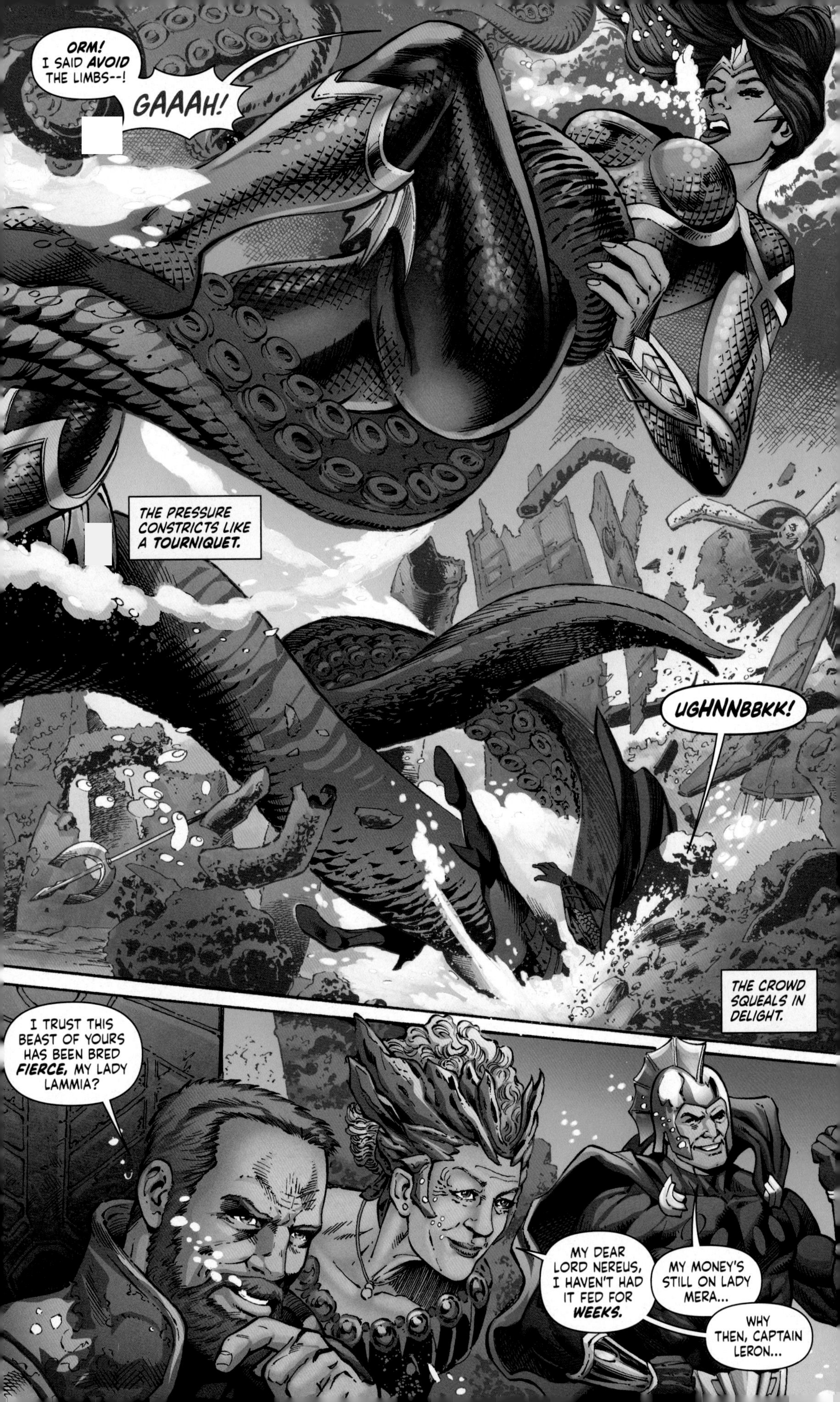
ORM! I SAID AVOID THE LIMBS--!
GAAAH!
THE PRESSURE CONSTRICTS LIKE A TOURNIQUET.
UGHNNBBKK!
THE CROWD SQUEALS IN DELIGHT.
I TRUST THIS BEAST OF YOURS HAS BEEN BRED FIERCE, MY LADY LAMMIA?
MY DEAR LORD NEREUS, I HAVEN'T HAD IT FED FOR WEEKS.
MY MONEY'S STILL ON LADY MERA...
WHY THEN, CAPTAIN LERON...

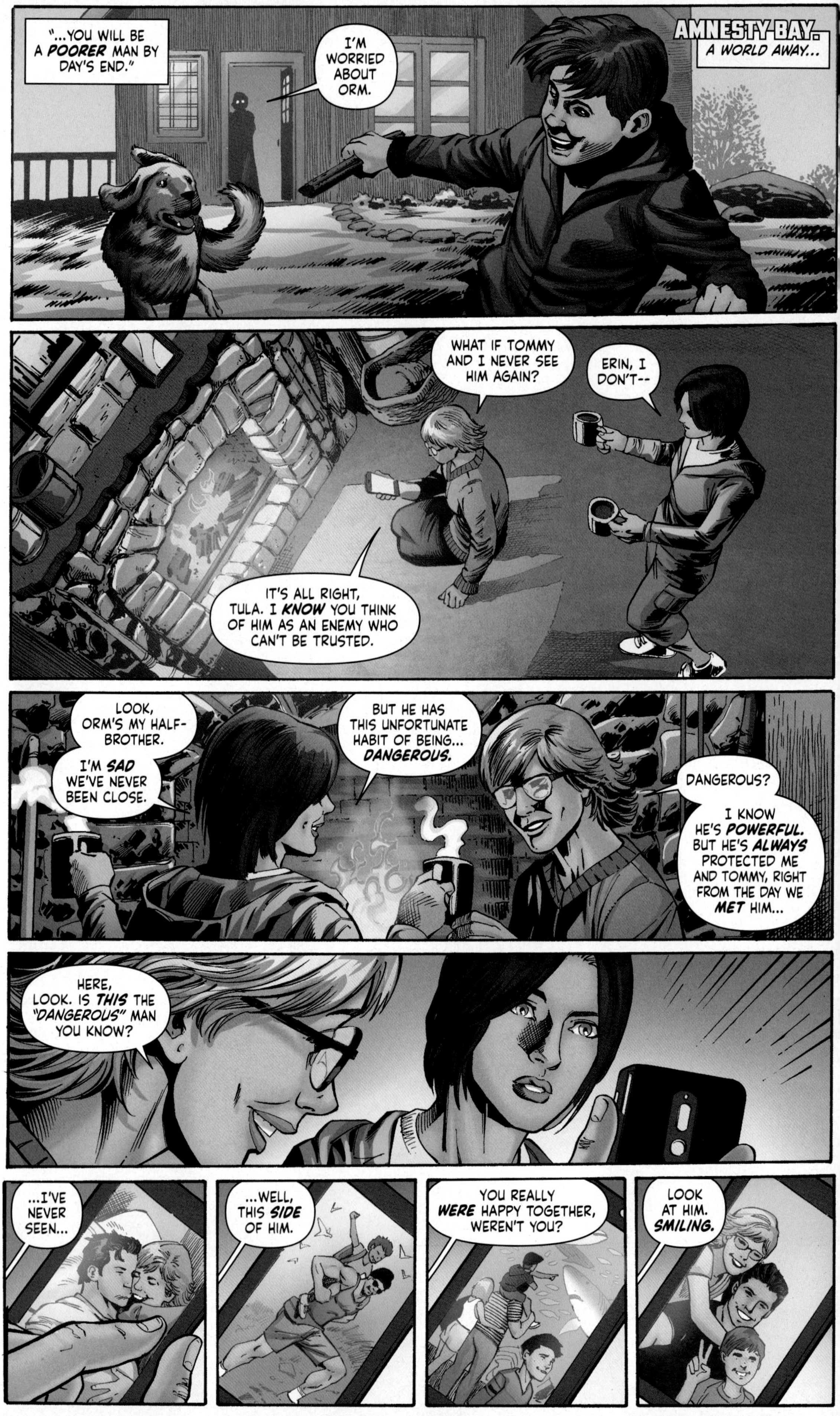

"...YOU WILL BE A POORER MAN BY DAY'S END."
AMNESTY BAY. A WORLD AWAY...
I'M WORRIED ABOUT ORM.
WHAT IF TOMMY AND I NEVER SEE HIM AGAIN?
ERIN, I DON'T--
IT'S ALL RIGHT, TULA. I KNOW YOU THINK OF HIM AS AN ENEMY WHO CAN'T BE TRUSTED.
LOOK, ORM'S MY HALF-BROTHER.
I'M SAD WE'VE NEVER BEEN CLOSE.
BUT HE HAS THIS UNFORTUNATE HABIT OF BEING... DANGEROUS.
DANGEROUS?
I KNOW HE'S POWERFUL. BUT HE'S ALWAYS PROTECTED ME AND TOMMY, RIGHT FROM THE DAY WE MET HIM...
HERE, LOOK. IS THIS THE "DANGEROUS" MAN YOU KNOW?
...I'VE NEVER SEEN...
...WELL, THIS SIDE OF HIM.
YOU REALLY WERE HAPPY TOGETHER, WEREN'T YOU?
LOOK AT HIM. SMILING.

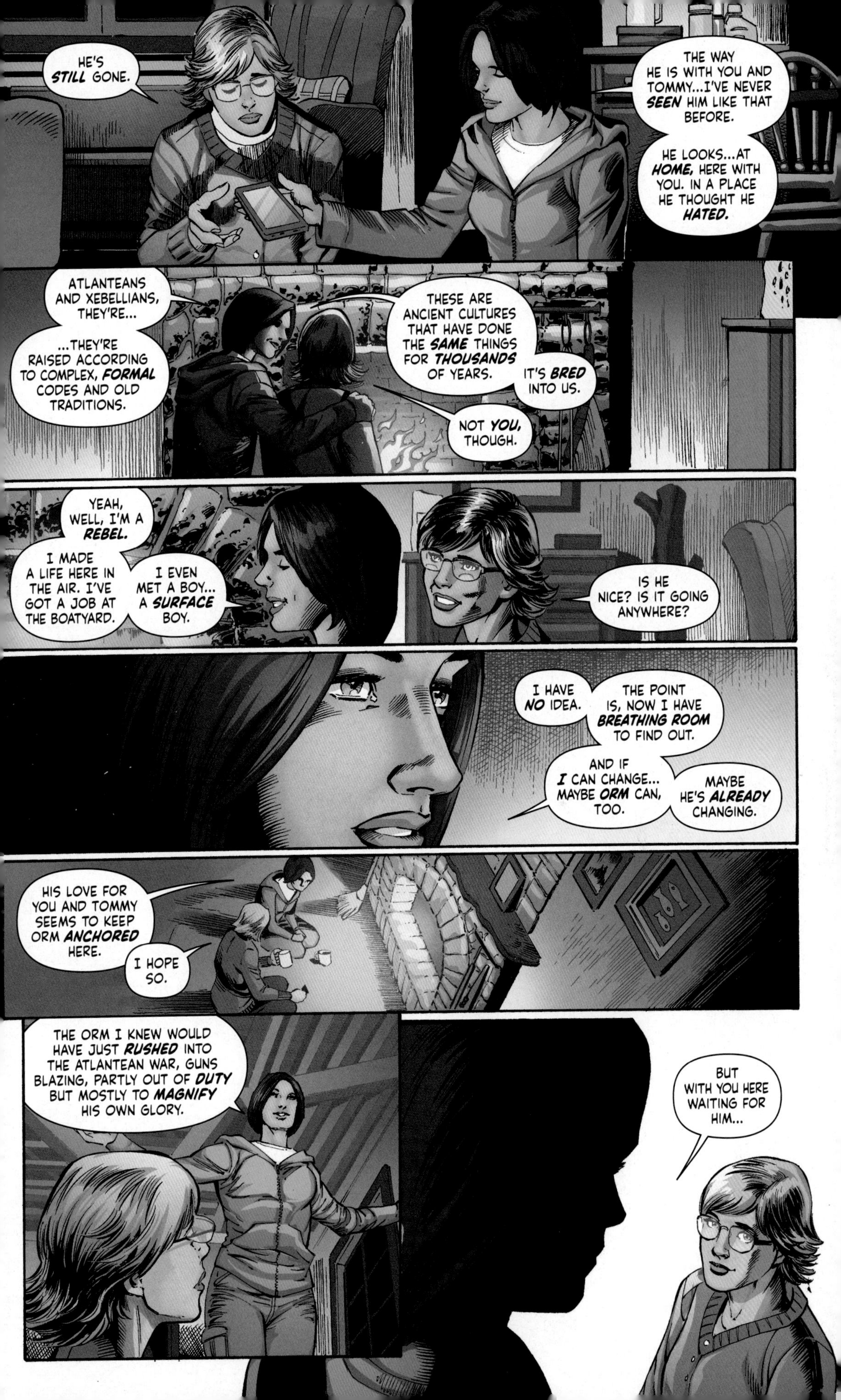
HE'S STILL GONE.
THE WAY HE IS WITH YOU AND TOMMY...I'VE NEVER SEEN HIM LIKE THAT BEFORE.
HE LOOKS...AT HOME, HERE WITH YOU. IN A PLACE HE THOUGHT HE HATED.
ATLANTEANS AND XEBELLIANS, THEY'RE...
...THEY'RE RAISED ACCORDING TO COMPLEX, FORMAL CODES AND OLD TRADITIONS.
THESE ARE ANCIENT CULTURES THAT HAVE DONE THE SAME THINGS FOR THOUSANDS OF YEARS.
IT'S BRED INTO US.
NOT YOU, THOUGH.
YEAH, WELL, I'M A REBEL.
I MADE A LIFE HERE IN THE AIR. I'VE GOT A JOB AT THE BOATYARD.
I EVEN MET A BOY... A SURFACE BOY.
IS HE NICE? IS IT GOING ANYWHERE?
I HAVE NO IDEA.
THE POINT IS, NOW I HAVE BREATHING ROOM TO FIND OUT.
AND IF I CAN CHANGE... MAYBE ORM CAN, TOO.
MAYBE HE'S ALREADY CHANGING.
HIS LOVE FOR YOU AND TOMMY SEEMS TO KEEP ORM ANCHORED HERE.
I HOPE SO.
THE ORM I KNEW WOULD HAVE JUST RUSHED INTO THE ATLANTEAN WAR, GUNS BLAZING, PARTLY OUT OF DUTY BUT MOSTLY TO MAGNIFY HIS OWN GLORY.
BUT WITH YOU HERE WAITING FOR HIM...

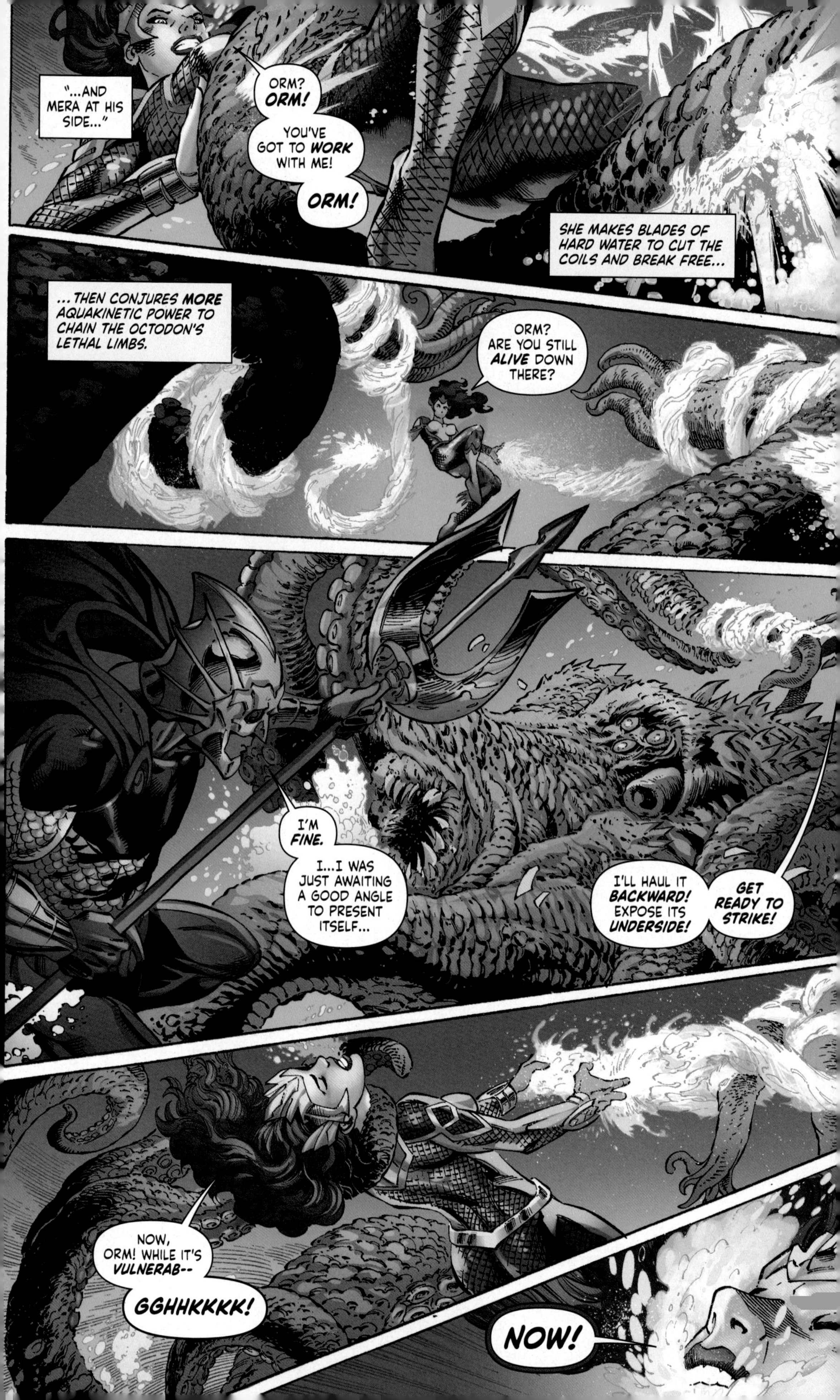

"...AND MERA AT HIS SIDE..."
ORM? ORM!
YOU'VE GOT TO WORK WITH ME!
ORM!
SHE MAKES BLADES OF HARD WATER TO CUT THE COILS AND BREAK FREE...
...THEN CONJURES MORE AQUAKINETIC POWER TO CHAIN THE OCTODON'S LETHAL LIMBS.
ORM? ARE YOU STILL ALIVE DOWN THERE?
I'M FINE.
I...I WAS JUST AWAITING A GOOD ANGLE TO PRESENT ITSELF...
I'LL HAUL IT BACKWARD! EXPOSE ITS UNDERSIDE!
GET READY TO STRIKE!
NOW, ORM! WHILE IT'S VULNERAB--
GGHHKKKK!
NOW!

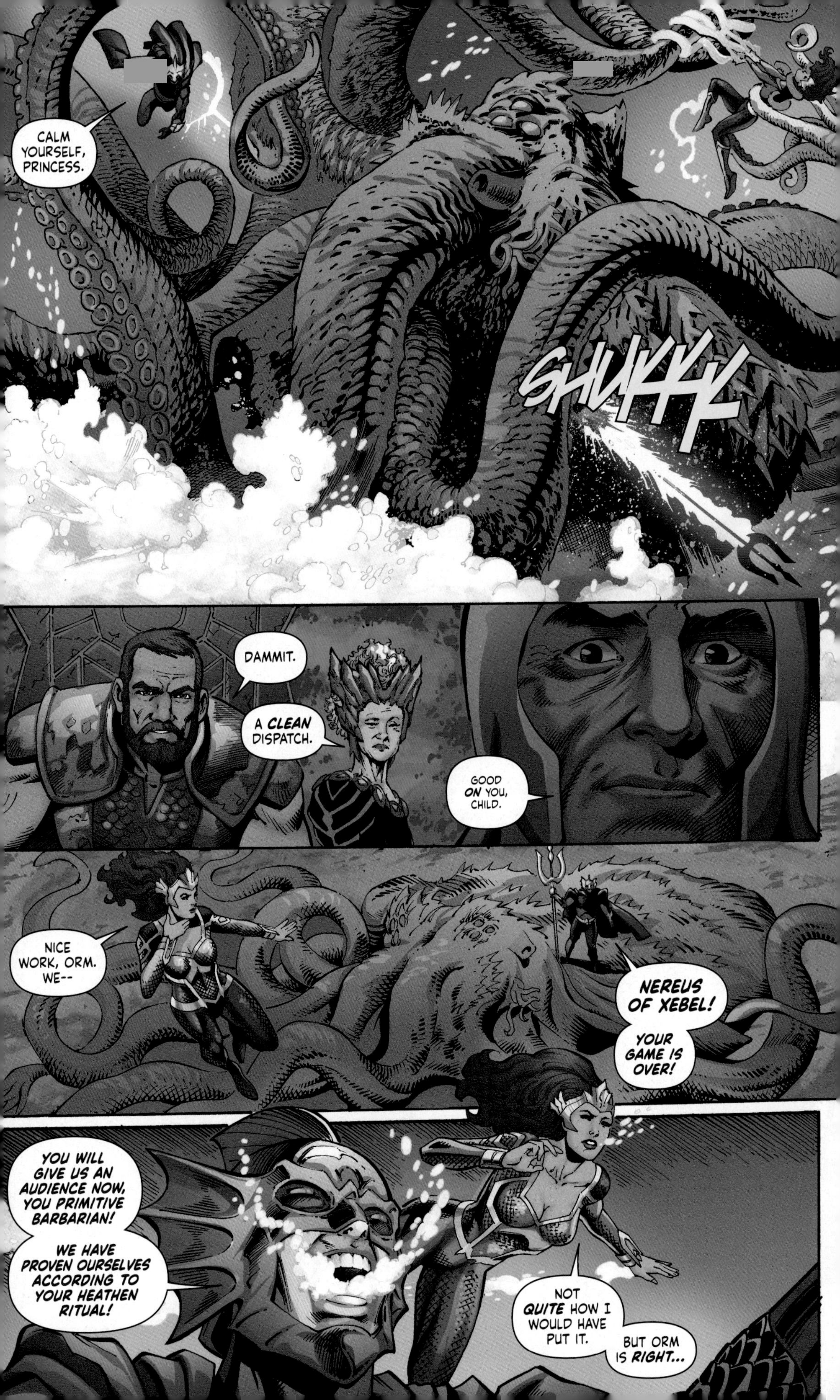

CALM YOURSELF, PRINCESS.
SHUKKK
DAMMIT.
A CLEAN DISPATCH.
GOOD ON YOU, CHILD.
NICE WORK, ORM. WE--
NEREUS OF XEBEL!
YOUR GAME IS OVER!
YOU WILL GIVE US AN AUDIENCE NOW, YOU PRIMITIVE BARBARIAN!
WE HAVE PROVEN OURSELVES ACCORDING TO YOUR HEATHEN RITUAL!
NOT QUITE HOW I WOULD HAVE PUT IT.
BUT ORM IS RIGHT...

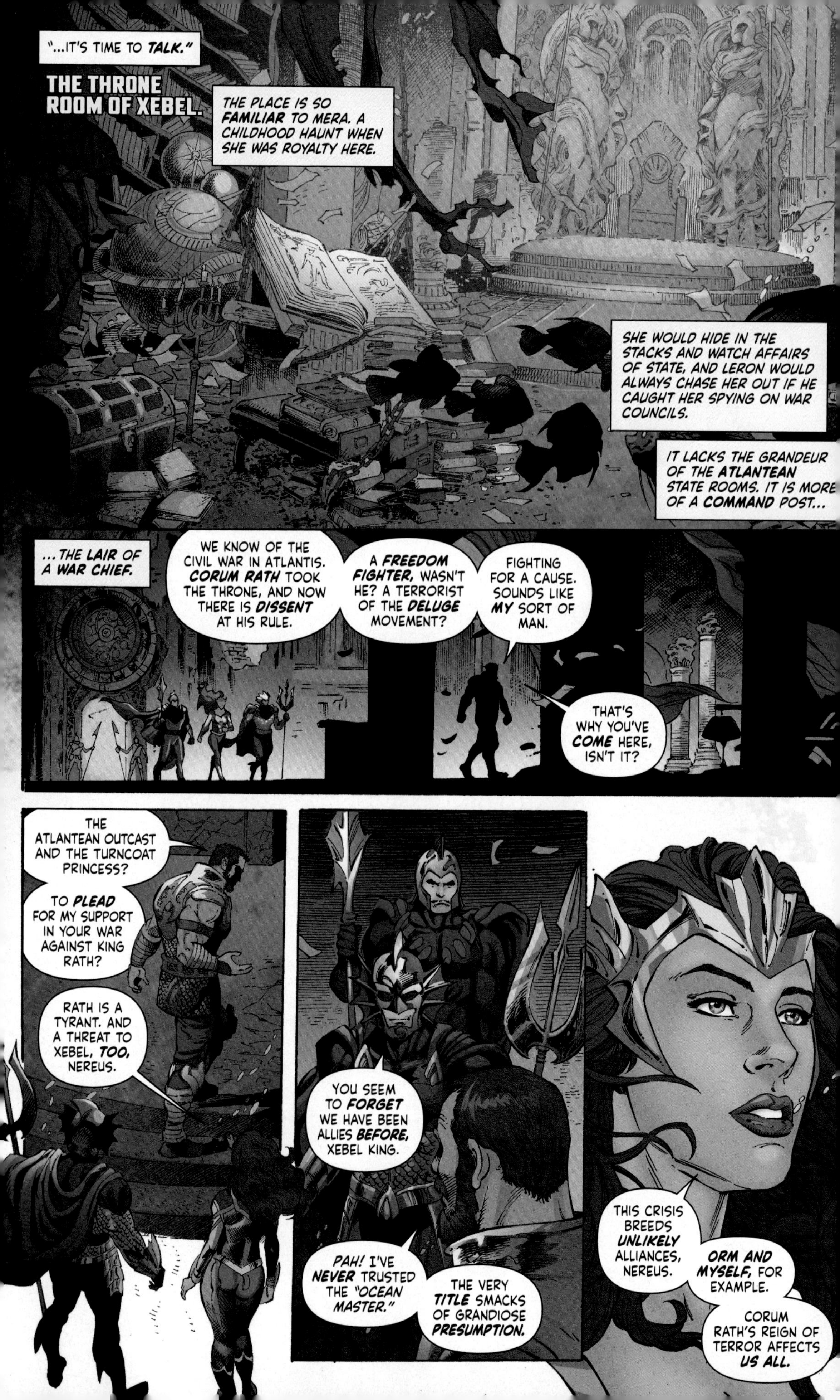
"...IT'S TIME TO TALK."
THE THRONE ROOM OF XEBEL.
THE PLACE IS SO FAMILIAR TO MERA. A CHILDHOOD HAUNT WHEN SHE WAS ROYALTY HERE.
SHE WOULD HIDE IN THE STACKS AND WATCH AFFAIRS OF STATE, AND LERON WOULD ALWAYS CHASE HER OUT IF HE CAUGHT HER SPYING ON WAR COUNCILS.
IT LACKS THE GRANDEUR OF THE ATLANTEAN STATE ROOMS. IT IS MORE OF A COMMAND POST...
...THE LAIR OF A WAR CHIEF.
WE KNOW OF THE CIVIL WAR IN ATLANTIS. CORUM RATH TOOK THE THRONE, AND NOW THERE IS DISSENT AT HIS RULE.
A FREEDOM FIGHTER, WASN'T HE? A TERRORIST OF THE DELUGE MOVEMENT?
FIGHTING FOR A CAUSE. SOUNDS LIKE MY SORT OF MAN.
THAT'S WHY YOU'VE COME HERE, ISN'T IT?
THE ATLANTEAN OUTCAST AND THE TURNCOAT PRINCESS?
TO PLEAD FOR MY SUPPORT IN YOUR WAR AGAINST KING RATH?
RATH IS A TYRANT. AND A THREAT TO XEBEL, TOO, NEREUS.
YOU SEEM TO FORGET WE HAVE BEEN ALLIES BEFORE, XEBEL KING.
PAH! I'VE NEVER TRUSTED THE "OCEAN MASTER."
THE VERY TITLE SMACKS OF GRANDIOSE PRESUMPTION.
THIS CRISIS BREEDS UNLIKELY ALLIANCES, NEREUS.
ORM AND MYSELF, FOR EXAMPLE.
CORUM RATH'S REIGN OF TERROR AFFECTS US ALL.

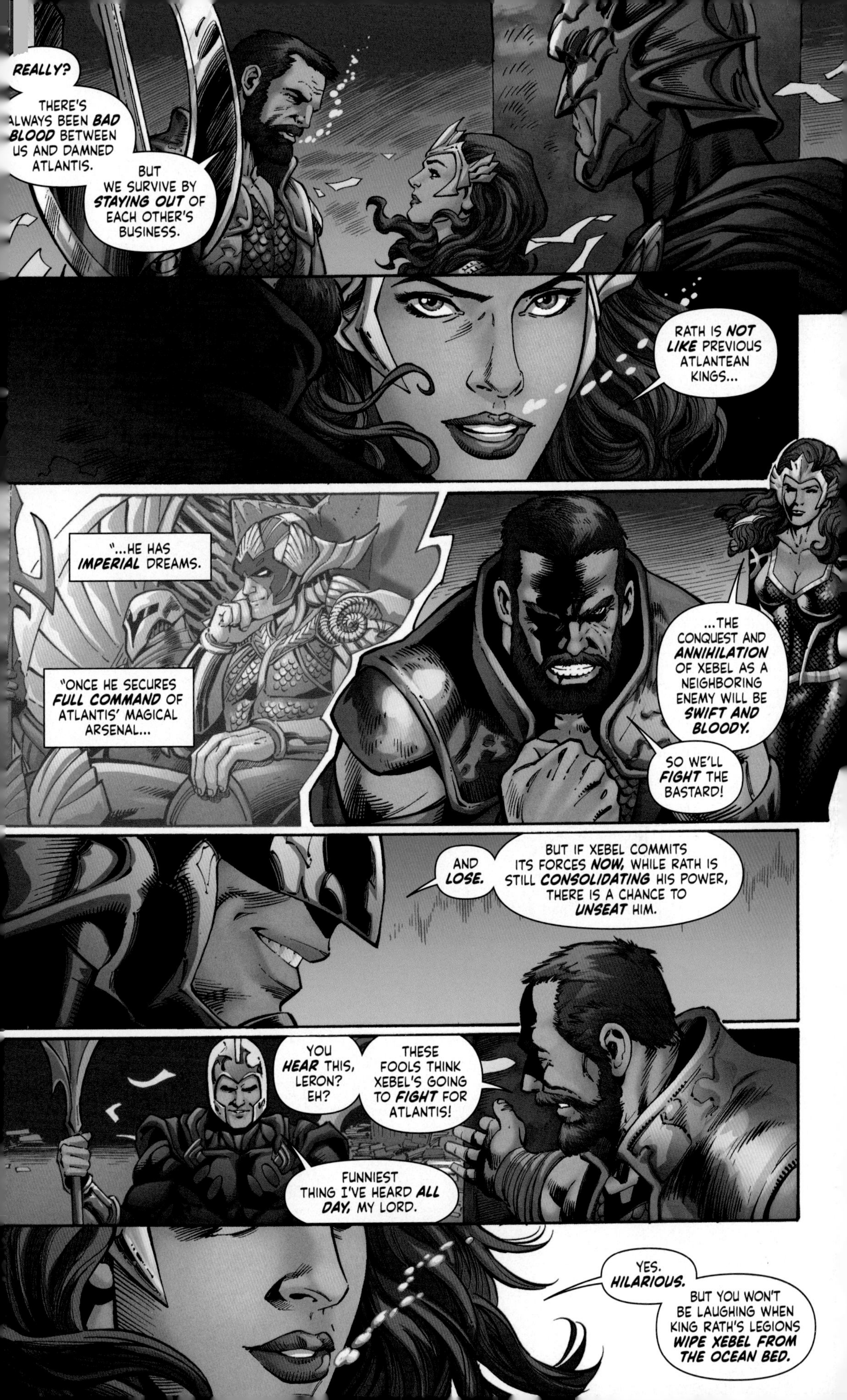
REALLY?
THERE'S ALWAYS BEEN BAD BLOOD BETWEEN US AND DAMNED ATLANTIS.
BUT WE SURVIVE BY STAYING OUT OF EACH OTHER'S BUSINESS.
RATH IS NOT LIKE PREVIOUS ATLANTEAN KINGS...
"...HE HAS IMPERIAL DREAMS.
"ONCE HE SECURES FULL COMMAND OF ATLANTIS' MAGICAL ARSENAL...
...THE CONQUEST AND ANNIHILATION OF XEBEL AS A NEIGHBORING ENEMY WILL BE SWIFT AND BLOODY.
SO WE'LL FIGHT THE BASTARD!
AND LOSE.
BUT IF XEBEL COMMITS ITS FORCES NOW, WHILE RATH IS STILL CONSOLIDATING HIS POWER, THERE IS A CHANCE TO UNSEAT HIM.
YOU HEAR THIS, LERON? EH?
THESE FOOLS THINK XEBEL'S GOING TO FIGHT FOR ATLANTIS!
FUNNIEST THING I'VE HEARD ALL DAY, MY LORD.
YES. HILARIOUS.
BUT YOU WON'T BE LAUGHING WHEN KING RATH'S LEGIONS WIPE XEBEL FROM THE OCEAN BED.

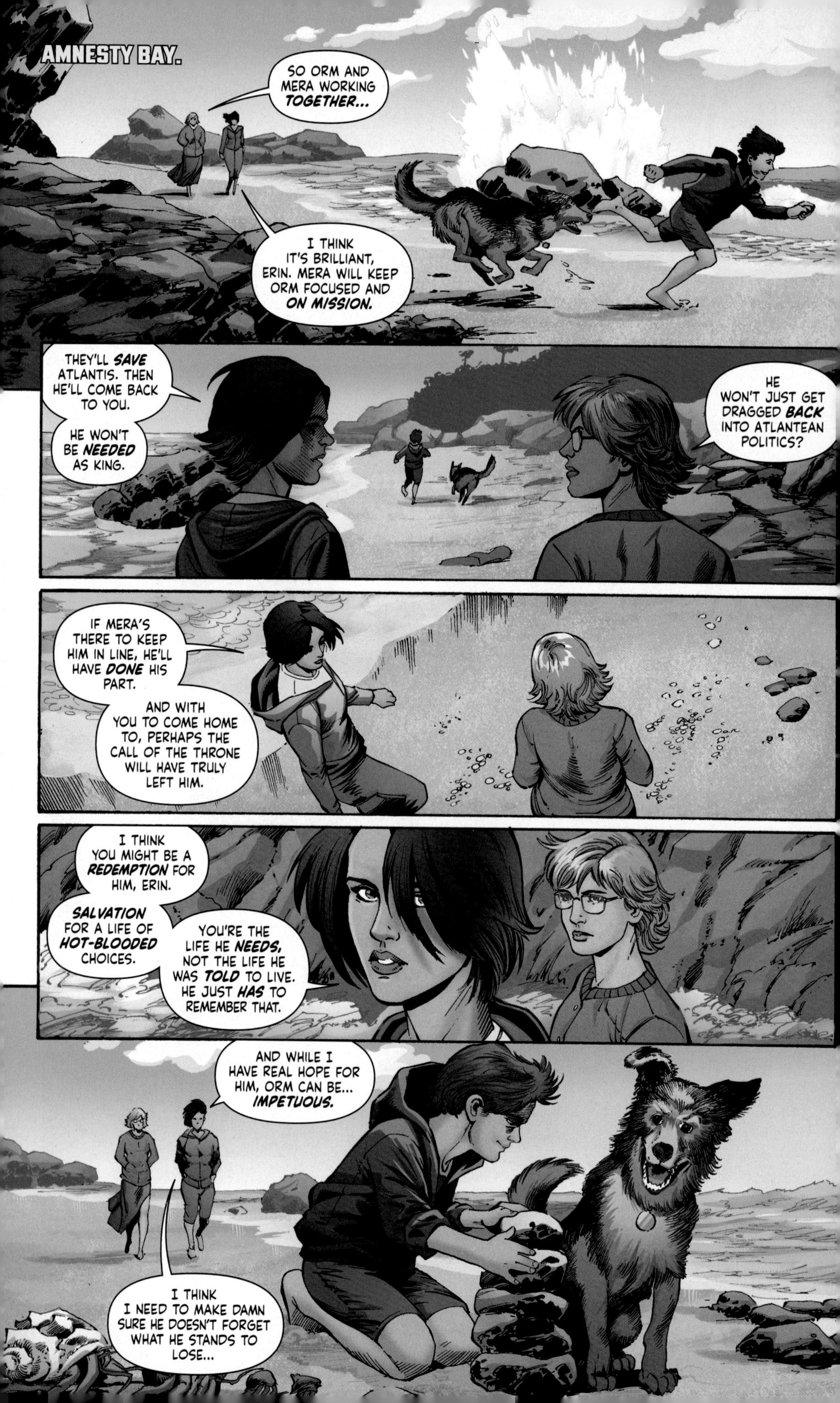
AMNESTY BAY.
SO ORM AND MERA WORKING TOGETHER...
I THINK IT'S BRILLIANT, ERIN. MERA WILL KEEP ORM FOCUSED AND ON MISSION.
THEY'LL SAVE ATLANTIS. THEN HE'LL COME BACK TO YOU.
HE WON'T BE NEEDED AS KING.
HE WON'T JUST GET DRAGGED BACK INTO ATLANTEAN POLITICS?
IF MERA'S THERE TO KEEP HIM IN LINE, HE'LL HAVE DONE HIS PART.
AND WITH YOU TO COME HOME TO, PERHAPS THE CALL OF THE THRONE WILL HAVE TRULY LEFT HIM.
I THINK YOU MIGHT BE A REDEMPTION FOR HIM, ERIN.
SALVATION FOR A LIFE OF HOT-BLOODED CHOICES.
YOU'RE THE LIFE HE NEEDS, NOT THE LIFE HE WAS TOLD TO LIVE. HE JUST HAS TO REMEMBER THAT.
AND WHILE I HAVE REAL HOPE FOR HIM, ORM CAN BE... IMPETUOUS.
I THINK I NEED TO MAKE DAMN SURE HE DOESN'T FORGET WHAT HE STANDS TO LOSE...

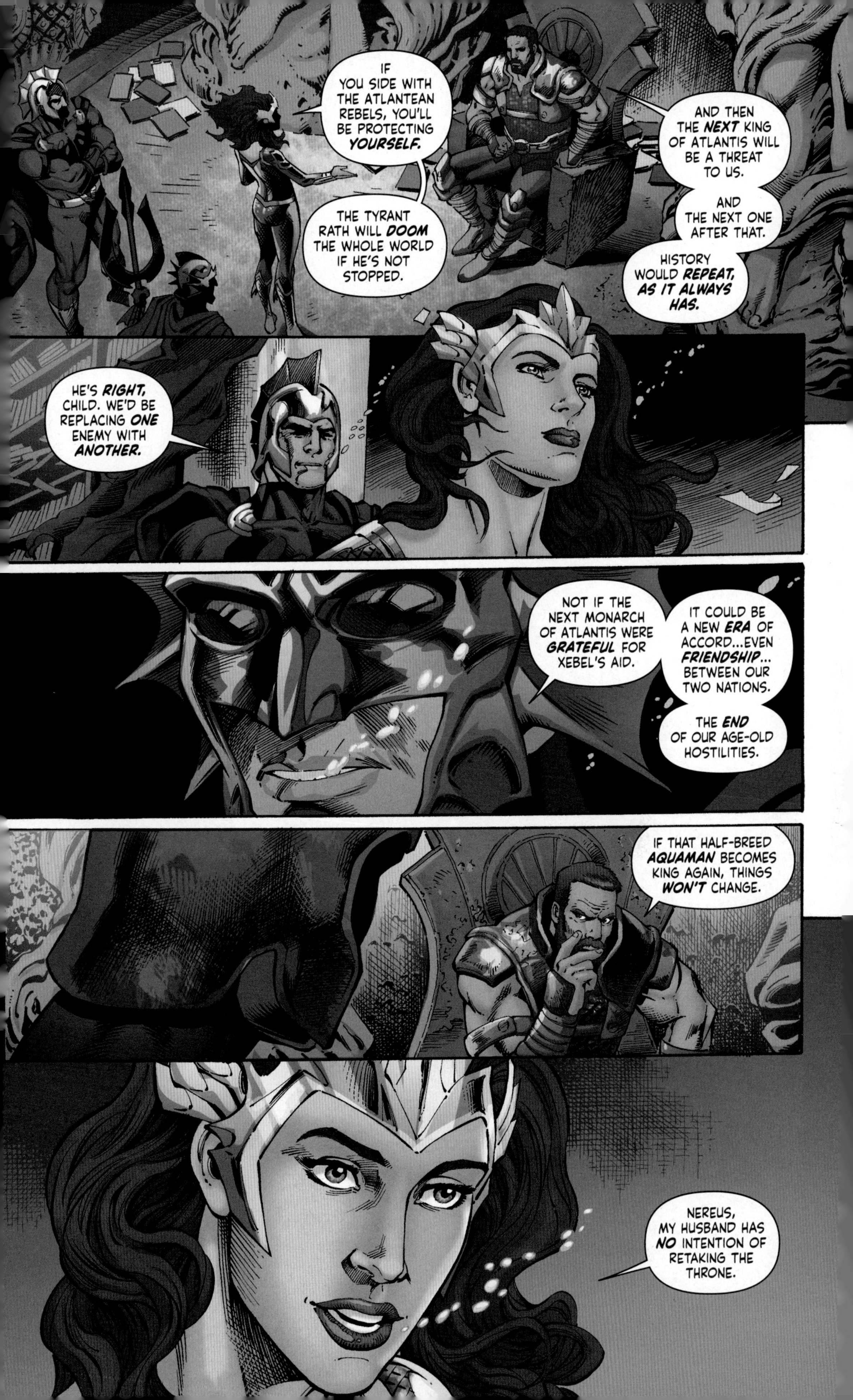

IF YOU SIDE WITH THE ATLANTEAN REBELS, YOU'LL BE PROTECTING **YOURSELF.**
THE TYRANT RATH WILL **DOOM** THE WHOLE WORLD IF HE'S NOT STOPPED.
AND THEN THE **NEXT** KING OF ATLANTIS WILL BE A THREAT TO US.
AND THE NEXT ONE AFTER THAT.
HISTORY WOULD **REPEAT, AS IT ALWAYS HAS.**
HE'S **RIGHT,** CHILD. WE'D BE REPLACING **ONE** ENEMY WITH **ANOTHER.**
NOT IF THE NEXT MONARCH OF ATLANTIS WERE **GRATEFUL** FOR XEBEL'S AID.
IT COULD BE A NEW **ERA** OF ACCORD...EVEN **FRIENDSHIP**... BETWEEN OUR TWO NATIONS.
THE **END** OF OUR AGE-OLD HOSTILITIES.
IF THAT HALF-BREED **AQUAMAN** BECOMES KING AGAIN, THINGS **WON'T** CHANGE.
NEREUS, MY HUSBAND HAS **NO** INTENTION OF RETAKING THE THRONE.

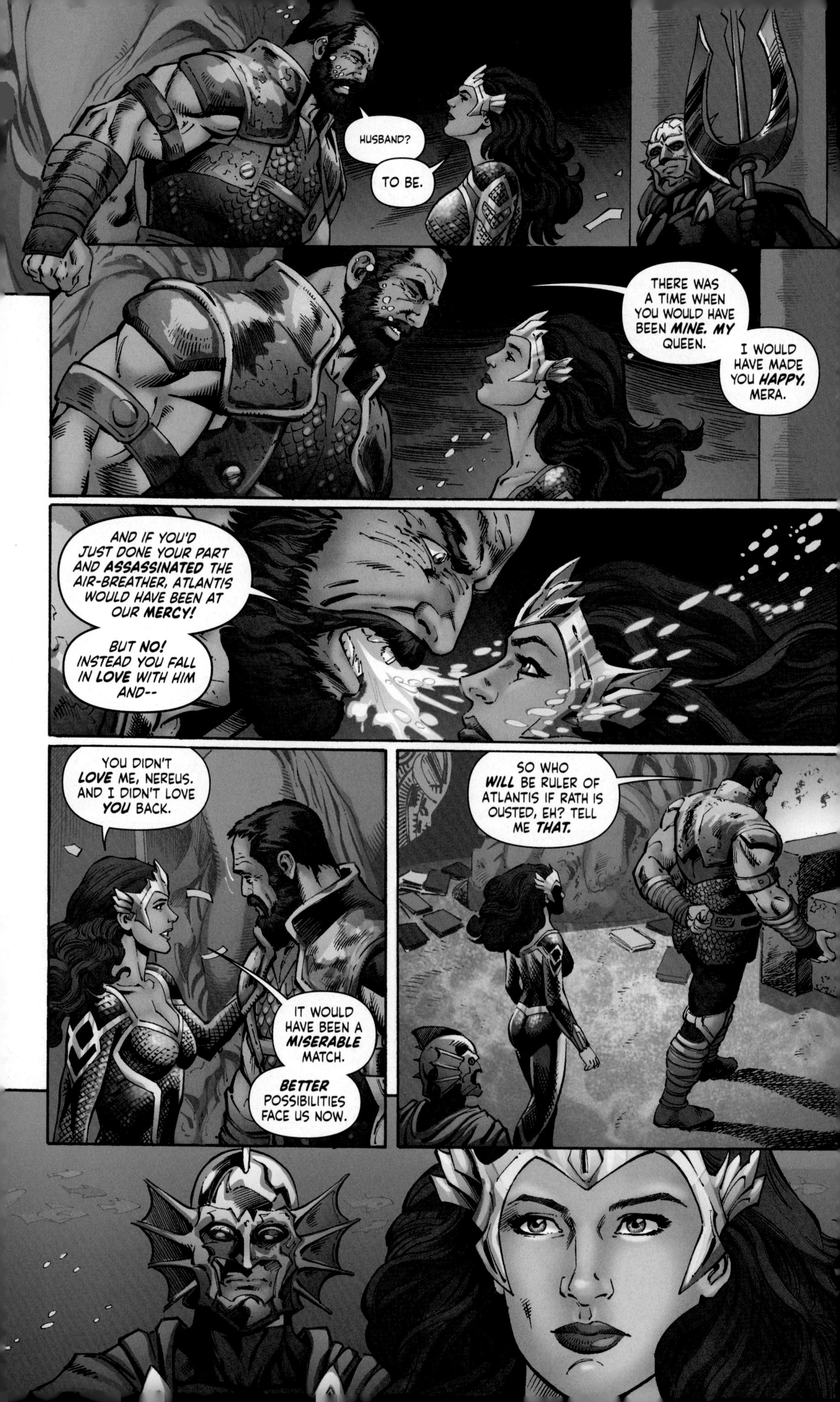
HUSBAND?
TO BE.
THERE WAS A TIME WHEN YOU WOULD HAVE BEEN MINE. MY QUEEN.
I WOULD HAVE MADE YOU HAPPY, MERA.
AND IF YOU'D JUST DONE YOUR PART AND ASSASSINATED THE AIR-BREATHER, ATLANTIS WOULD HAVE BEEN AT OUR MERCY!
BUT NO! INSTEAD YOU FALL IN LOVE WITH HIM AND--
YOU DIDN'T LOVE ME, NEREUS. AND I DIDN'T LOVE YOU BACK.
IT WOULD HAVE BEEN A MISERABLE MATCH.
BETTER POSSIBILITIES FACE US NOW.
SO WHO WILL BE RULER OF ATLANTIS IF RATH IS OUSTED, EH? TELL ME THAT.

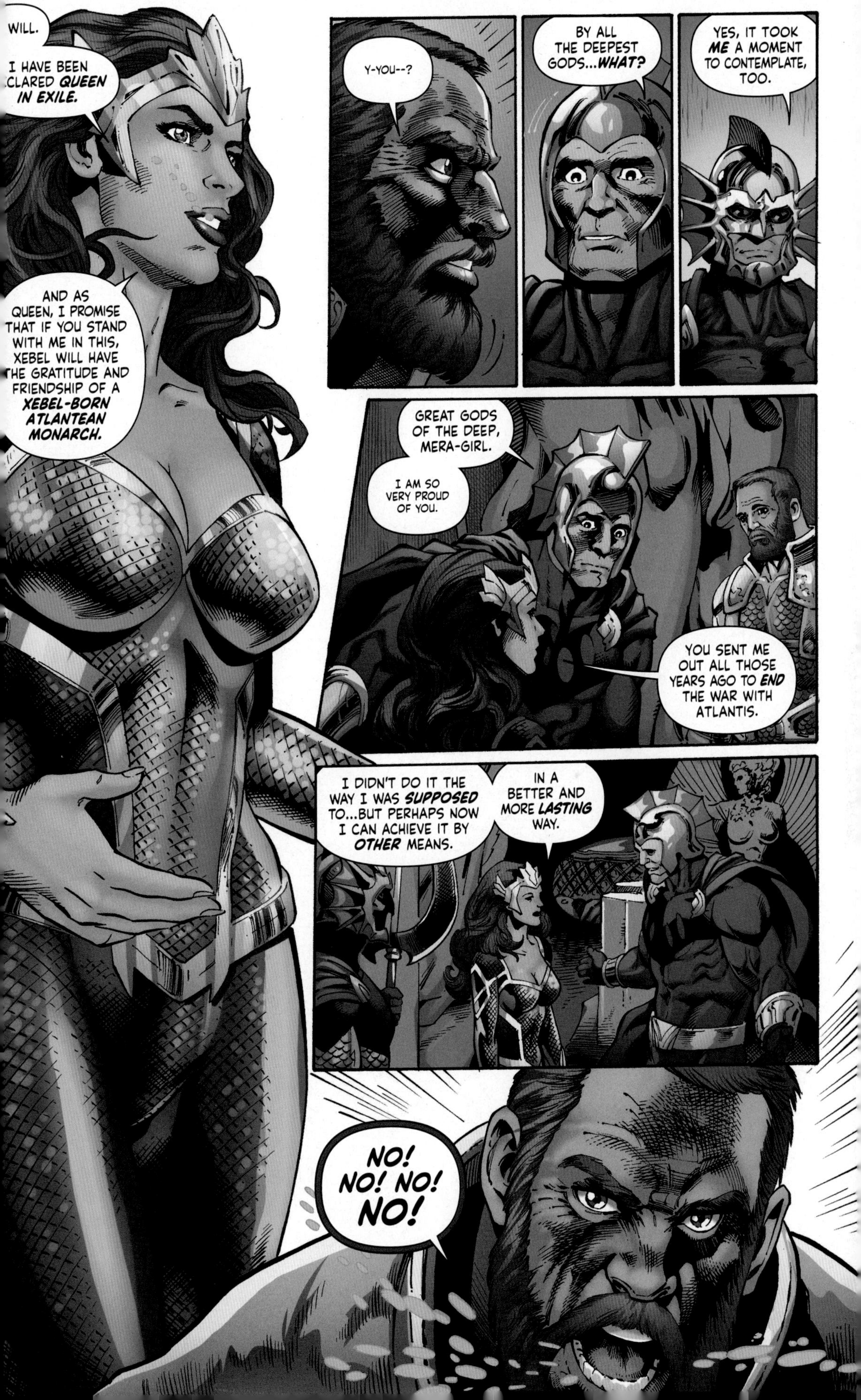
WILL.
I HAVE BEEN
CLARED QUEEN IN EXILE.
AND AS QUEEN, I PROMISE THAT IF YOU STAND WITH ME IN THIS, XEBEL WILL HAVE THE GRATITUDE AND FRIENDSHIP OF A XEBEL-BORN ATLANTEAN MONARCH.
Y-YOU--?
BY ALL THE DEEPEST GODS...WHAT?
YES, IT TOOK ME A MOMENT TO CONTEMPLATE, TOO.
GREAT GODS OF THE DEEP, MERA-GIRL.
I AM SO VERY PROUD OF YOU.
YOU SENT ME OUT ALL THOSE YEARS AGO TO END THE WAR WITH ATLANTIS.
I DIDN'T DO IT THE WAY I WAS SUPPOSED TO...BUT PERHAPS NOW I CAN ACHIEVE IT BY OTHER MEANS.
IN A BETTER AND MORE LASTING WAY.
NO! NO! NO! NO!

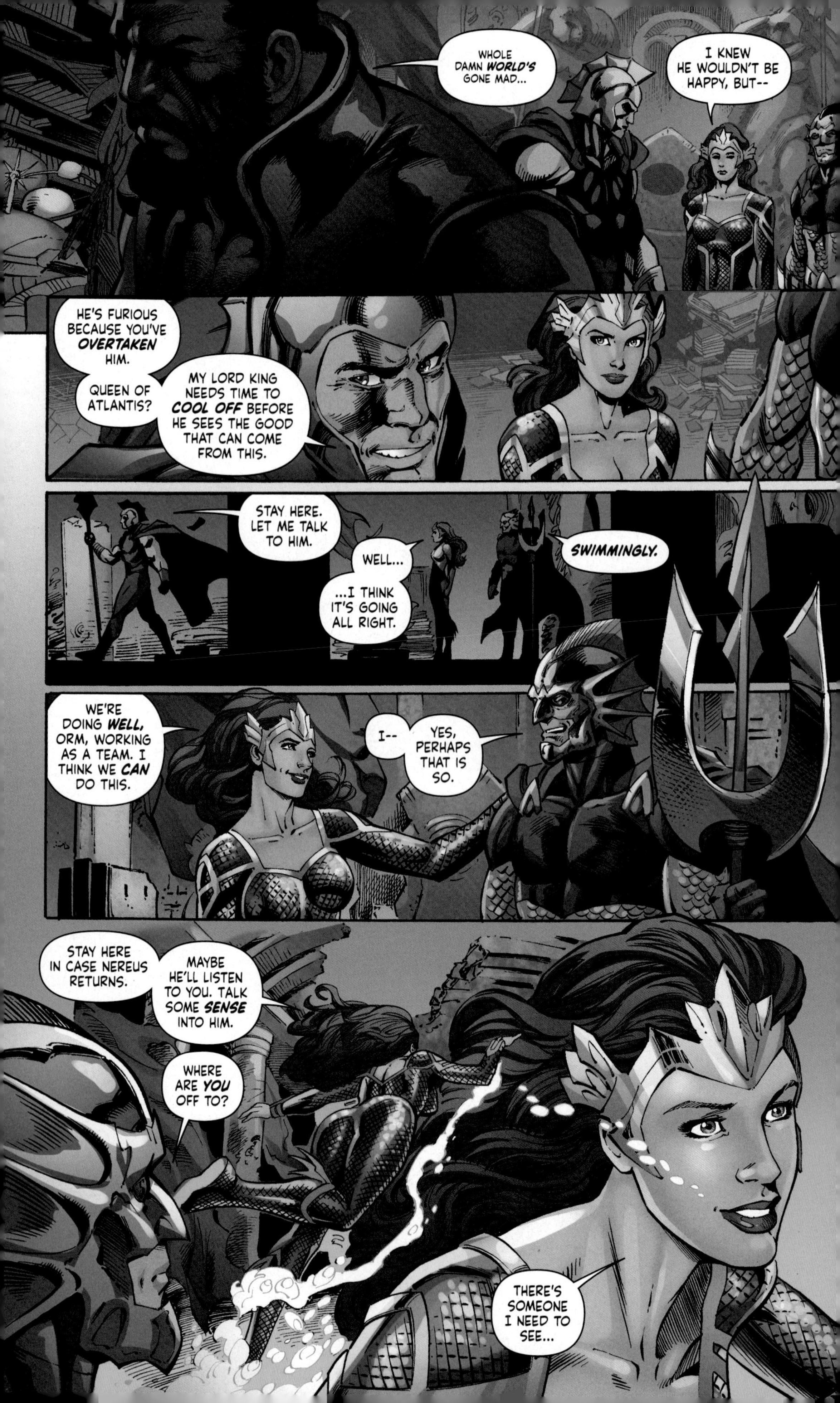
WHOLE DAMN WORLD'S GONE MAD...
I KNEW HE WOULDN'T BE HAPPY, BUT--
HE'S FURIOUS BECAUSE YOU'VE OVERTAKEN HIM.
QUEEN OF ATLANTIS?
MY LORD KING NEEDS TIME TO COOL OFF BEFORE HE SEES THE GOOD THAT CAN COME FROM THIS.
STAY HERE. LET ME TALK TO HIM.
WELL...
...I THINK IT'S GOING ALL RIGHT.
SWIMMINGLY.
WE'RE DOING WELL, ORM, WORKING AS A TEAM. I THINK WE CAN DO THIS.
I--
YES, PERHAPS THAT IS SO.
STAY HERE IN CASE NEREUS RETURNS.
MAYBE HE'LL LISTEN TO YOU. TALK SOME SENSE INTO HIM.
WHERE ARE YOU OFF TO?
THERE'S SOMEONE I NEED TO SEE...

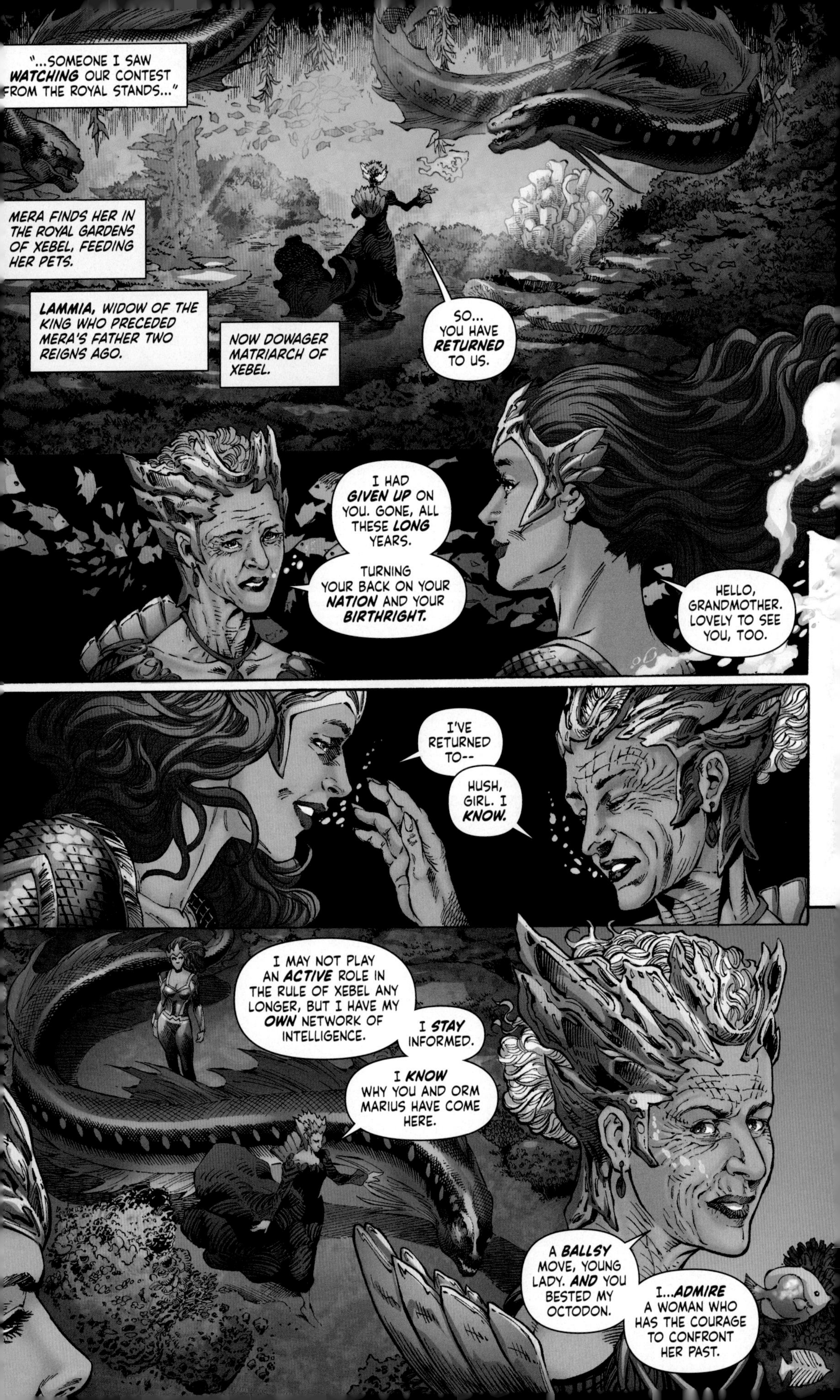

"...SOMEONE I SAW WATCHING OUR CONTEST FROM THE ROYAL STANDS..."
MERA FINDS HER IN THE ROYAL GARDENS OF XEBEL, FEEDING HER PETS.
LAMMIA, WIDOW OF THE KING WHO PRECEDED MERA'S FATHER TWO REIGNS AGO.
NOW DOWAGER MATRIARCH OF XEBEL.
SO... YOU HAVE RETURNED TO US.
I HAD GIVEN UP ON YOU. GONE, ALL THESE LONG YEARS.
TURNING YOUR BACK ON YOUR NATION AND YOUR BIRTHRIGHT.
HELLO, GRANDMOTHER. LOVELY TO SEE YOU, TOO.
I'VE RETURNED TO--
HUSH, GIRL. I KNOW.
I MAY NOT PLAY AN ACTIVE ROLE IN THE RULE OF XEBEL ANY LONGER, BUT I HAVE MY OWN NETWORK OF INTELLIGENCE.
I STAY INFORMED.
I KNOW WHY YOU AND ORM MARIUS HAVE COME HERE.
A BALLSY MOVE, YOUNG LADY. AND YOU BESTED MY OCTODON.
I...ADMIRE A WOMAN WHO HAS THE COURAGE TO CONFRONT HER PAST.

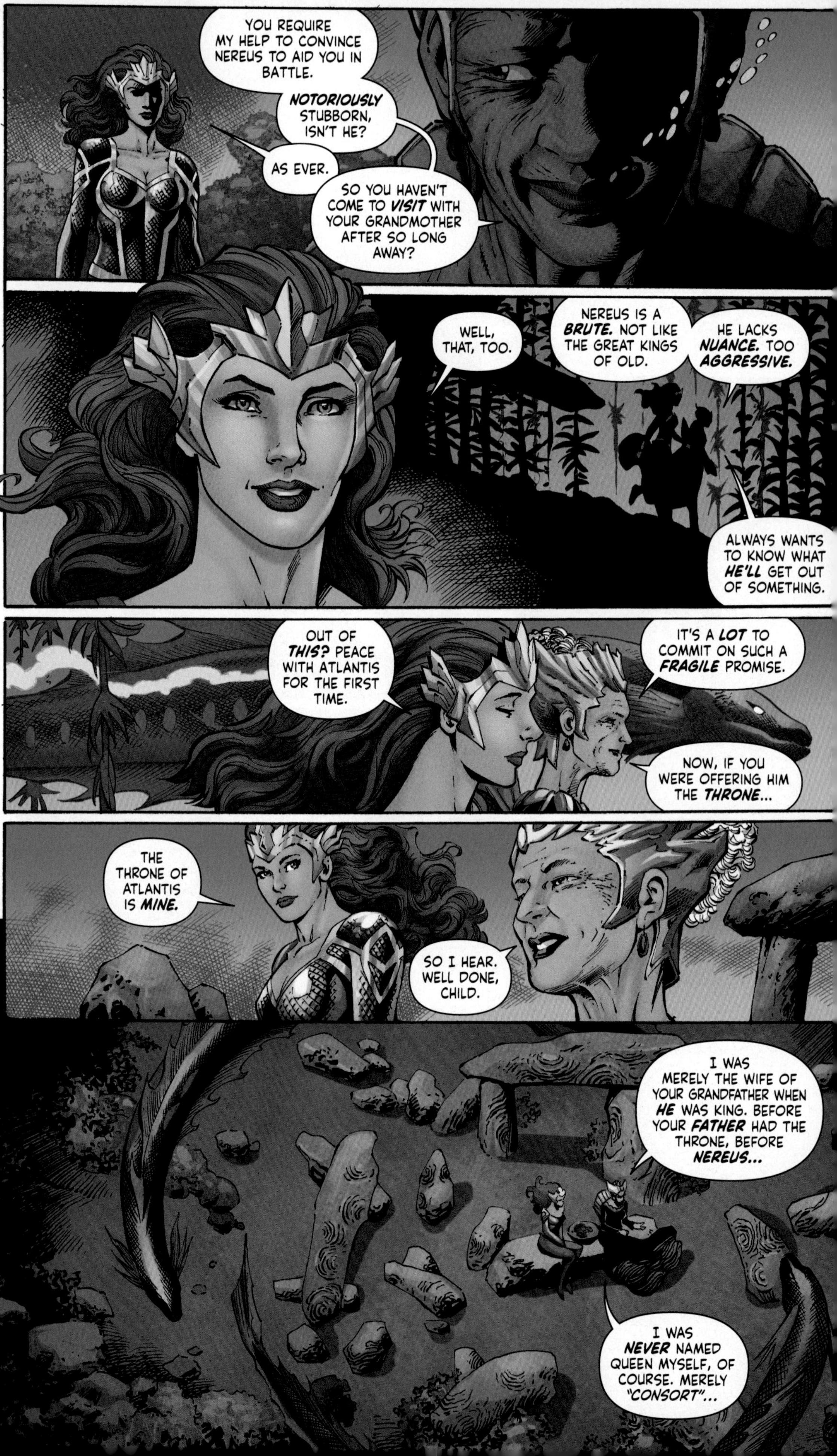

YOU REQUIRE MY HELP TO CONVINCE NEREUS TO AID YOU IN BATTLE.
NOTORIOUSLY STUBBORN, ISN'T HE?
AS EVER.
SO YOU HAVEN'T COME TO VISIT WITH YOUR GRANDMOTHER AFTER SO LONG AWAY?
WELL, THAT, TOO.
NEREUS IS A BRUTE. NOT LIKE THE GREAT KINGS OF OLD.
HE LACKS NUANCE. TOO AGGRESSIVE.
ALWAYS WANTS TO KNOW WHAT HE'LL GET OUT OF SOMETHING.
OUT OF THIS? PEACE WITH ATLANTIS FOR THE FIRST TIME.
IT'S A LOT TO COMMIT ON SUCH A FRAGILE PROMISE.
NOW, IF YOU WERE OFFERING HIM THE THRONE...
THE THRONE OF ATLANTIS IS MINE.
SO I HEAR. WELL DONE, CHILD.
I WAS MERELY THE WIFE OF YOUR GRANDFATHER WHEN HE WAS KING. BEFORE YOUR FATHER HAD THE THRONE, BEFORE NEREUS...
I WAS NEVER NAMED QUEEN MYSELF, OF COURSE. MERELY "CONSORT"...

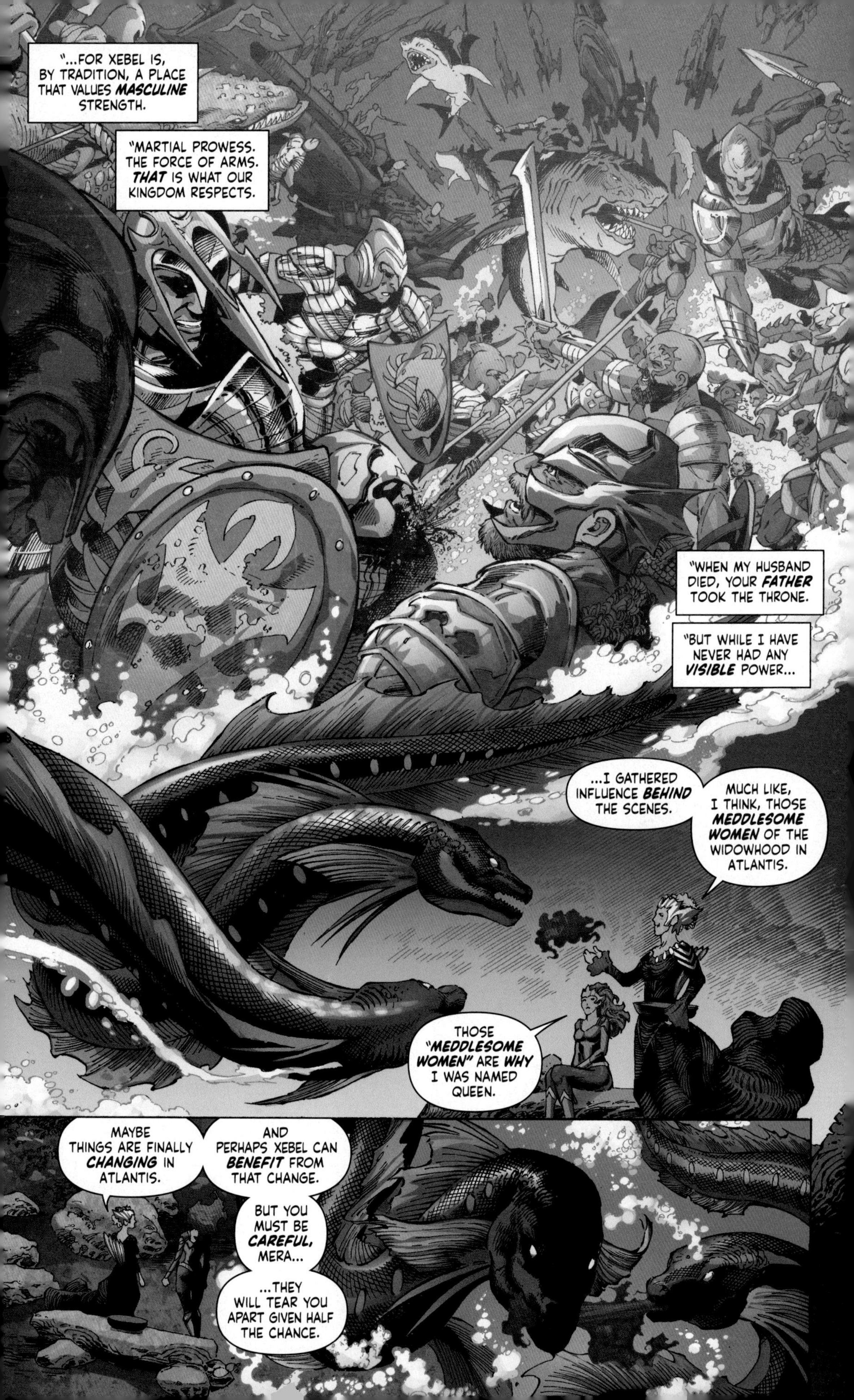
"...FOR XEBEL IS, BY TRADITION, A PLACE THAT VALUES MASCULINE STRENGTH.
"MARTIAL PROWESS. THE FORCE OF ARMS. THAT IS WHAT OUR KINGDOM RESPECTS.
"WHEN MY HUSBAND DIED, YOUR FATHER TOOK THE THRONE.
"BUT WHILE I HAVE NEVER HAD ANY VISIBLE POWER...
...I GATHERED INFLUENCE BEHIND THE SCENES.
MUCH LIKE, I THINK, THOSE MEDDLESOME WOMEN OF THE WIDOWHOOD IN ATLANTIS.
THOSE "MEDDLESOME WOMEN" ARE WHY I WAS NAMED QUEEN.
MAYBE THINGS ARE FINALLY CHANGING IN ATLANTIS.
AND PERHAPS XEBEL CAN BENEFIT FROM THAT CHANGE.
BUT YOU MUST BE CAREFUL, MERA...
...THEY WILL TEAR YOU APART GIVEN HALF THE CHANCE.

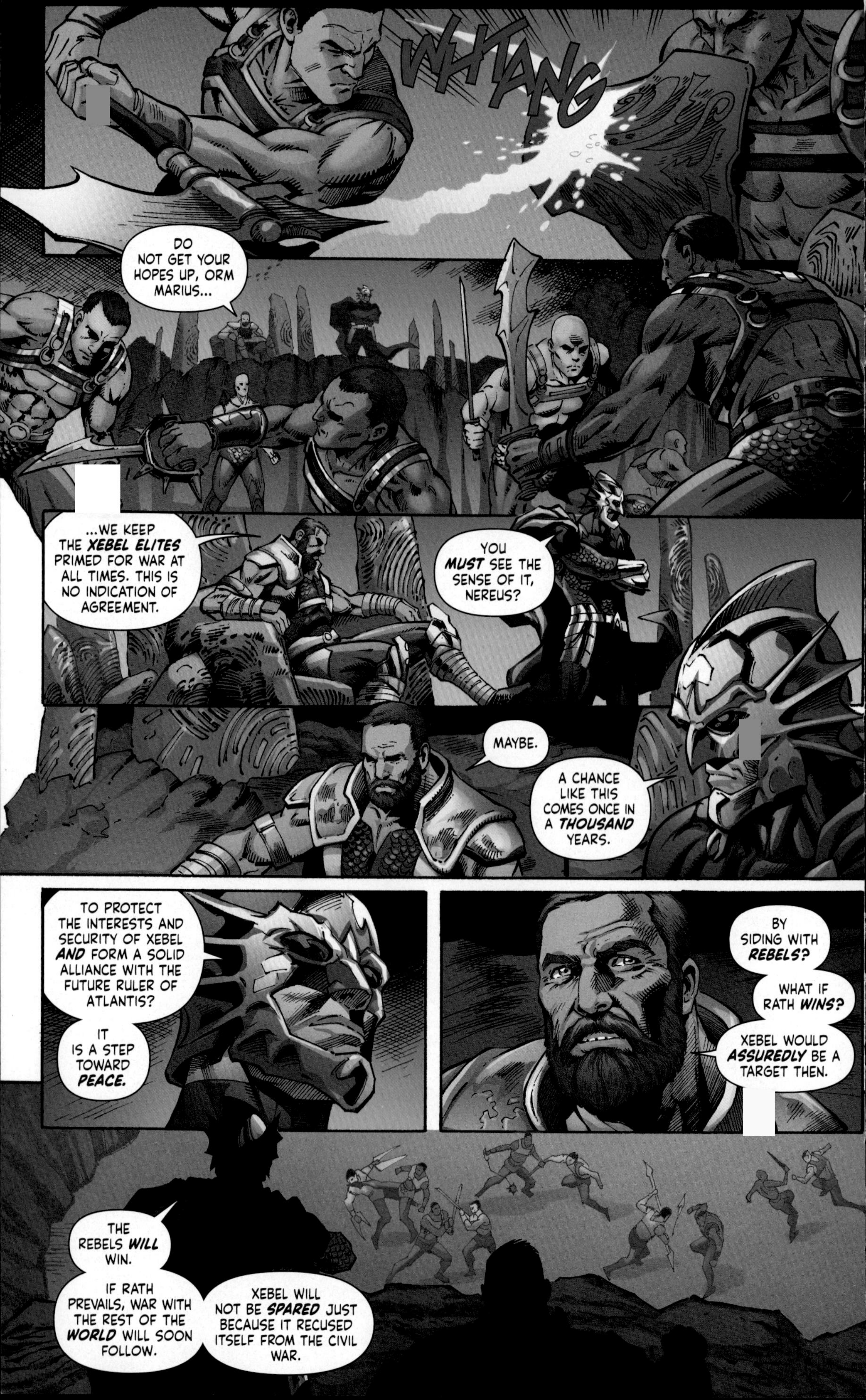

WHTANG
DO NOT GET YOUR HOPES UP, ORM MARIUS...
...WE KEEP THE XEBEL ELITES PRIMED FOR WAR AT ALL TIMES. THIS IS NO INDICATION OF AGREEMENT.
YOU MUST SEE THE SENSE OF IT, NEREUS?
MAYBE.
A CHANCE LIKE THIS COMES ONCE IN A THOUSAND YEARS.
TO PROTECT THE INTERESTS AND SECURITY OF XEBEL AND FORM A SOLID ALLIANCE WITH THE FUTURE RULER OF ATLANTIS?
IT IS A STEP TOWARD PEACE.
BY SIDING WITH REBELS?
WHAT IF RATH WINS?
XEBEL WOULD ASSUREDLY BE A TARGET THEN.
THE REBELS WILL WIN.
IF RATH PREVAILS, WAR WITH THE REST OF THE WORLD WILL SOON FOLLOW.
XEBEL WILL NOT BE SPARED JUST BECAUSE IT RECUSED ITSELF FROM THE CIVIL WAR.

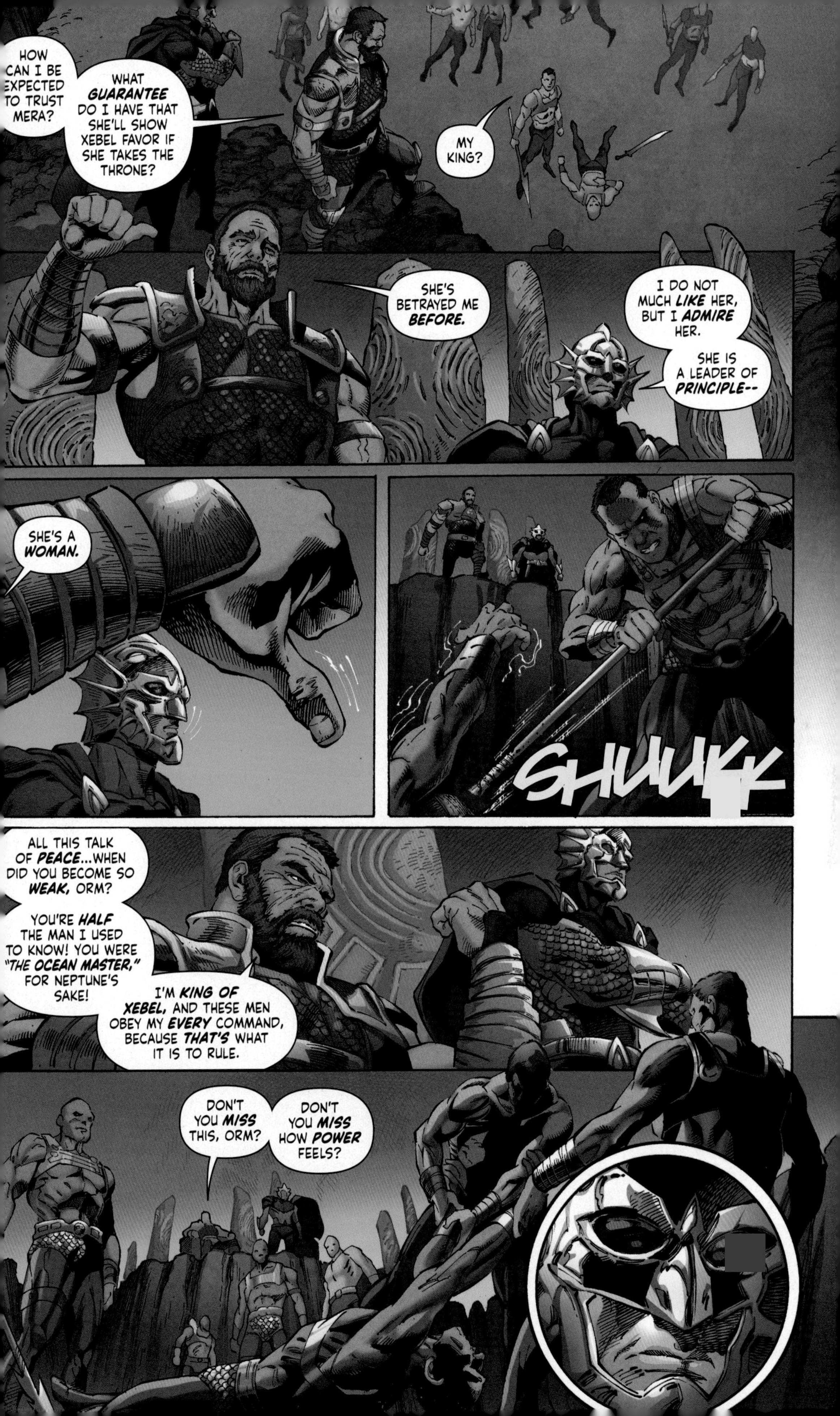
HOW CAN I BE EXPECTED TO TRUST MERA?
WHAT GUARANTEE DO I HAVE THAT SHE'LL SHOW XEBEL FAVOR IF SHE TAKES THE THRONE?
MY KING?
SHE'S BETRAYED ME BEFORE.
I DO NOT MUCH LIKE HER, BUT I ADMIRE HER.
SHE IS A LEADER OF PRINCIPLE--
SHE'S A WOMAN.
SHUUKK
ALL THIS TALK OF PEACE...WHEN DID YOU BECOME SO WEAK, ORM?
YOU'RE HALF THE MAN I USED TO KNOW! YOU WERE "THE OCEAN MASTER," FOR NEPTUNE'S SAKE!
I'M KING OF XEBEL, AND THESE MEN OBEY MY EVERY COMMAND, BECAUSE THAT'S WHAT IT IS TO RULE.
DON'T YOU MISS THIS, ORM?
DON'T YOU MISS HOW POWER FEELS?

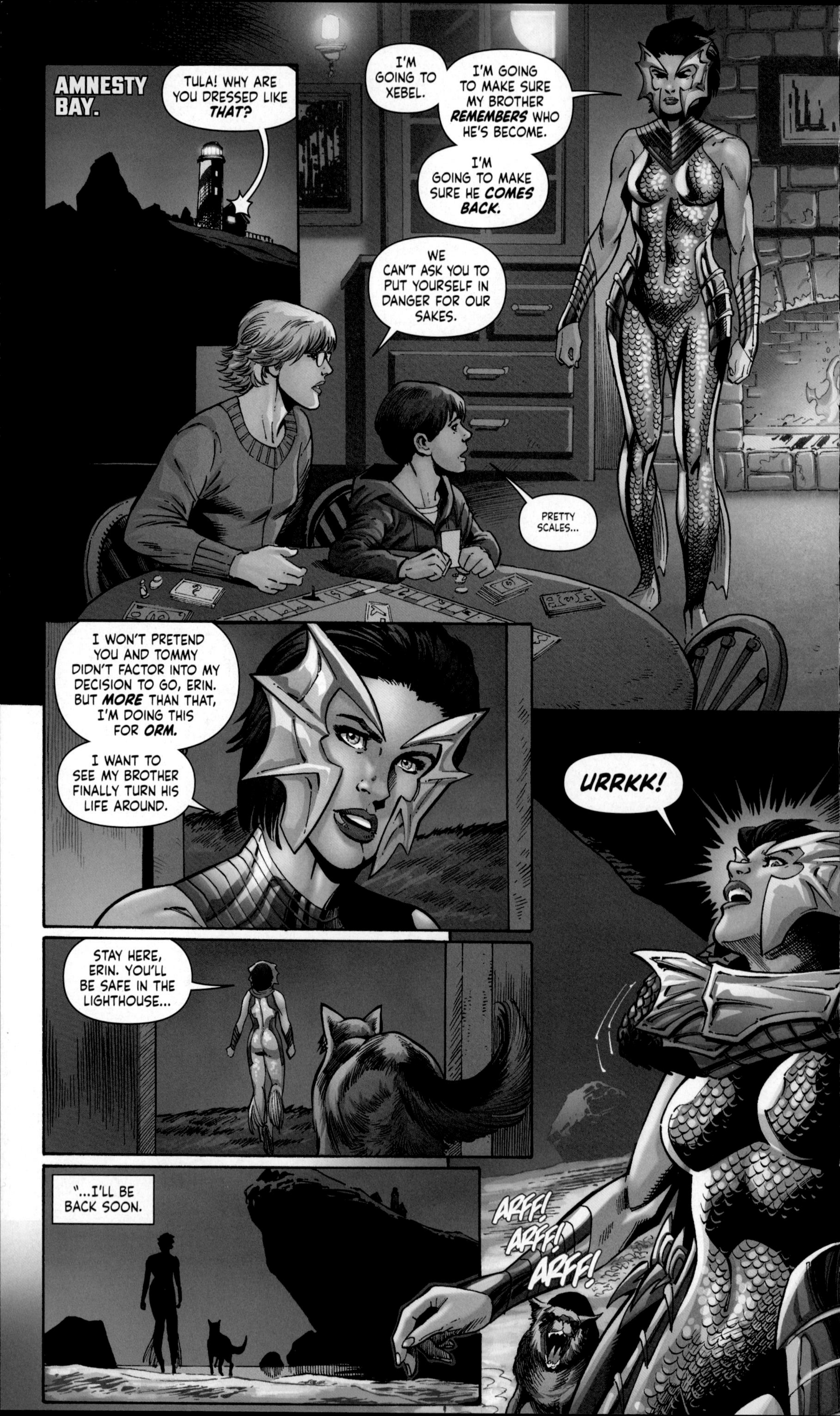
AMNESTY BAY.
TULA! WHY ARE YOU DRESSED LIKE THAT?
I'M GOING TO XEBEL.
I'M GOING TO MAKE SURE MY BROTHER REMEMBERS WHO HE'S BECOME.
I'M GOING TO MAKE SURE HE COMES BACK.
WE CAN'T ASK YOU TO PUT YOURSELF IN DANGER FOR OUR SAKES.
PRETTY SCALES...
I WON'T PRETEND YOU AND TOMMY DIDN'T FACTOR INTO MY DECISION TO GO, ERIN. BUT MORE THAN THAT, I'M DOING THIS FOR ORM.
I WANT TO SEE MY BROTHER FINALLY TURN HIS LIFE AROUND.
STAY HERE, ERIN. YOU'LL BE SAFE IN THE LIGHTHOUSE...
"...I'LL BE BACK SOON.
URRKK!
ARFF! ARFF! ARFF!

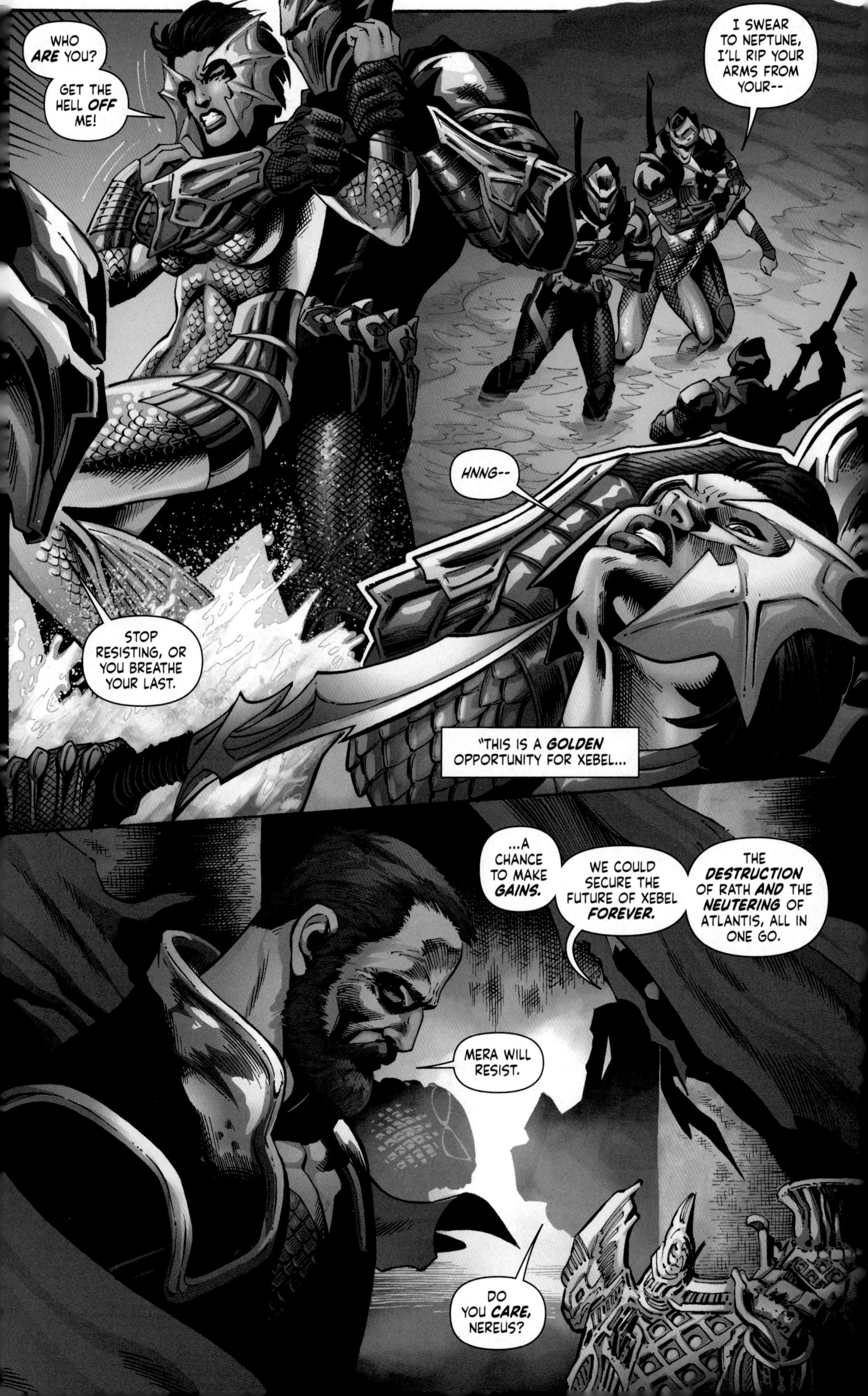
WHO *ARE* YOU?
GET THE HELL *OFF* ME!
I SWEAR TO NEPTUNE, I'LL RIP YOUR ARMS FROM YOUR--
HNNG--
STOP RESISTING, OR YOU BREATHE YOUR LAST.
"THIS IS A *GOLDEN* OPPORTUNITY FOR XEBEL...
...A CHANCE TO MAKE *GAINS.*
WE COULD SECURE THE FUTURE OF XEBEL *FOREVER.*
THE *DESTRUCTION* OF RATH *AND* THE *NEUTERING* OF ATLANTIS, ALL IN ONE GO.
MERA WILL RESIST.
DO YOU *CARE,* NEREUS?

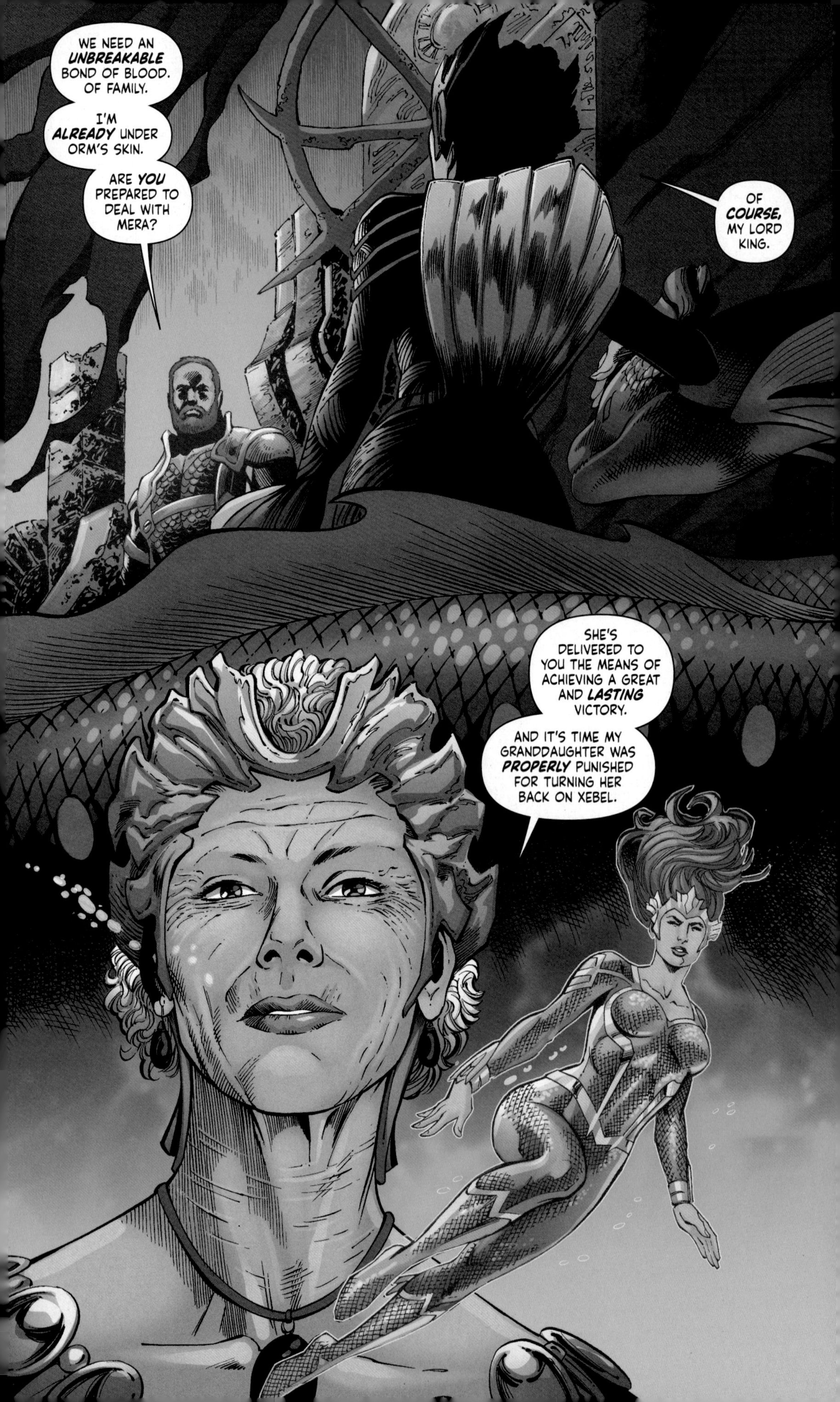
WE NEED AN UNBREAKABLE BOND OF BLOOD. OF FAMILY.
I'M ALREADY UNDER ORM'S SKIN.
ARE YOU PREPARED TO DEAL WITH MERA?
OF COURSE, MY LORD KING.
SHE'S DELIVERED TO YOU THE MEANS OF ACHIEVING A GREAT AND LASTING VICTORY.
AND IT'S TIME MY GRANDDAUGHTER WAS PROPERLY PUNISHED FOR TURNING HER BACK ON XEBEL.

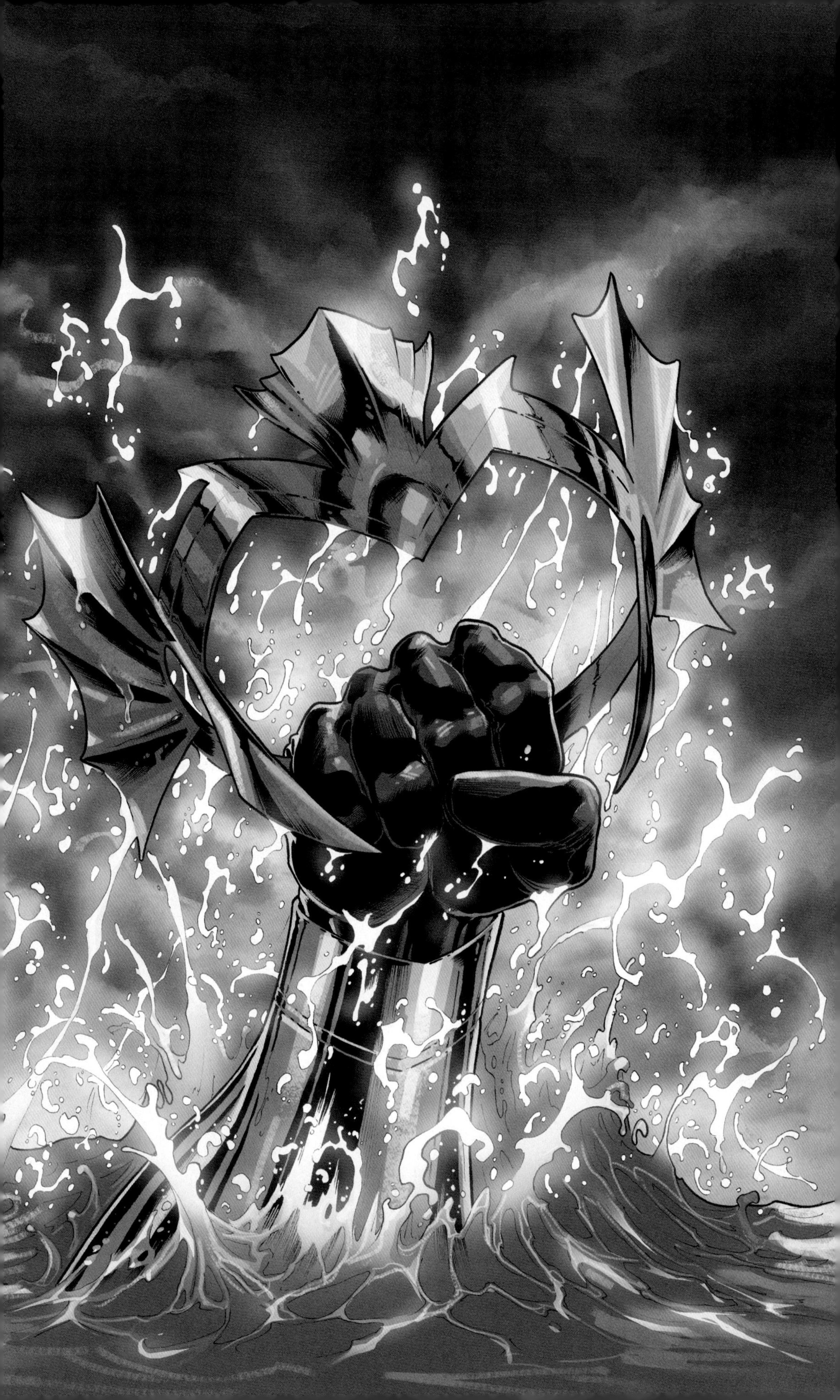

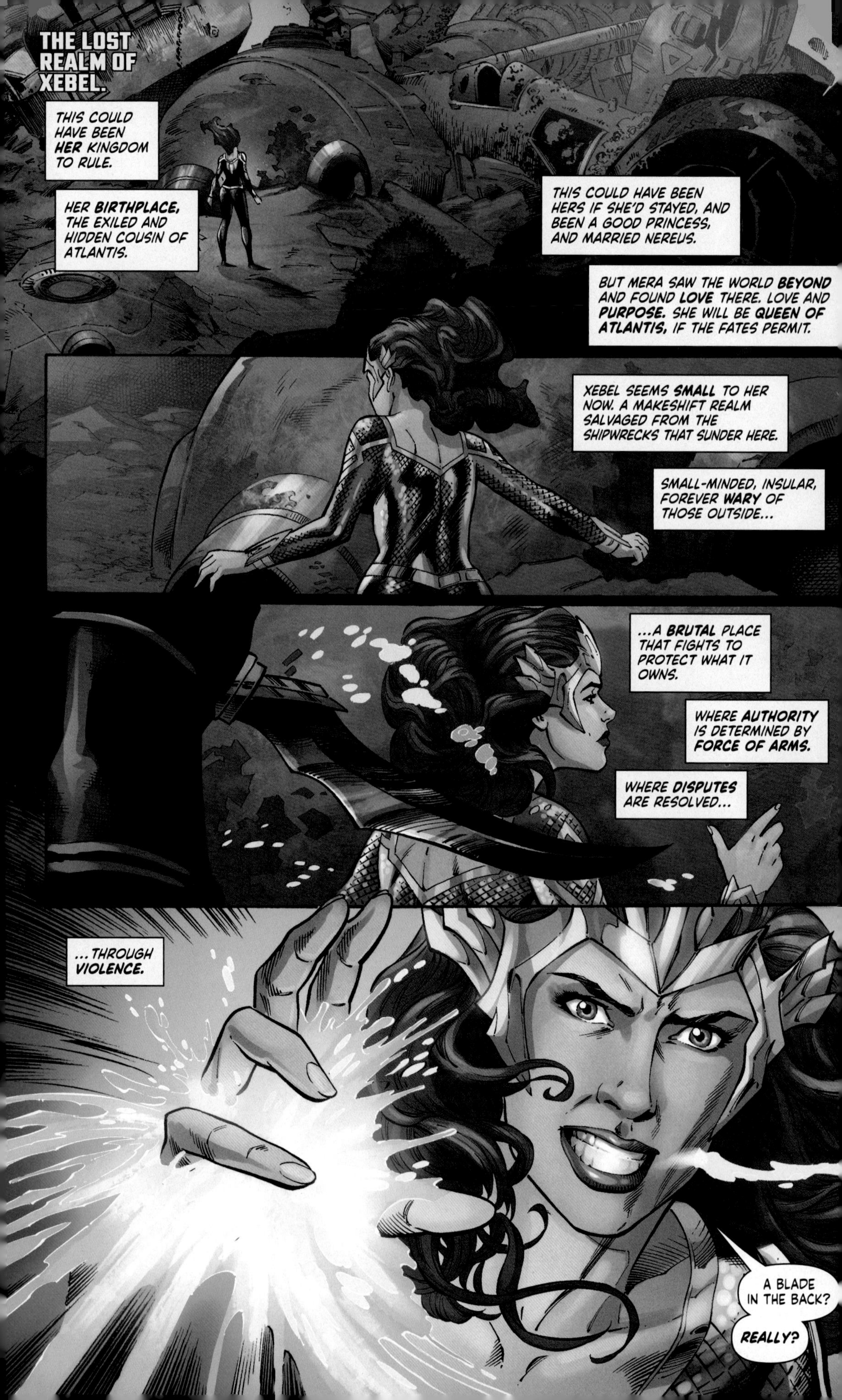
THE LOST REALM OF XEBEL.
THIS COULD HAVE BEEN HER KINGDOM TO RULE.
HER BIRTHPLACE, THE EXILED AND HIDDEN COUSIN OF ATLANTIS.
THIS COULD HAVE BEEN HERS IF SHE'D STAYED, AND BEEN A GOOD PRINCESS, AND MARRIED NEREUS.
BUT MERA SAW THE WORLD BEYOND AND FOUND LOVE THERE. LOVE AND PURPOSE. SHE WILL BE QUEEN OF ATLANTIS, IF THE FATES PERMIT.
XEBEL SEEMS SMALL TO HER NOW. A MAKESHIFT REALM SALVAGED FROM THE SHIPWRECKS THAT SUNDER HERE.
SMALL-MINDED, INSULAR, FOREVER WARY OF THOSE OUTSIDE...
...A BRUTAL PLACE THAT FIGHTS TO PROTECT WHAT IT OWNS.
WHERE AUTHORITY IS DETERMINED BY FORCE OF ARMS.
WHERE DISPUTES ARE RESOLVED...
...THROUGH VIOLENCE.
A BLADE IN THE BACK?
REALLY?

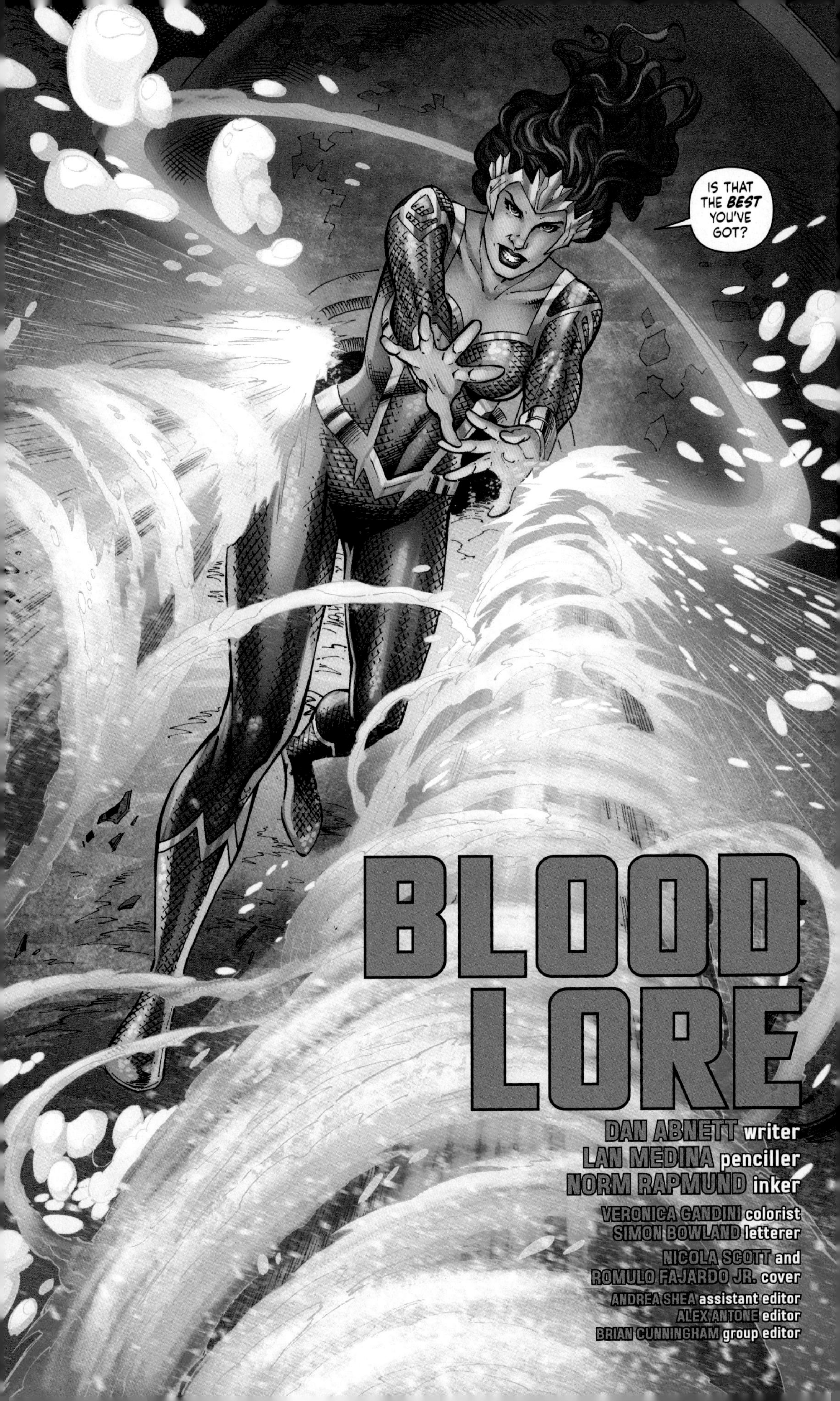

IS THAT THE BEST YOU'VE GOT?
BLOOD LORE
DAN ABNETT writer
LAN MEDINA penciller
NORM RAPMUND inker
VERONICA GANDINI colorist
SIMON BOWLAND letterer
NICOLA SCOTT and ROMULO FAJARDO JR. cover
ANDREA SHEA assistant editor
ALEX ANTONE editor
BRIAN CUNNINGHAM group editor

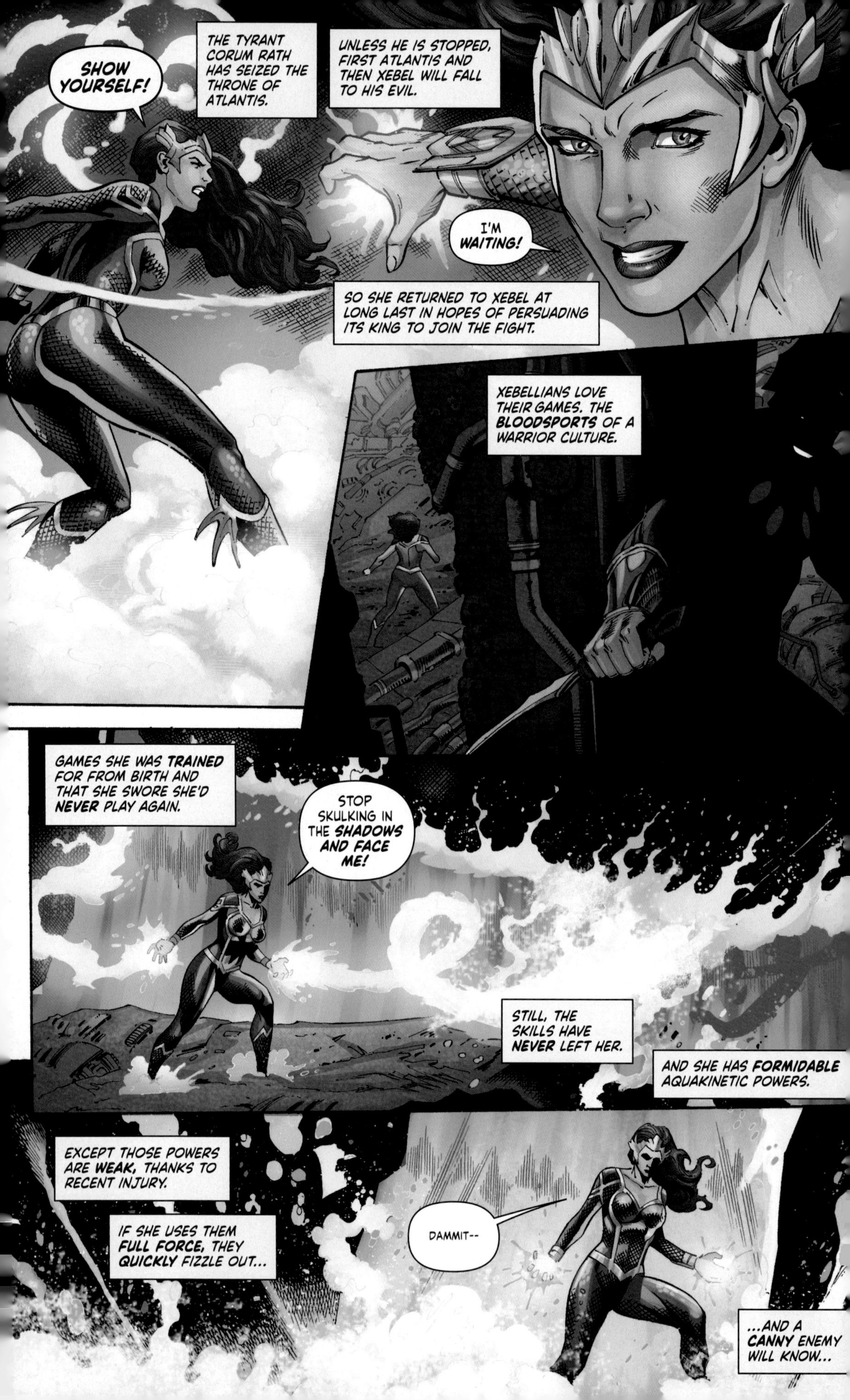
SHOW YOURSELF!
THE TYRANT CORUM RATH HAS SEIZED THE THRONE OF ATLANTIS.
UNLESS HE IS STOPPED, FIRST ATLANTIS AND THEN XEBEL WILL FALL TO HIS EVIL.
I'M WAITING!
SO SHE RETURNED TO XEBEL AT LONG LAST IN HOPES OF PERSUADING ITS KING TO JOIN THE FIGHT.
XEBELLIANS LOVE THEIR GAMES. THE BLOODSPORTS OF A WARRIOR CULTURE.
GAMES SHE WAS TRAINED FOR FROM BIRTH AND THAT SHE SWORE SHE'D NEVER PLAY AGAIN.
STOP SKULKING IN THE SHADOWS AND FACE ME!
STILL, THE SKILLS HAVE NEVER LEFT HER.
AND SHE HAS FORMIDABLE AQUAKINETIC POWERS.
EXCEPT THOSE POWERS ARE WEAK, THANKS TO RECENT INJURY.
IF SHE USES THEM FULL FORCE, THEY QUICKLY FIZZLE OUT...
DAMMIT--
...AND A CANNY ENEMY WILL KNOW...

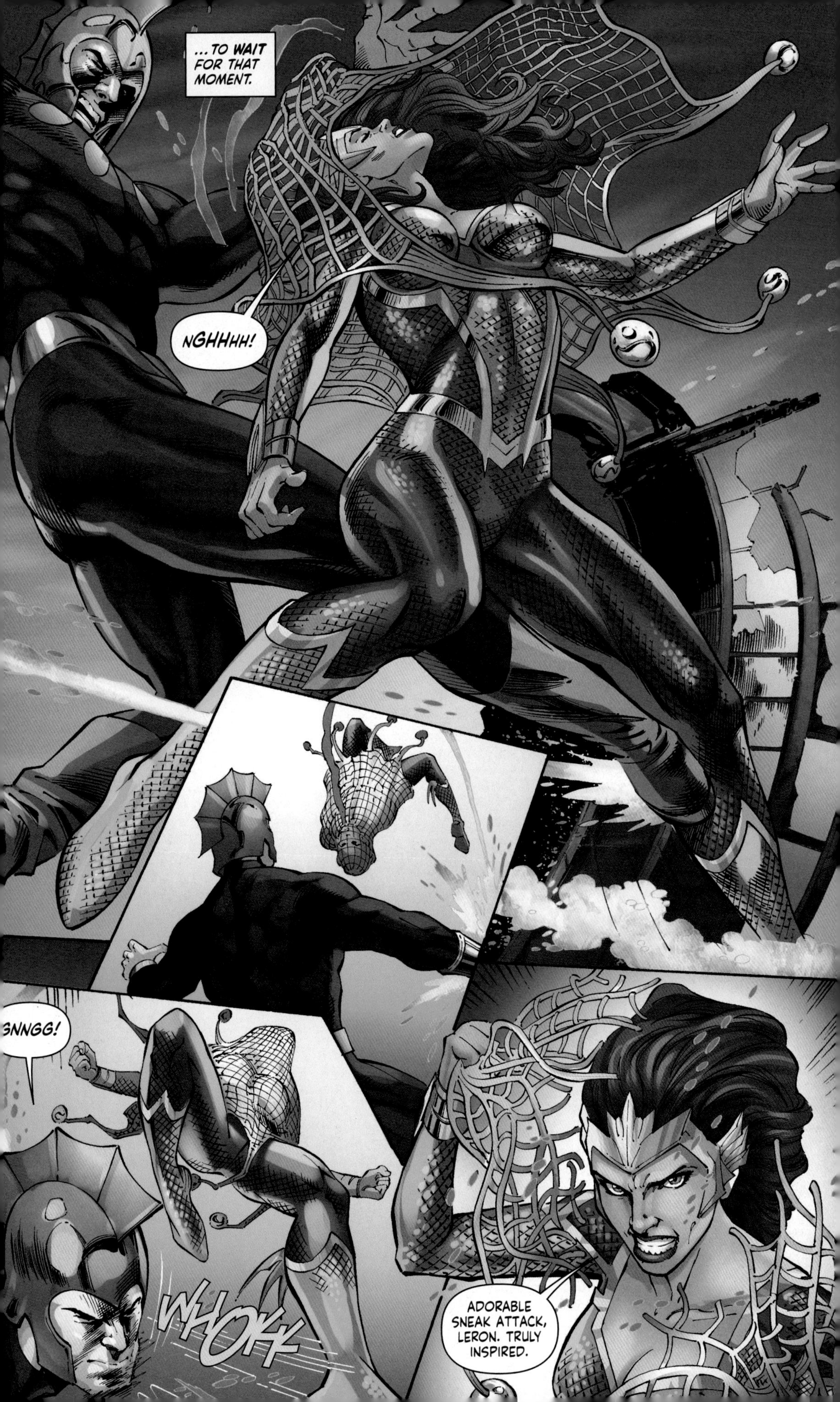
...TO WAIT FOR THAT MOMENT.
NGHHHH!
GNNGG!
WHOKK
ADORABLE SNEAK ATTACK, LERON. TRULY INSPIRED.

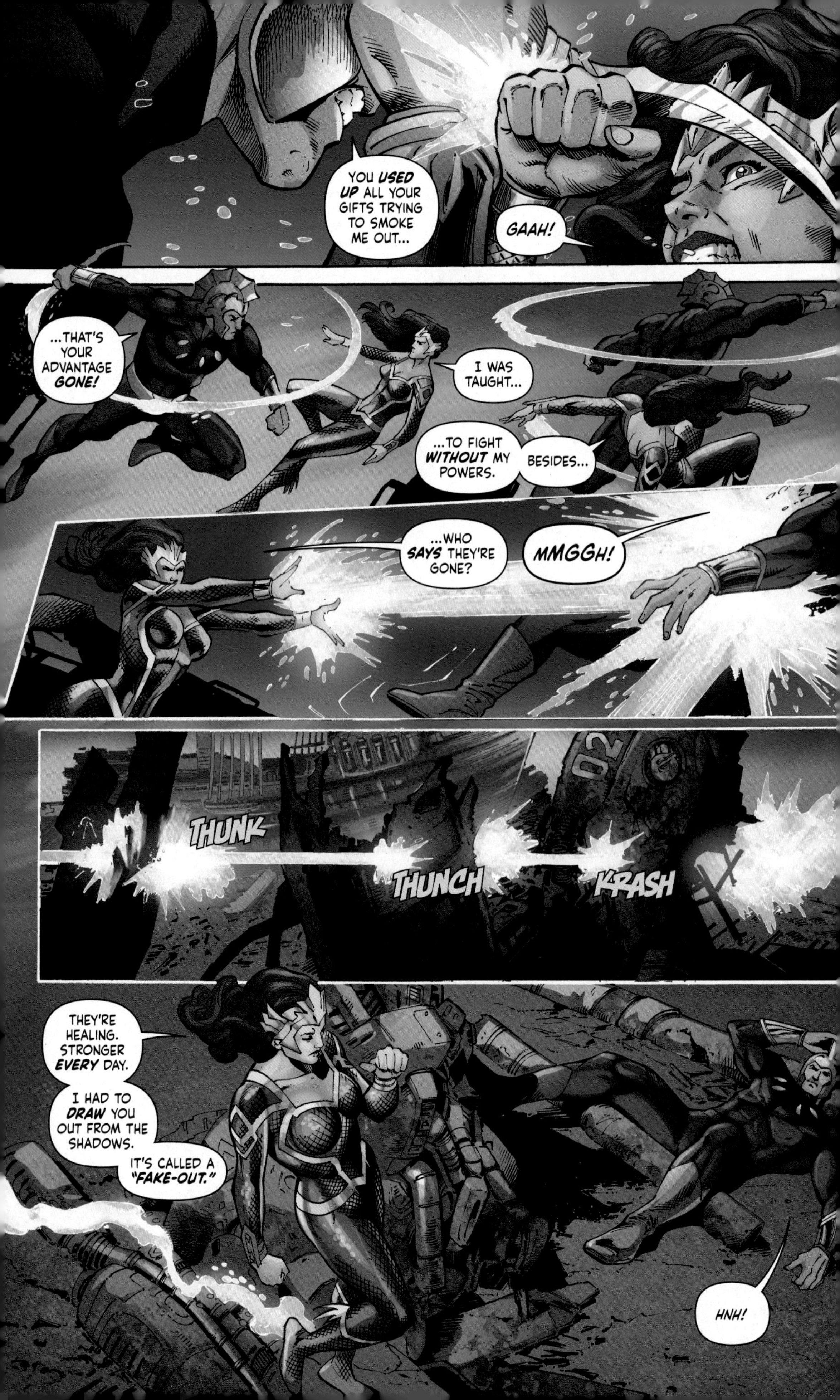
YOU USED UP ALL YOUR GIFTS TRYING TO SMOKE ME OUT...
GAAH!
...THAT'S YOUR ADVANTAGE GONE!
I WAS TAUGHT...
...TO FIGHT WITHOUT MY POWERS.
BESIDES...
...WHO SAYS THEY'RE GONE?
MMGGH!
THUNK
THUNCH
KRASH
THEY'RE HEALING. STRONGER EVERY DAY.
I HAD TO DRAW YOU OUT FROM THE SHADOWS.
IT'S CALLED A "FAKE-OUT."
HNH!

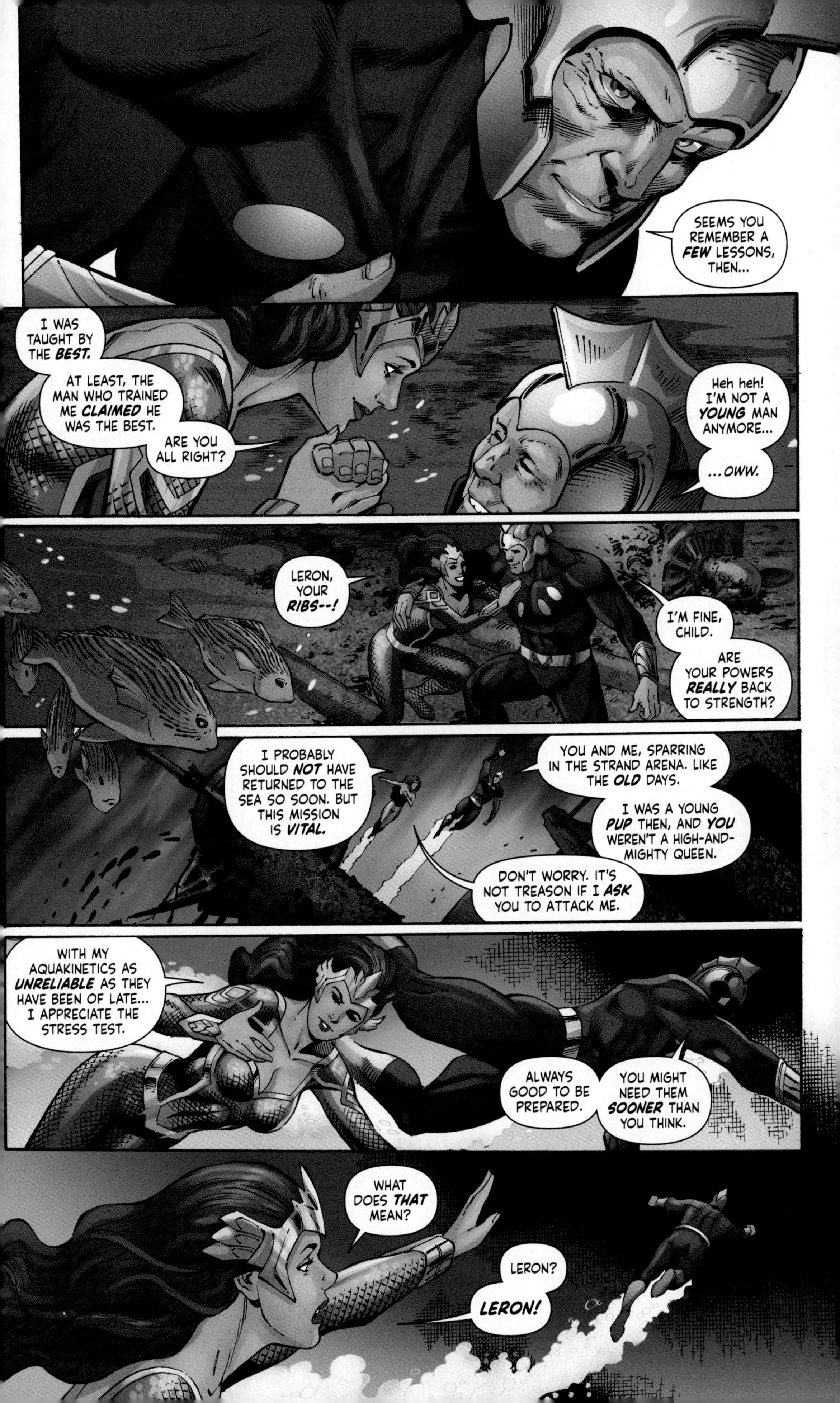
SEEMS YOU REMEMBER A FEW LESSONS, THEN...
I WAS TAUGHT BY THE BEST.
AT LEAST, THE MAN WHO TRAINED ME CLAIMED HE WAS THE BEST.
ARE YOU ALL RIGHT?
Heh heh! I'M NOT A YOUNG MAN ANYMORE...
...OWW.
LERON, YOUR RIBS--!
I'M FINE, CHILD.
ARE YOUR POWERS REALLY BACK TO STRENGTH?
I PROBABLY SHOULD NOT HAVE RETURNED TO THE SEA SO SOON. BUT THIS MISSION IS VITAL.
YOU AND ME, SPARRING IN THE STRAND ARENA. LIKE THE OLD DAYS.
I WAS A YOUNG PUP THEN, AND YOU WEREN'T A HIGH-AND-MIGHTY QUEEN.
DON'T WORRY. IT'S NOT TREASON IF I ASK YOU TO ATTACK ME.
WITH MY AQUAKINETICS AS UNRELIABLE AS THEY HAVE BEEN OF LATE... I APPRECIATE THE STRESS TEST.
ALWAYS GOOD TO BE PREPARED.
YOU MIGHT NEED THEM SOONER THAN YOU THINK.
WHAT DOES THAT MEAN?
LERON?
LERON!

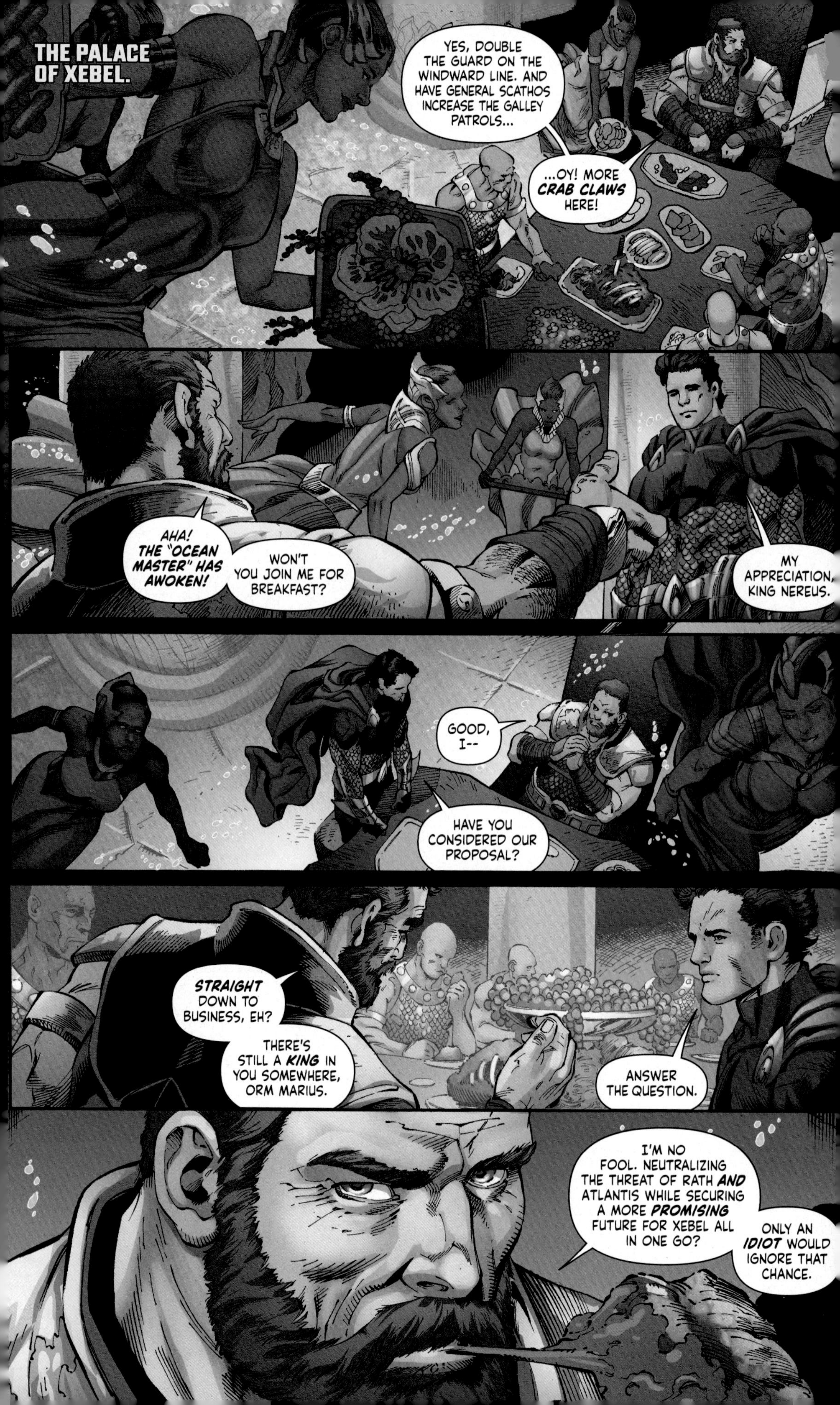

THE PALACE OF XEBEL.
YES, DOUBLE THE GUARD ON THE WINDWARD LINE. AND HAVE GENERAL SCATHOS INCREASE THE GALLEY PATROLS...
...OY! MORE CRAB CLAWS HERE!
AHA! THE "OCEAN MASTER" HAS AWOKEN!
WON'T YOU JOIN ME FOR BREAKFAST?
MY APPRECIATION, KING NEREUS.
GOOD, I--
HAVE YOU CONSIDERED OUR PROPOSAL?
STRAIGHT DOWN TO BUSINESS, EH?
THERE'S STILL A KING IN YOU SOMEWHERE, ORM MARIUS.
ANSWER THE QUESTION.
I'M NO FOOL. NEUTRALIZING THE THREAT OF RATH AND ATLANTIS WHILE SECURING A MORE PROMISING FUTURE FOR XEBEL ALL IN ONE GO?
ONLY AN IDIOT WOULD IGNORE THAT CHANCE.

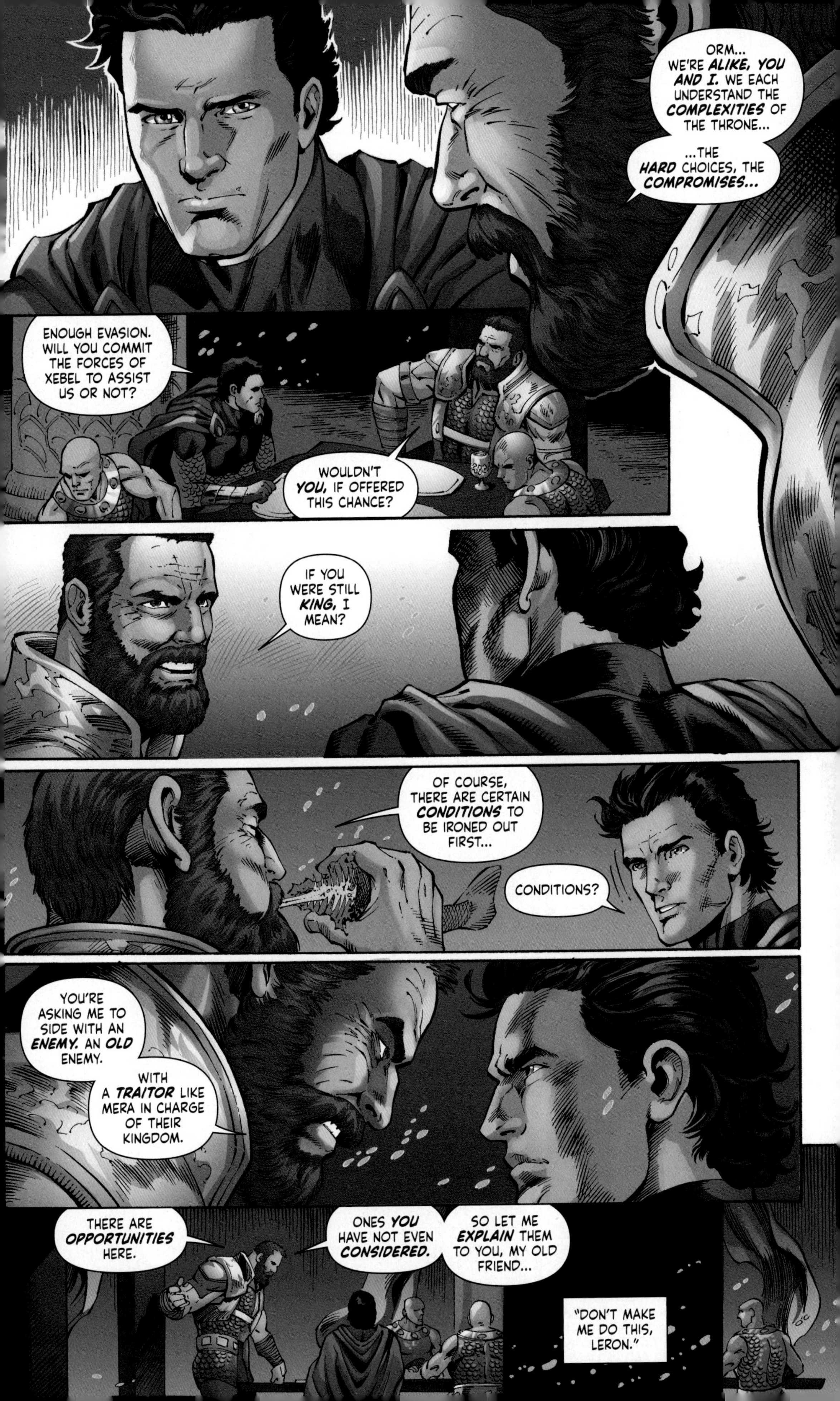
ORM... WE'RE ALIKE, YOU AND I. WE EACH UNDERSTAND THE COMPLEXITIES OF THE THRONE...
...THE HARD CHOICES, THE COMPROMISES...
ENOUGH EVASION. WILL YOU COMMIT THE FORCES OF XEBEL TO ASSIST US OR NOT?
WOULDN'T YOU, IF OFFERED THIS CHANCE?
IF YOU WERE STILL KING, I MEAN?
OF COURSE, THERE ARE CERTAIN CONDITIONS TO BE IRONED OUT FIRST...
CONDITIONS?
YOU'RE ASKING ME TO SIDE WITH AN ENEMY. AN OLD ENEMY.
WITH A TRAITOR LIKE MERA IN CHARGE OF THEIR KINGDOM.
THERE ARE OPPORTUNITIES HERE.
ONES YOU HAVE NOT EVEN CONSIDERED.
SO LET ME EXPLAIN THEM TO YOU, MY OLD FRIEND...
"DON'T MAKE ME DO THIS, LERON."

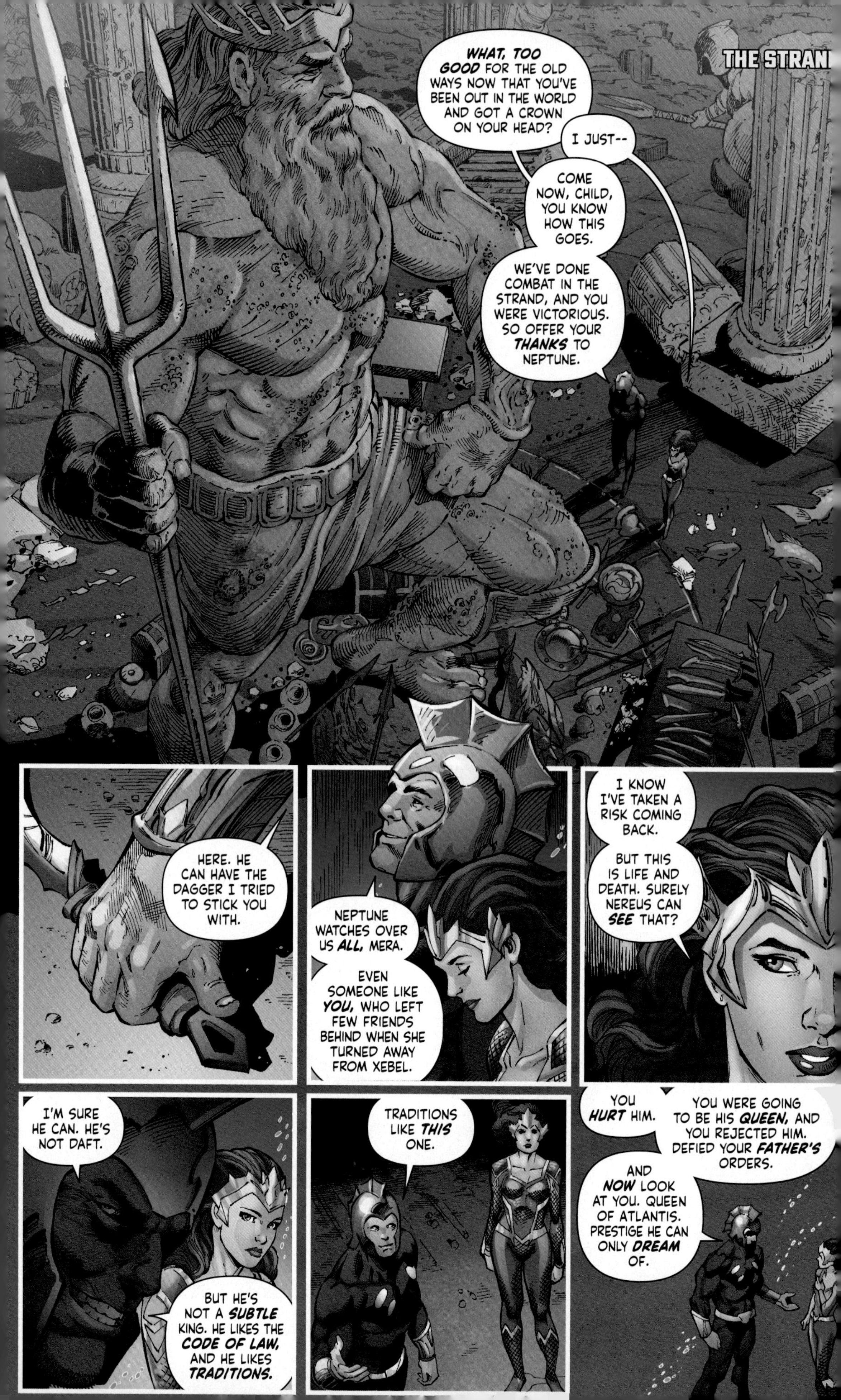
THE STRAN
WHAT, TOO GOOD FOR THE OLD WAYS NOW THAT YOU'VE BEEN OUT IN THE WORLD AND GOT A CROWN ON YOUR HEAD?
I JUST--
COME NOW, CHILD, YOU KNOW HOW THIS GOES.
WE'VE DONE COMBAT IN THE STRAND, AND YOU WERE VICTORIOUS. SO OFFER YOUR THANKS TO NEPTUNE.
HERE. HE CAN HAVE THE DAGGER I TRIED TO STICK YOU WITH.
NEPTUNE WATCHES OVER US ALL, MERA.
EVEN SOMEONE LIKE YOU, WHO LEFT FEW FRIENDS BEHIND WHEN SHE TURNED AWAY FROM XEBEL.
I KNOW I'VE TAKEN A RISK COMING BACK.
BUT THIS IS LIFE AND DEATH. SURELY NEREUS CAN SEE THAT?
I'M SURE HE CAN. HE'S NOT DAFT.
BUT HE'S NOT A SUBTLE KING. HE LIKES THE CODE OF LAW, AND HE LIKES TRADITIONS.
TRADITIONS LIKE THIS ONE.
YOU HURT HIM.
YOU WERE GOING TO BE HIS QUEEN, AND YOU REJECTED HIM. DEFIED YOUR FATHER'S ORDERS.
AND NOW LOOK AT YOU. QUEEN OF ATLANTIS. PRESTIGE HE CAN ONLY DREAM OF.

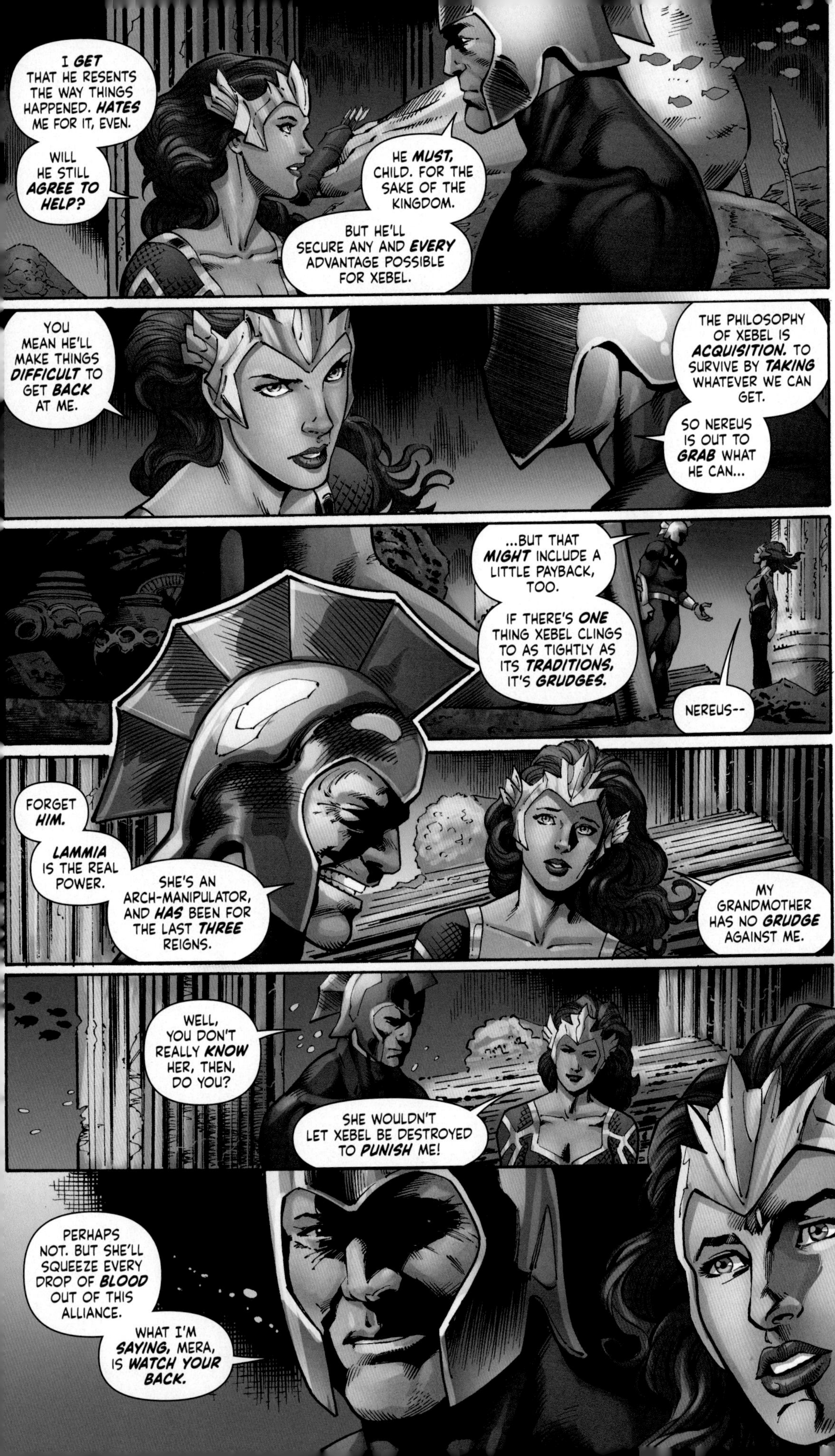

I GET THAT HE RESENTS THE WAY THINGS HAPPENED. HATES ME FOR IT, EVEN.
WILL HE STILL AGREE TO HELP?
HE MUST, CHILD. FOR THE SAKE OF THE KINGDOM.
BUT HE'LL SECURE ANY AND EVERY ADVANTAGE POSSIBLE FOR XEBEL.
YOU MEAN HE'LL MAKE THINGS DIFFICULT TO GET BACK AT ME.
THE PHILOSOPHY OF XEBEL IS ACQUISITION. TO SURVIVE BY TAKING WHATEVER WE CAN GET.
SO NEREUS IS OUT TO GRAB WHAT HE CAN...
...BUT THAT MIGHT INCLUDE A LITTLE PAYBACK, TOO.
IF THERE'S ONE THING XEBEL CLINGS TO AS TIGHTLY AS ITS TRADITIONS, IT'S GRUDGES.
NEREUS--
FORGET HIM.
LAMMIA IS THE REAL POWER.
SHE'S AN ARCH-MANIPULATOR, AND HAS BEEN FOR THE LAST THREE REIGNS.
MY GRANDMOTHER HAS NO GRUDGE AGAINST ME.
WELL, YOU DON'T REALLY KNOW HER, THEN, DO YOU?
SHE WOULDN'T LET XEBEL BE DESTROYED TO PUNISH ME!
PERHAPS NOT. BUT SHE'LL SQUEEZE EVERY DROP OF BLOOD OUT OF THIS ALLIANCE.
WHAT I'M SAYING, MERA, IS WATCH YOUR BACK.

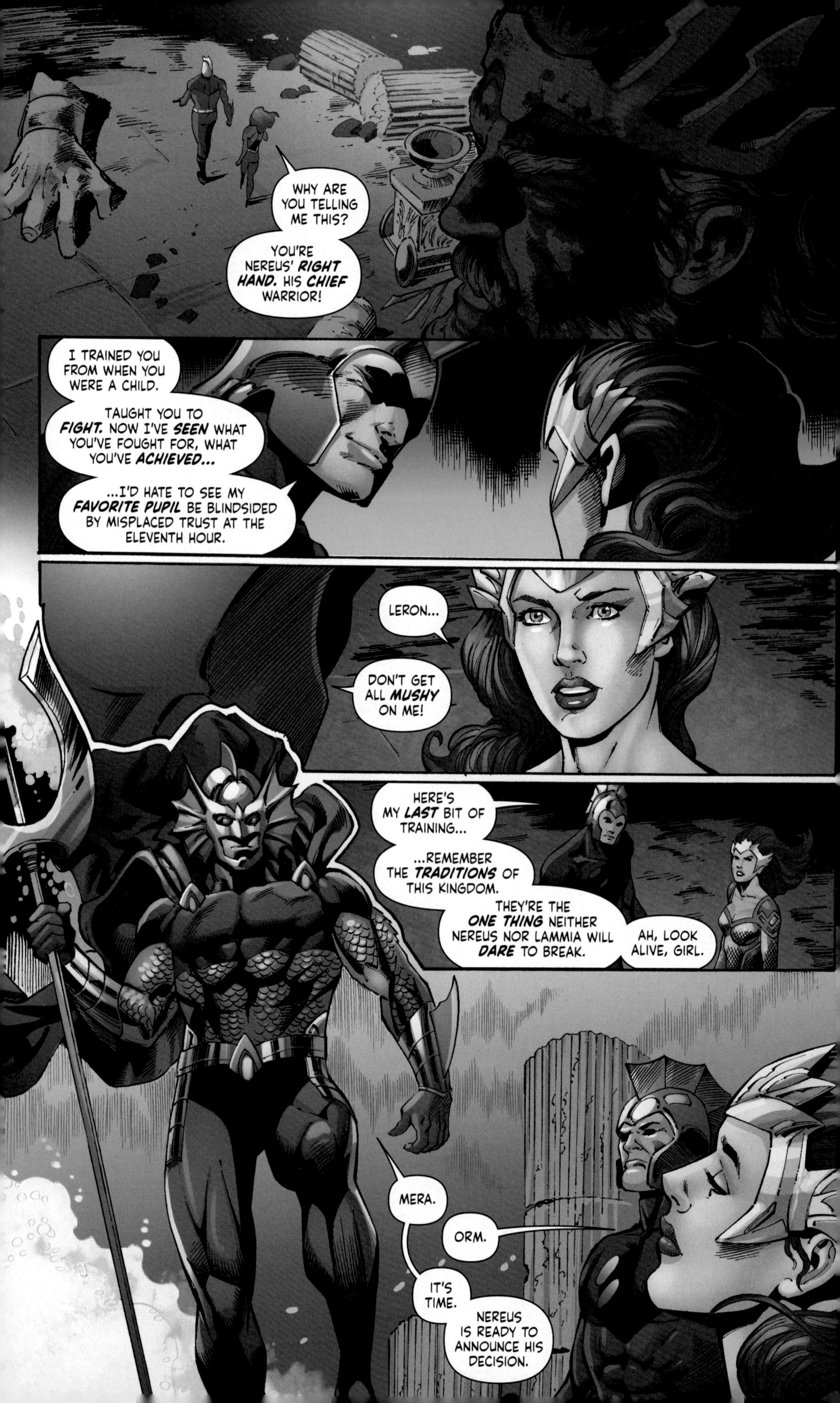
WHY ARE YOU TELLING ME THIS?
YOU'RE NEREUS' RIGHT HAND. HIS CHIEF WARRIOR!
I TRAINED YOU FROM WHEN YOU WERE A CHILD.
TAUGHT YOU TO FIGHT. NOW I'VE SEEN WHAT YOU'VE FOUGHT FOR, WHAT YOU'VE ACHIEVED...
...I'D HATE TO SEE MY FAVORITE PUPIL BE BLINDSIDED BY MISPLACED TRUST AT THE ELEVENTH HOUR.
LERON...
DON'T GET ALL MUSHY ON ME!
HERE'S MY LAST BIT OF TRAINING...
...REMEMBER THE TRADITIONS OF THIS KINGDOM.
THEY'RE THE ONE THING NEITHER NEREUS NOR LAMMIA WILL DARE TO BREAK.
AH, LOOK ALIVE, GIRL.
MERA.
ORM.
IT'S TIME.
NEREUS IS READY TO ANNOUNCE HIS DECISION.

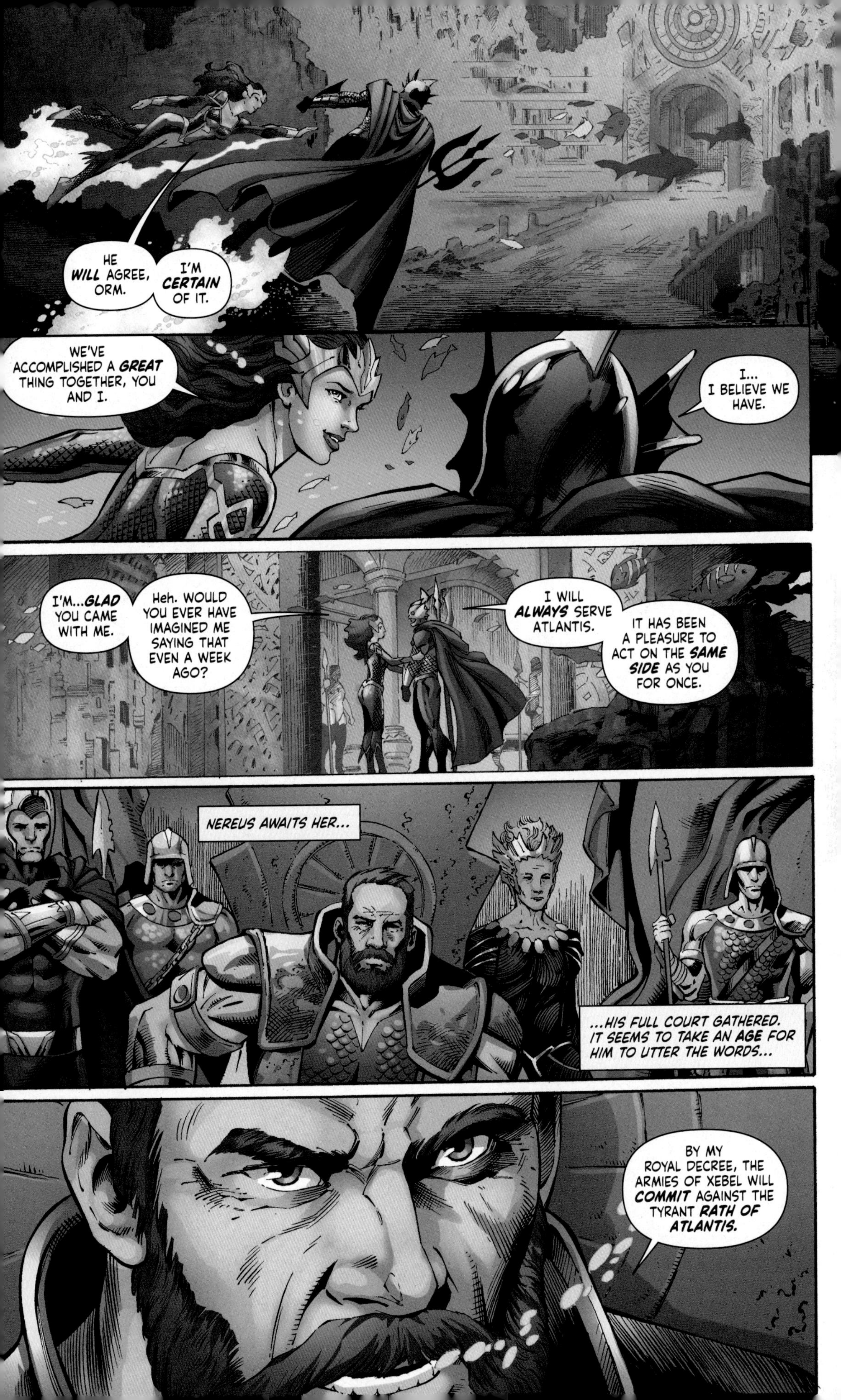
HE WILL AGREE, ORM.
I'M CERTAIN OF IT.
WE'VE ACCOMPLISHED A GREAT THING TOGETHER, YOU AND I.
I... I BELIEVE WE HAVE.
I'M...GLAD YOU CAME WITH ME.
Heh. WOULD YOU EVER HAVE IMAGINED ME SAYING THAT EVEN A WEEK AGO?
I WILL ALWAYS SERVE ATLANTIS.
IT HAS BEEN A PLEASURE TO ACT ON THE SAME SIDE AS YOU FOR ONCE.
NEREUS AWAITS HER...
...HIS FULL COURT GATHERED. IT SEEMS TO TAKE AN AGE FOR HIM TO UTTER THE WORDS...
BY MY ROYAL DECREE, THE ARMIES OF XEBEL WILL COMMIT AGAINST THE TYRANT RATH OF ATLANTIS.

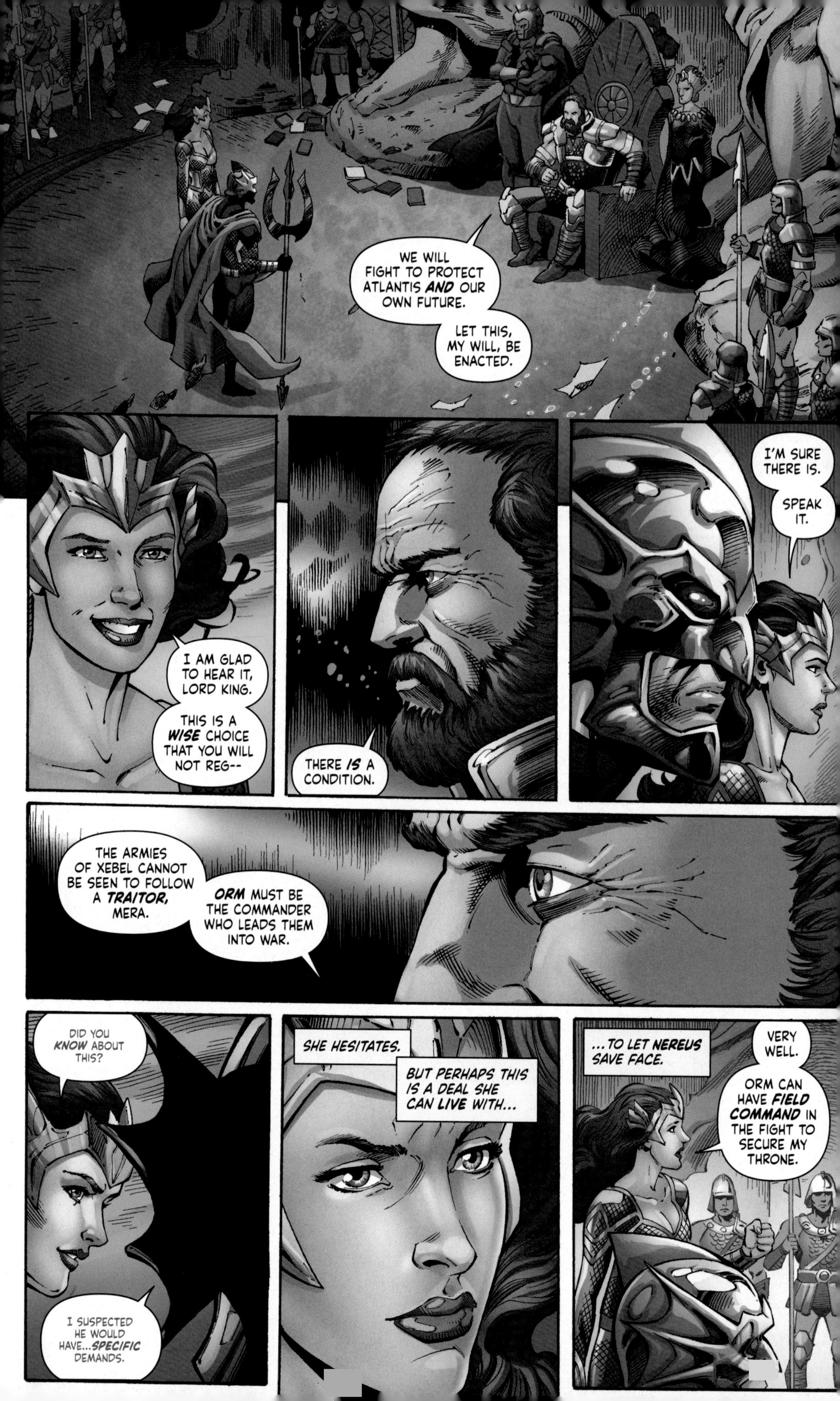
WE WILL FIGHT TO PROTECT ATLANTIS AND OUR OWN FUTURE.
LET THIS, MY WILL, BE ENACTED.
I AM GLAD TO HEAR IT, LORD KING.
THIS IS A WISE CHOICE THAT YOU WILL NOT REG--
THERE IS A CONDITION.
I'M SURE THERE IS.
SPEAK IT.
THE ARMIES OF XEBEL CANNOT BE SEEN TO FOLLOW A TRAITOR, MERA.
ORM MUST BE THE COMMANDER WHO LEADS THEM INTO WAR.
DID YOU KNOW ABOUT THIS?
I SUSPECTED HE WOULD HAVE...SPECIFIC DEMANDS.
SHE HESITATES.
BUT PERHAPS THIS IS A DEAL SHE CAN LIVE WITH...
...TO LET NEREUS SAVE FACE.
VERY WELL.
ORM CAN HAVE FIELD COMMAND IN THE FIGHT TO SECURE MY THRONE.

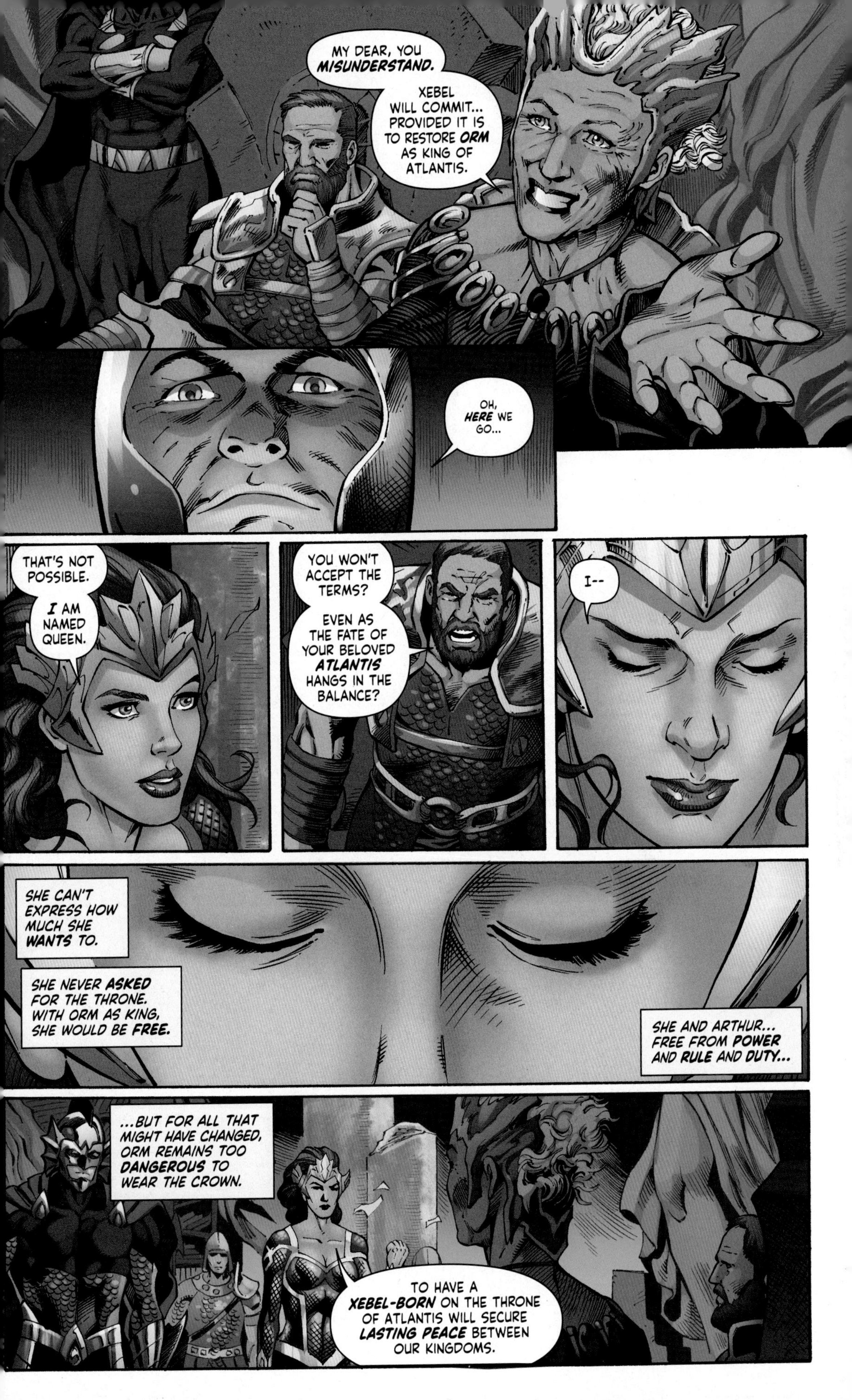

MY DEAR, YOU MISUNDERSTAND.
XEBEL WILL COMMIT... PROVIDED IT IS TO RESTORE ORM AS KING OF ATLANTIS.
OH, HERE WE GO...
THAT'S NOT POSSIBLE.
I AM NAMED QUEEN.
YOU WON'T ACCEPT THE TERMS?
EVEN AS THE FATE OF YOUR BELOVED ATLANTIS HANGS IN THE BALANCE?
I--
SHE CAN'T EXPRESS HOW MUCH SHE WANTS TO.
SHE NEVER ASKED FOR THE THRONE. WITH ORM AS KING, SHE WOULD BE FREE.
SHE AND ARTHUR... FREE FROM POWER AND RULE AND DUTY...
...BUT FOR ALL THAT MIGHT HAVE CHANGED, ORM REMAINS TOO DANGEROUS TO WEAR THE CROWN.
TO HAVE A XEBEL-BORN ON THE THRONE OF ATLANTIS WILL SECURE LASTING PEACE BETWEEN OUR KINGDOMS.

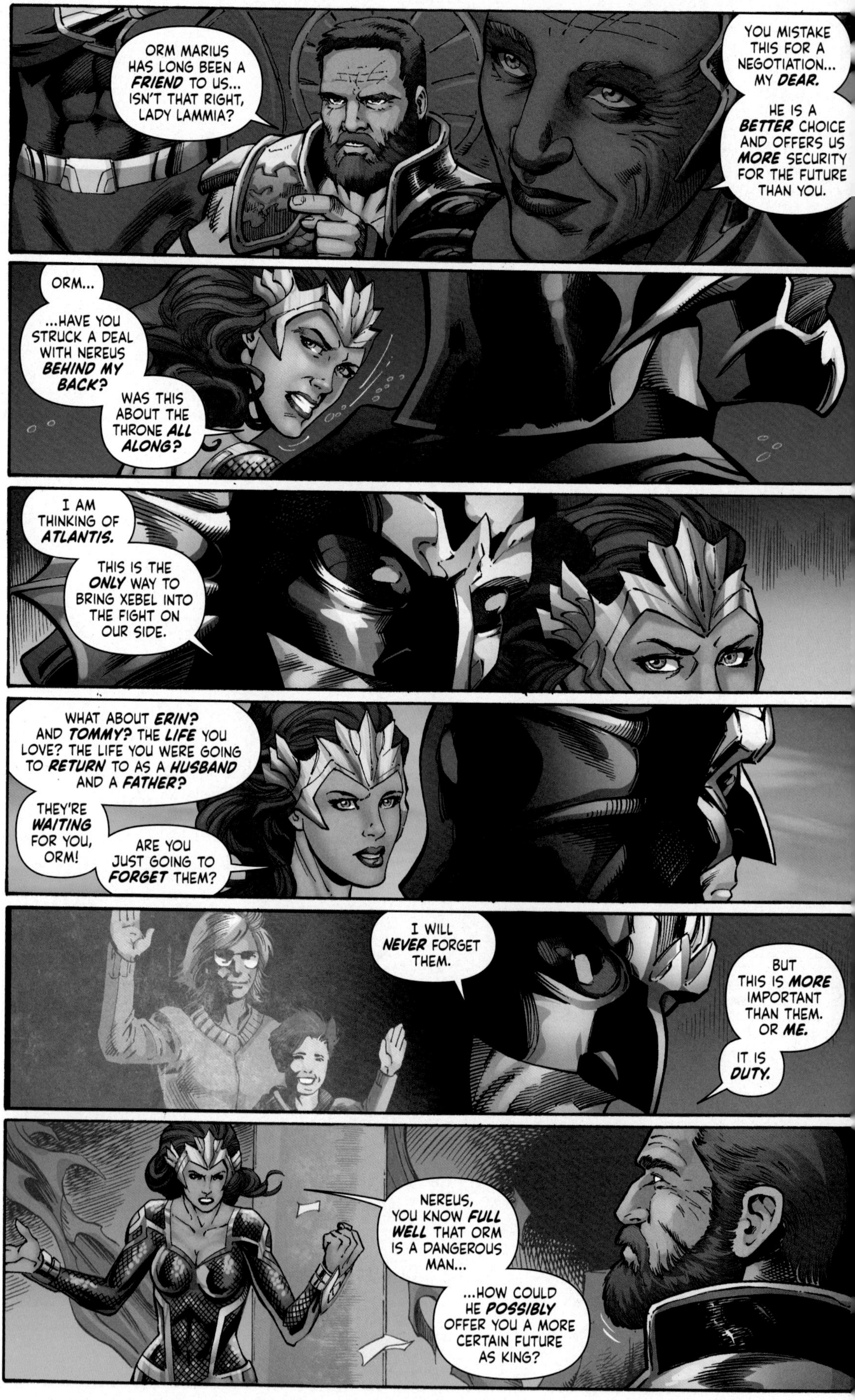
ORM MARIUS HAS LONG BEEN A FRIEND TO US... ISN'T THAT RIGHT, LADY LAMMIA?
YOU MISTAKE THIS FOR A NEGOTIATION... MY DEAR.
HE IS A BETTER CHOICE AND OFFERS US MORE SECURITY FOR THE FUTURE THAN YOU.
ORM...
...HAVE YOU STRUCK A DEAL WITH NEREUS BEHIND MY BACK?
WAS THIS ABOUT THE THRONE ALL ALONG?
I AM THINKING OF ATLANTIS.
THIS IS THE ONLY WAY TO BRING XEBEL INTO THE FIGHT ON OUR SIDE.
WHAT ABOUT ERIN? AND TOMMY? THE LIFE YOU LOVE? THE LIFE YOU WERE GOING TO RETURN TO AS A HUSBAND AND A FATHER?
THEY'RE WAITING FOR YOU, ORM!
ARE YOU JUST GOING TO FORGET THEM?
I WILL NEVER FORGET THEM.
BUT THIS IS MORE IMPORTANT THAN THEM. OR ME.
IT IS DUTY.
NEREUS, YOU KNOW FULL WELL THAT ORM IS A DANGEROUS MAN...
...HOW COULD HE POSSIBLY OFFER YOU A MORE CERTAIN FUTURE AS KING?

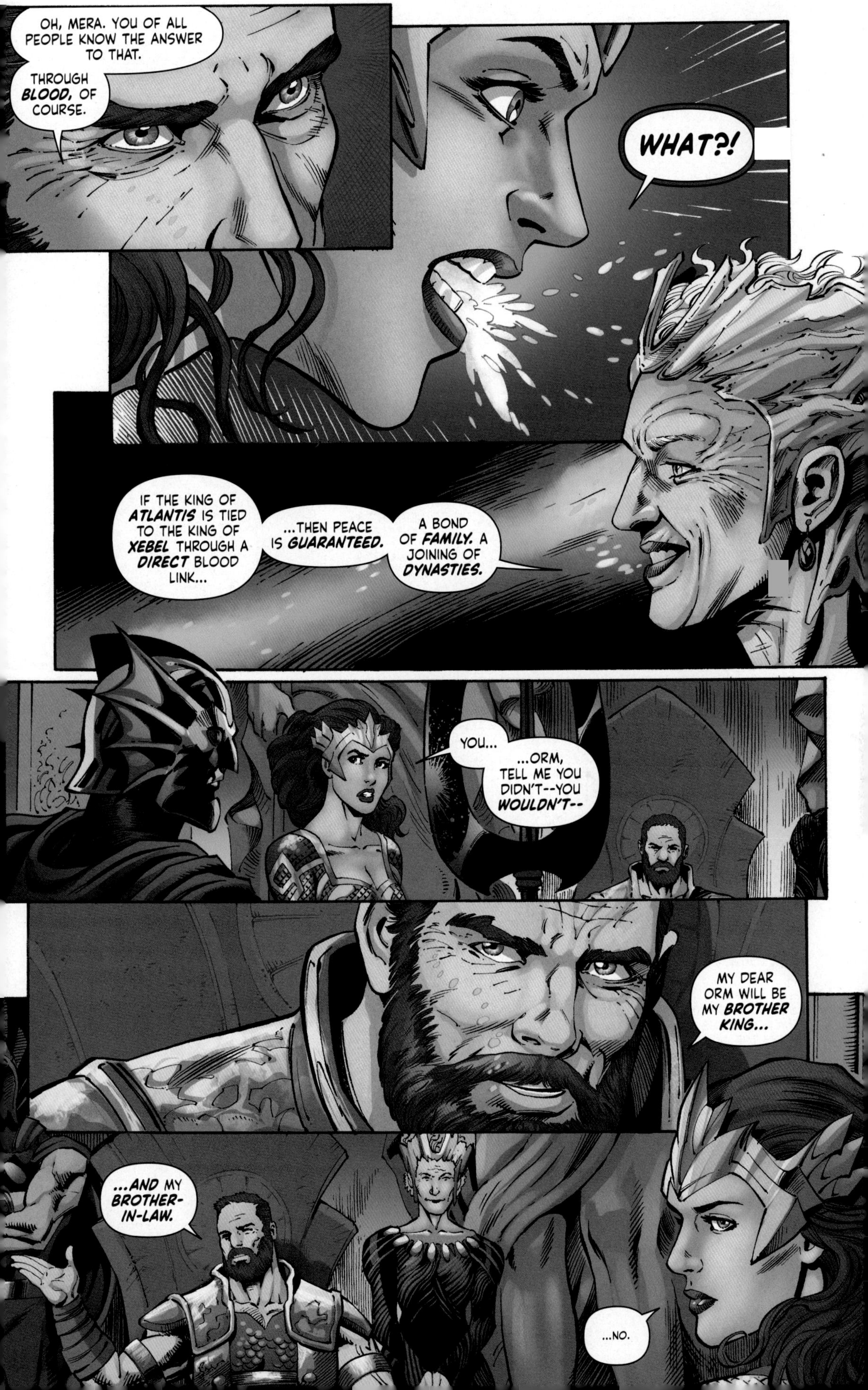
OH, MERA. YOU OF ALL PEOPLE KNOW THE ANSWER TO THAT.
THROUGH BLOOD, OF COURSE.
WHAT?!
IF THE KING OF ATLANTIS IS TIED TO THE KING OF XEBEL THROUGH A DIRECT BLOOD LINK...
...THEN PEACE IS GUARANTEED.
A BOND OF FAMILY. A JOINING OF DYNASTIES.
YOU...
...ORM, TELL ME YOU DIDN'T--YOU WOULDN'T--
MY DEAR ORM WILL BE MY BROTHER KING...
...AND MY BROTHER-IN-LAW.
...NO.

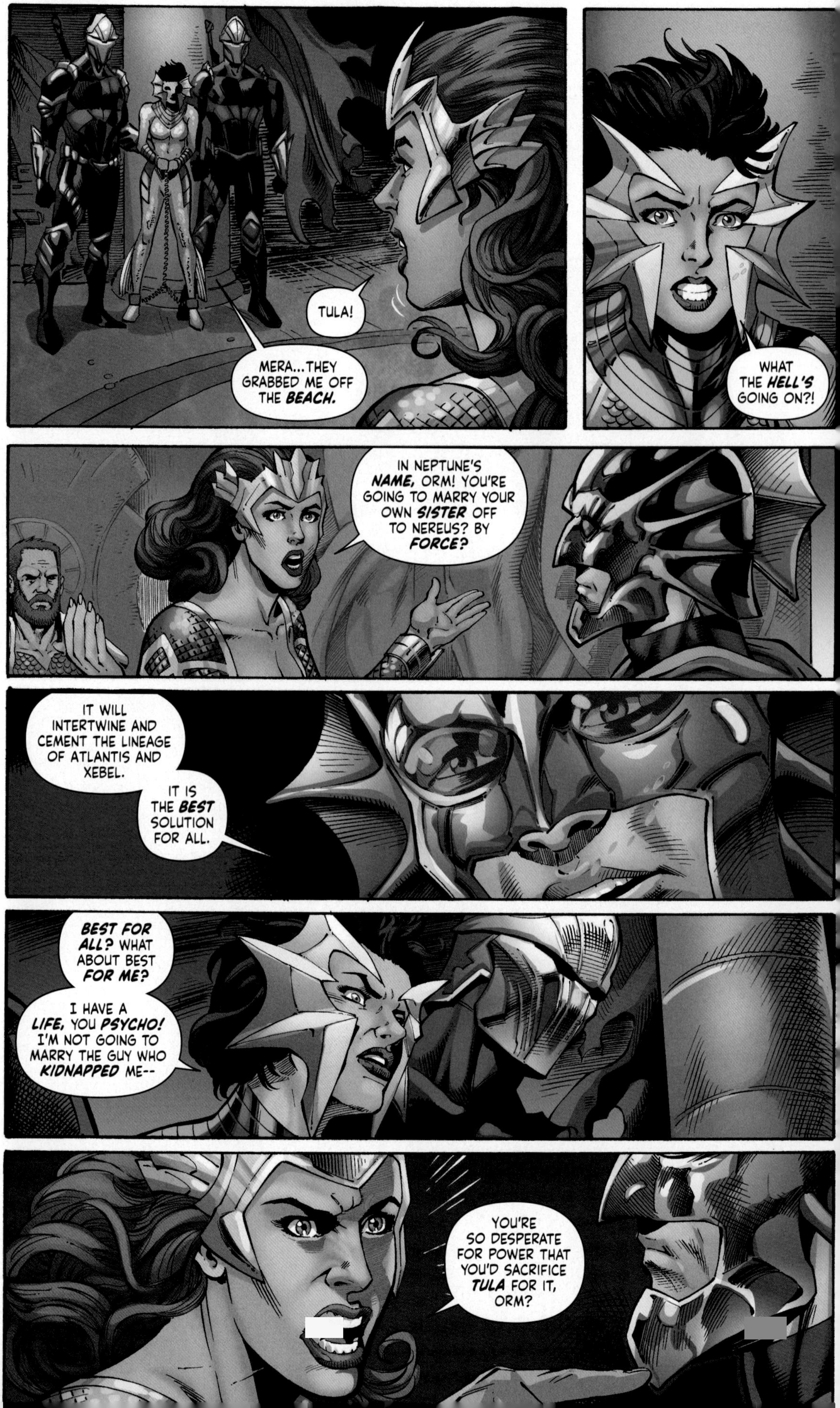

TULA!
MERA...THEY GRABBED ME OFF THE BEACH.
WHAT THE HELL'S GOING ON?!
IN NEPTUNE'S NAME, ORM! YOU'RE GOING TO MARRY YOUR OWN SISTER OFF TO NEREUS? BY FORCE?
IT WILL INTERTWINE AND CEMENT THE LINEAGE OF ATLANTIS AND XEBEL.
IT IS THE BEST SOLUTION FOR ALL.
BEST FOR ALL? WHAT ABOUT BEST FOR ME?
I HAVE A LIFE, YOU PSYCHO! I'M NOT GOING TO MARRY THE GUY WHO KIDNAPPED ME--
YOU'RE SO DESPERATE FOR POWER THAT YOU'D SACRIFICE TULA FOR IT, ORM?

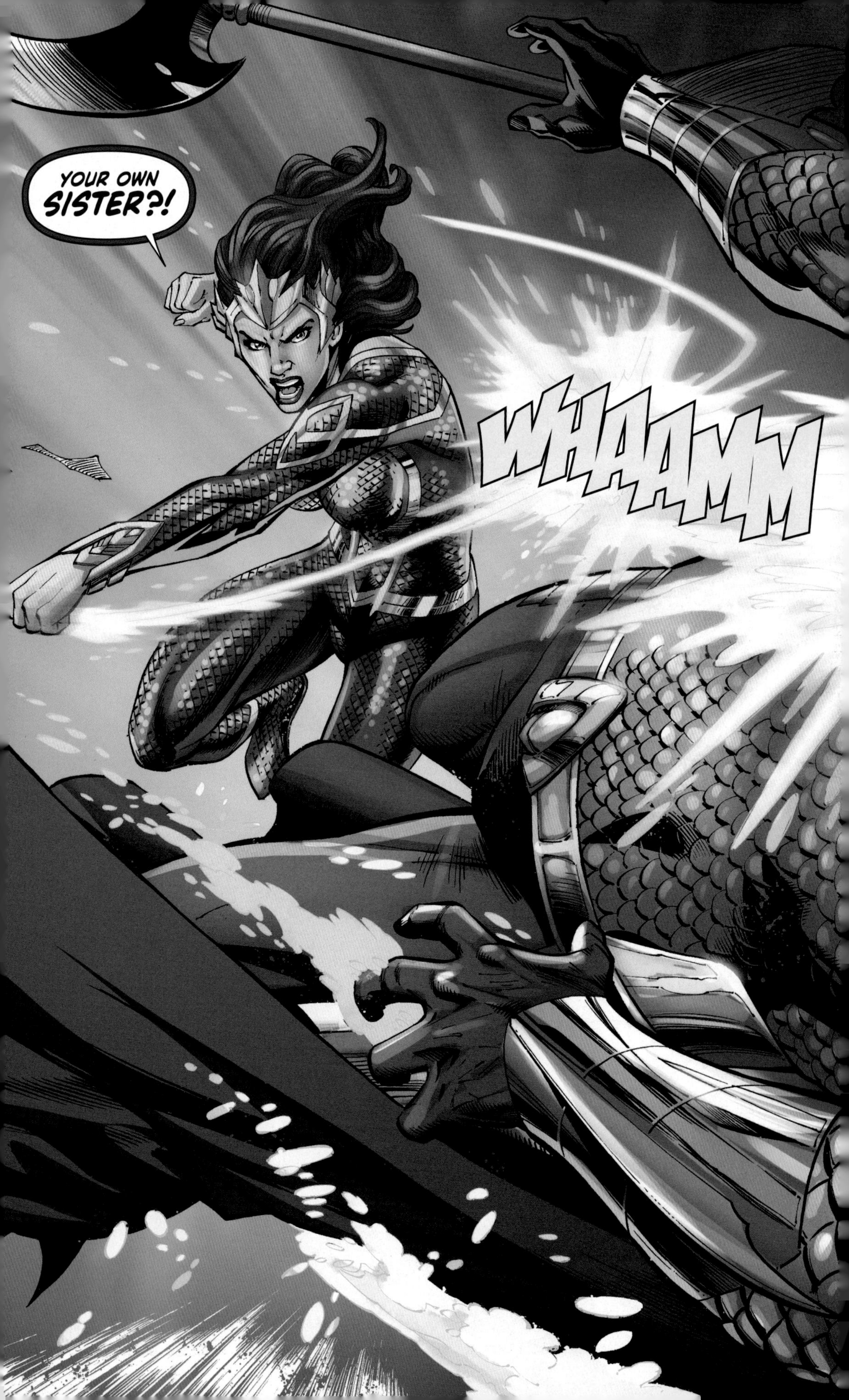
YOUR OWN SISTER?!
WHAAMM

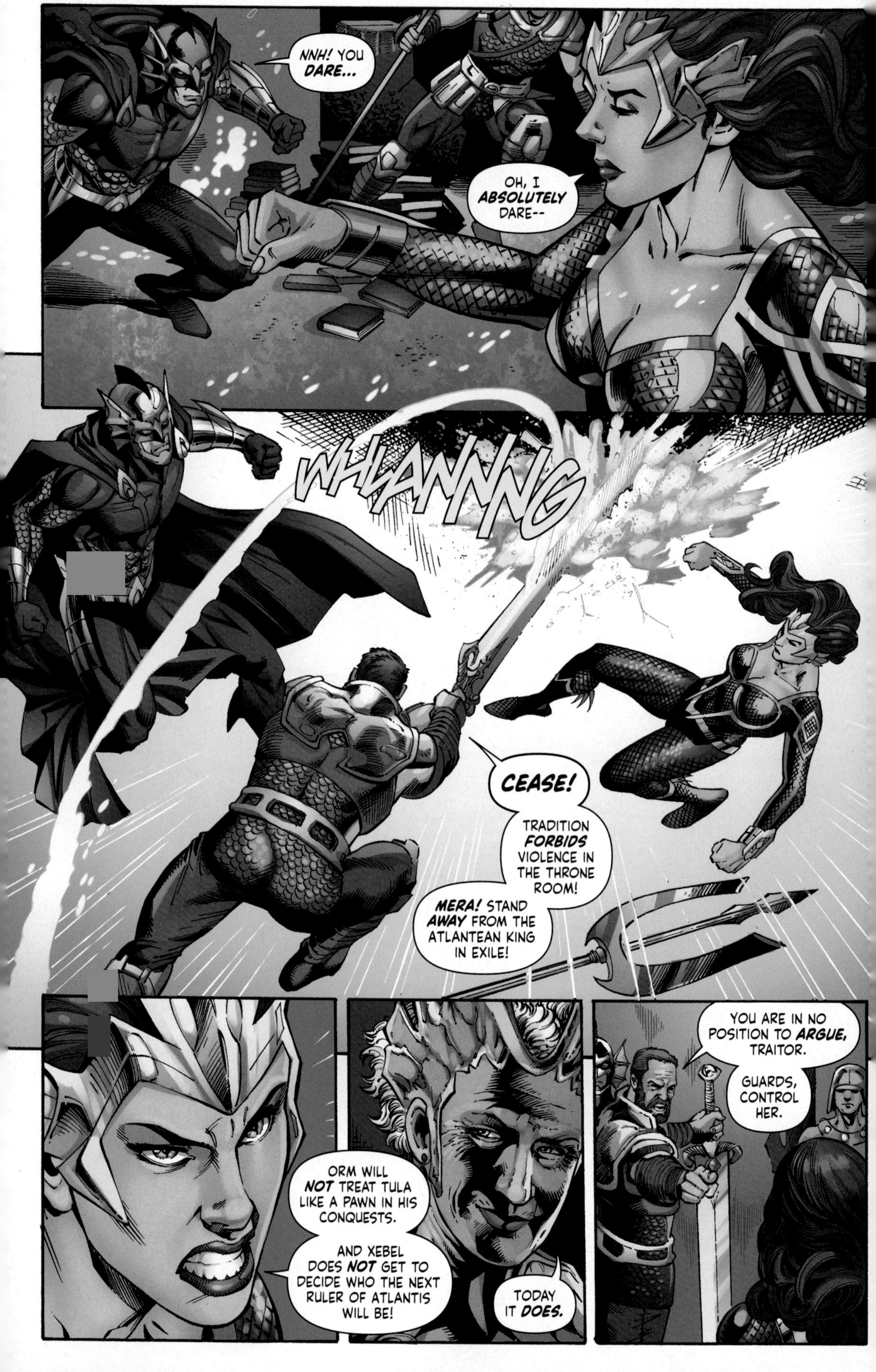
NNH! YOU DARE...
OH, I ABSOLUTELY DARE--
WHLANNNG
CEASE!
TRADITION FORBIDS VIOLENCE IN THE THRONE ROOM!
MERA! STAND AWAY FROM THE ATLANTEAN KING IN EXILE!
ORM WILL NOT TREAT TULA LIKE A PAWN IN HIS CONQUESTS.
AND XEBEL DOES NOT GET TO DECIDE WHO THE NEXT RULER OF ATLANTIS WILL BE!
TODAY IT DOES.
YOU ARE IN NO POSITION TO ARGUE, TRAITOR.
GUARDS, CONTROL HER.

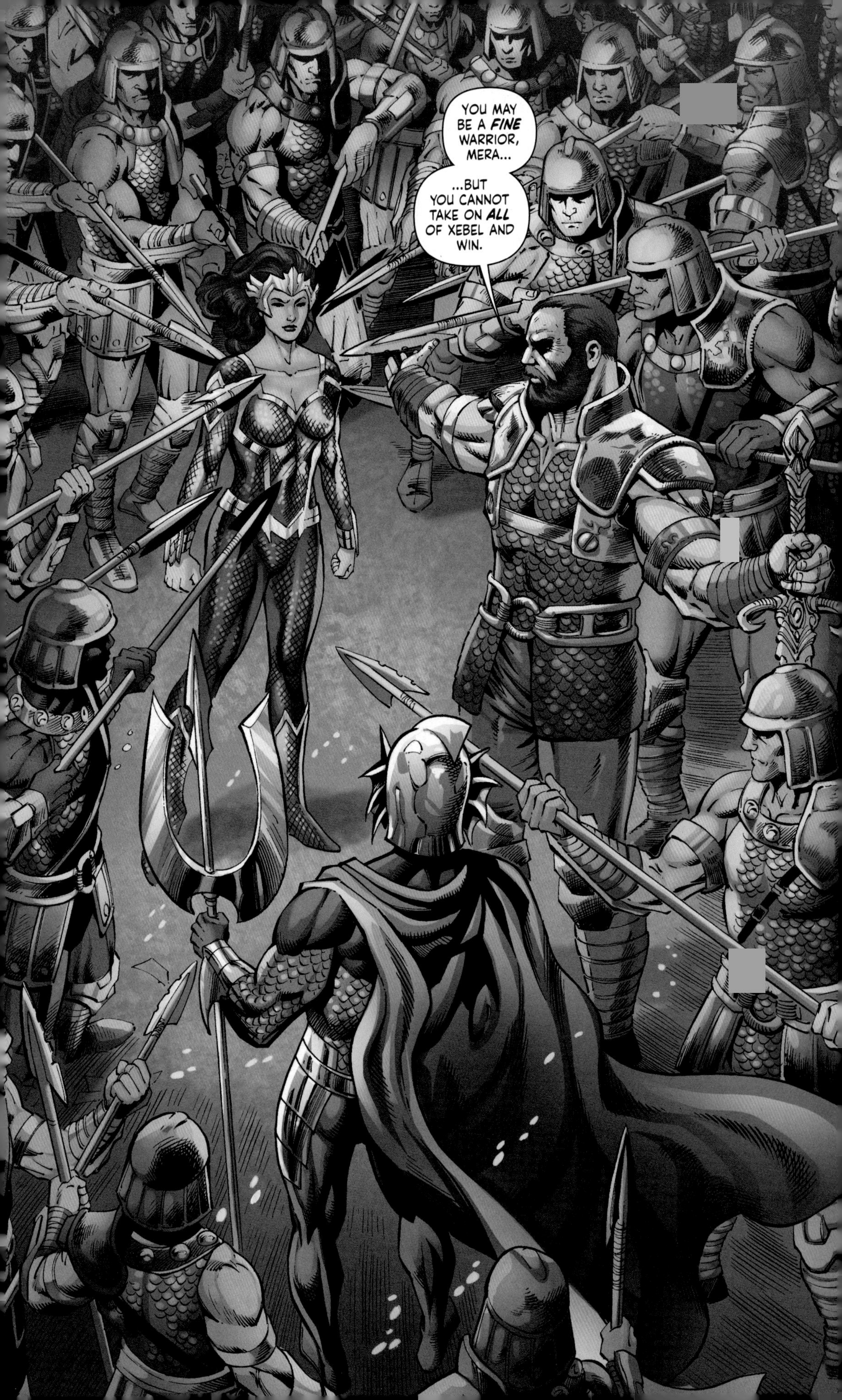
YOU MAY BE A ***FINE*** WARRIOR, MERA...
...BUT YOU CANNOT TAKE ON ***ALL*** OF XEBEL AND WIN.

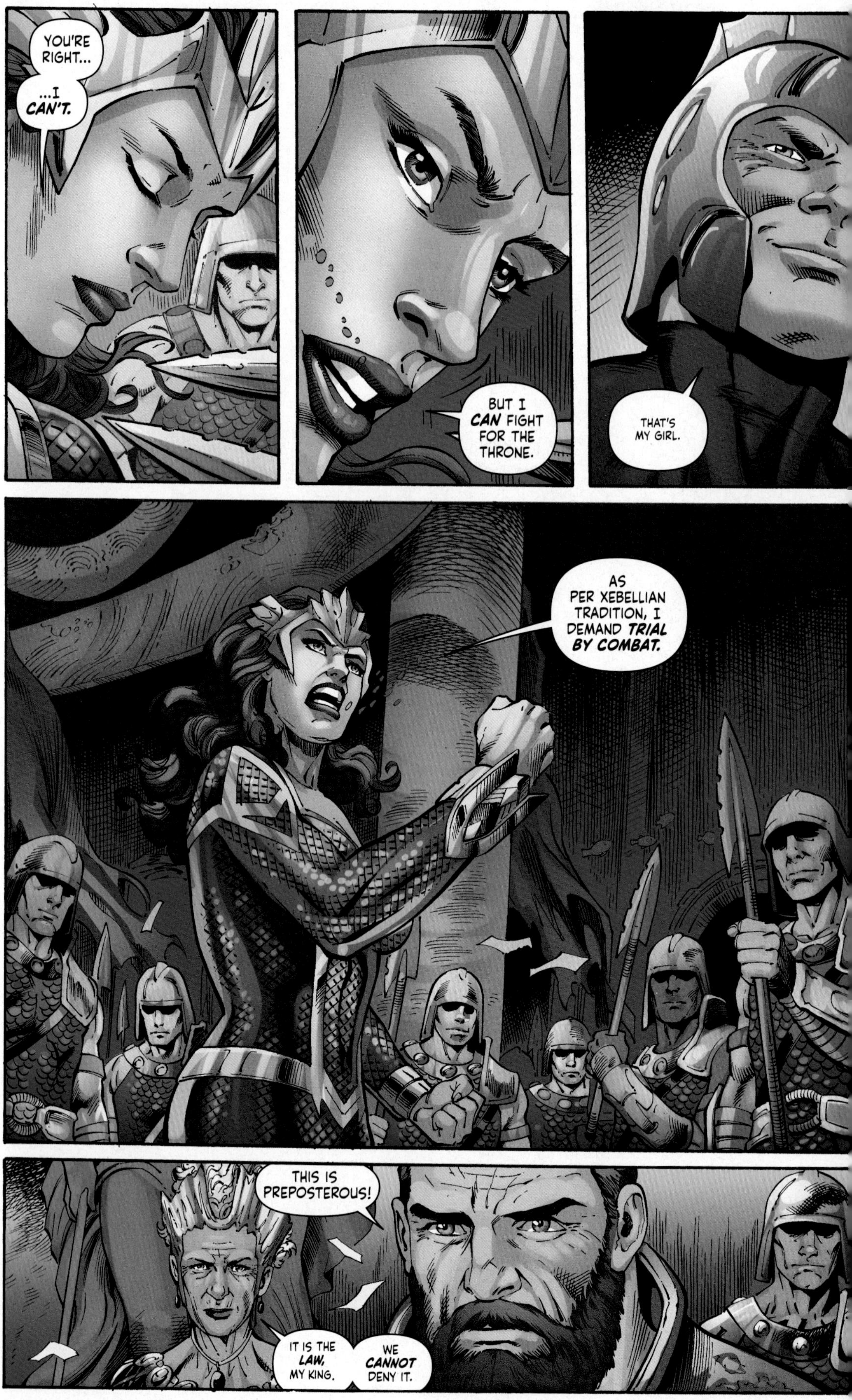
YOU'RE RIGHT...
...I CAN'T.
BUT I CAN FIGHT FOR THE THRONE.
THAT'S MY GIRL.
AS PER XEBELLIAN TRADITION, I DEMAND TRIAL BY COMBAT.
THIS IS PREPOSTEROUS!
IT IS THE LAW, MY KING.
WE CANNOT DENY IT.

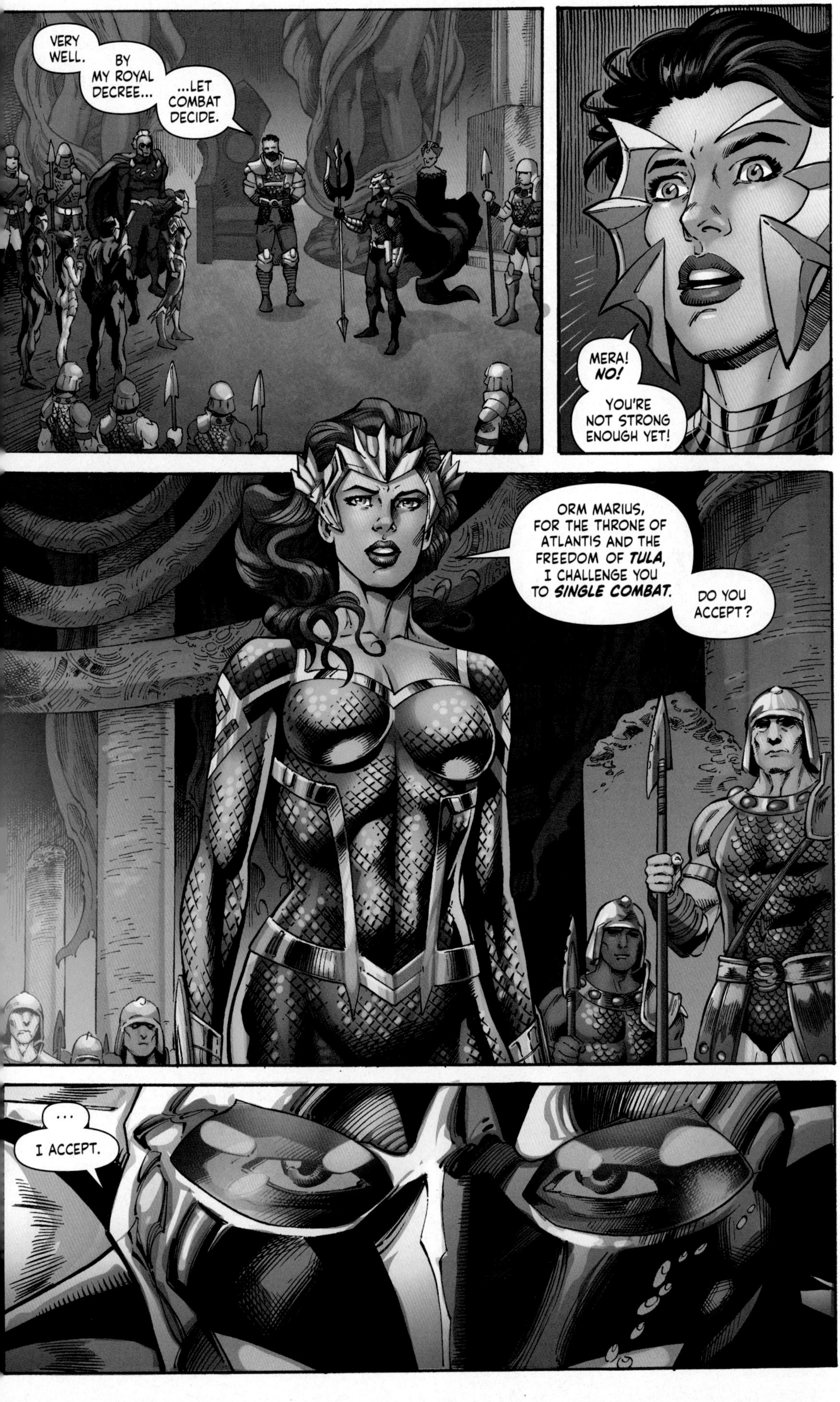

VERY WELL.
BY MY ROYAL DECREE...
...LET COMBAT DECIDE.
MERA! NO!
YOU'RE NOT STRONG ENOUGH YET!
ORM MARIUS, FOR THE THRONE OF ATLANTIS AND THE FREEDOM OF TULA, I CHALLENGE YOU TO SINGLE COMBAT.
DO YOU ACCEPT?
...
I ACCEPT.

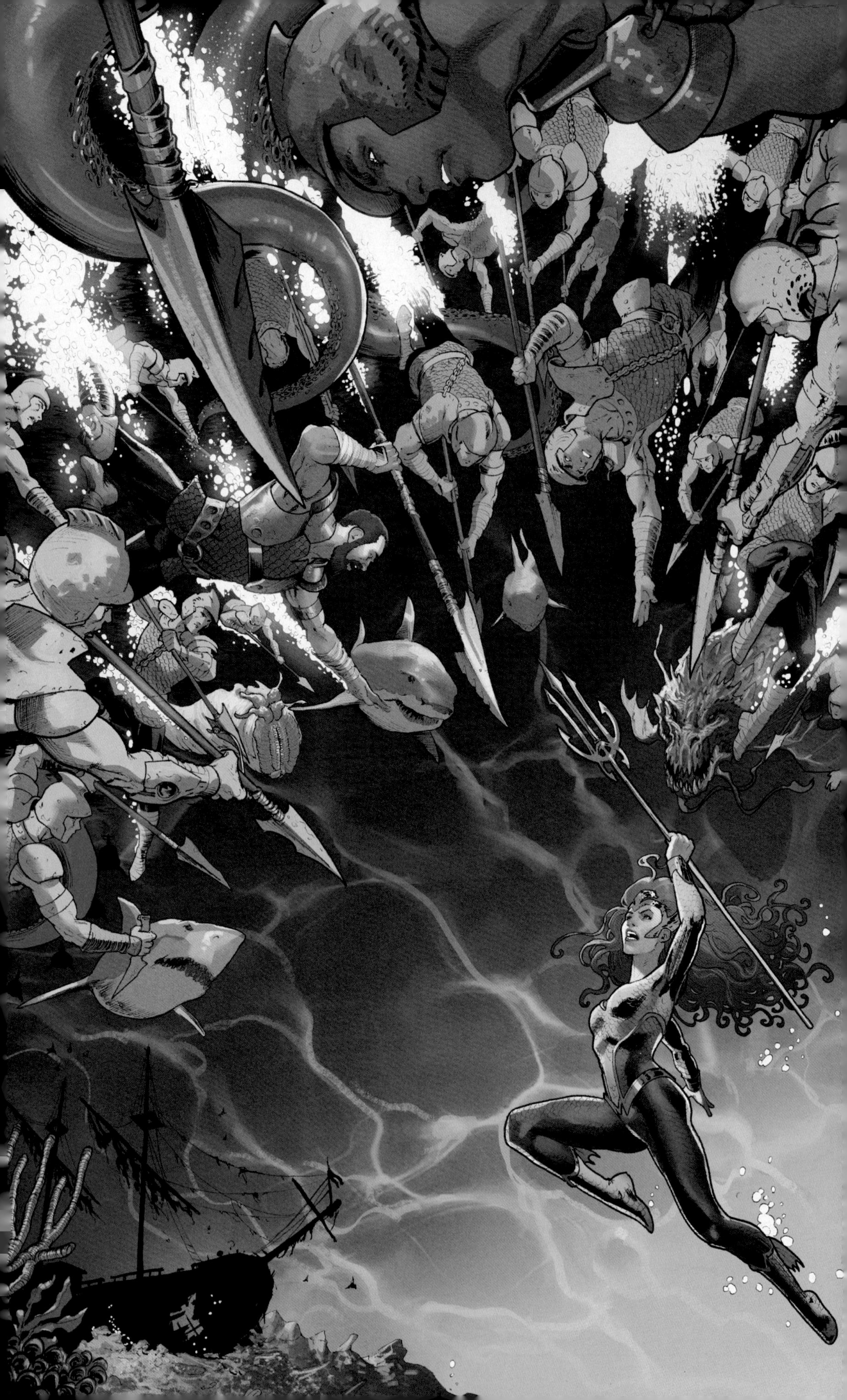

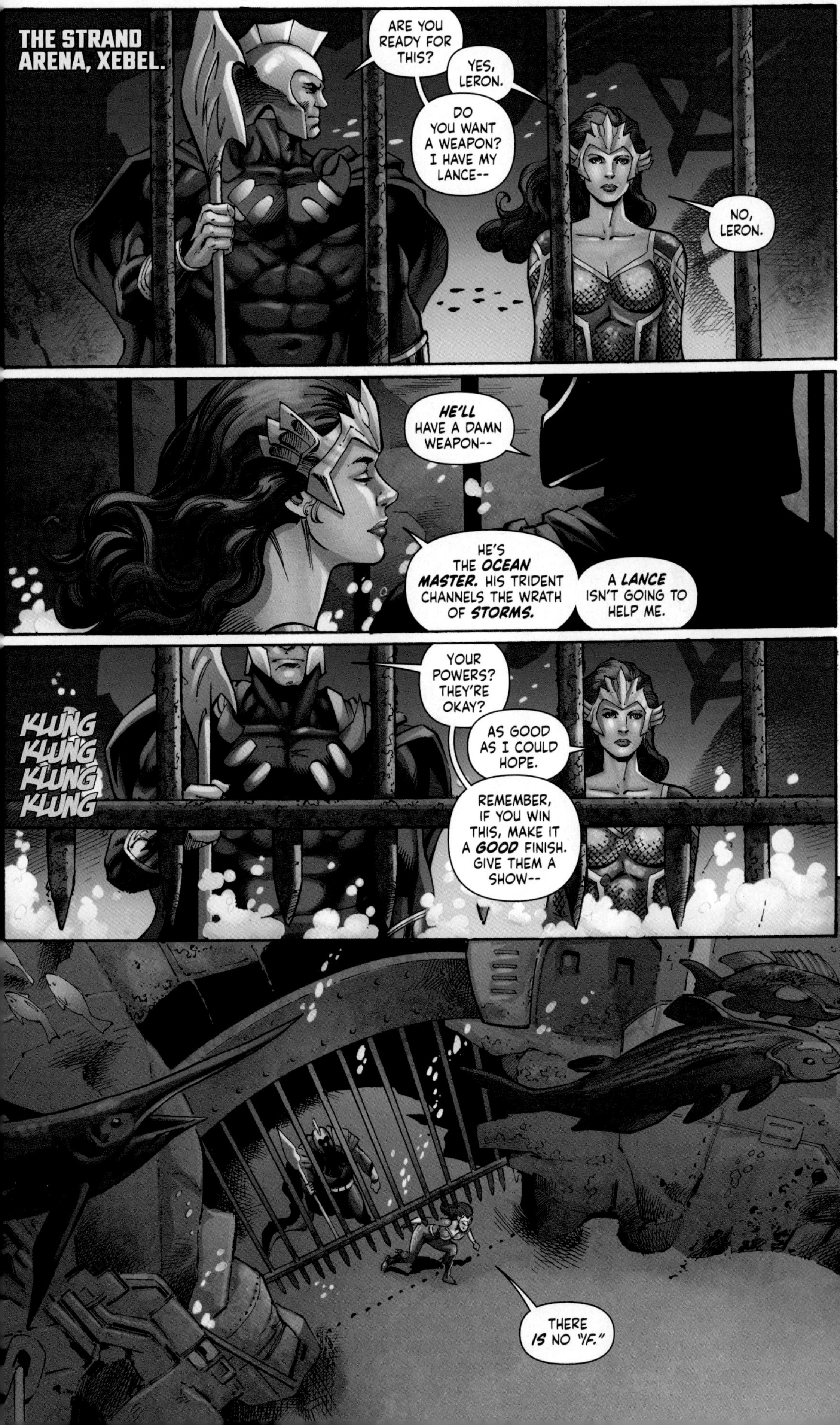
THE STRAND ARENA, XEBEL.
ARE YOU READY FOR THIS?
YES, LERON.
DO YOU WANT A WEAPON? I HAVE MY LANCE--
NO, LERON.
HE'LL HAVE A DAMN WEAPON--
HE'S THE OCEAN MASTER. HIS TRIDENT CHANNELS THE WRATH OF STORMS.
A LANCE ISN'T GOING TO HELP ME.
YOUR POWERS? THEY'RE OKAY?
AS GOOD AS I COULD HOPE.
KLUNG KLUNG KLUNG KLUNG
REMEMBER, IF YOU WIN THIS, MAKE IT A GOOD FINISH. GIVE THEM A SHOW--
THERE IS NO "IF."

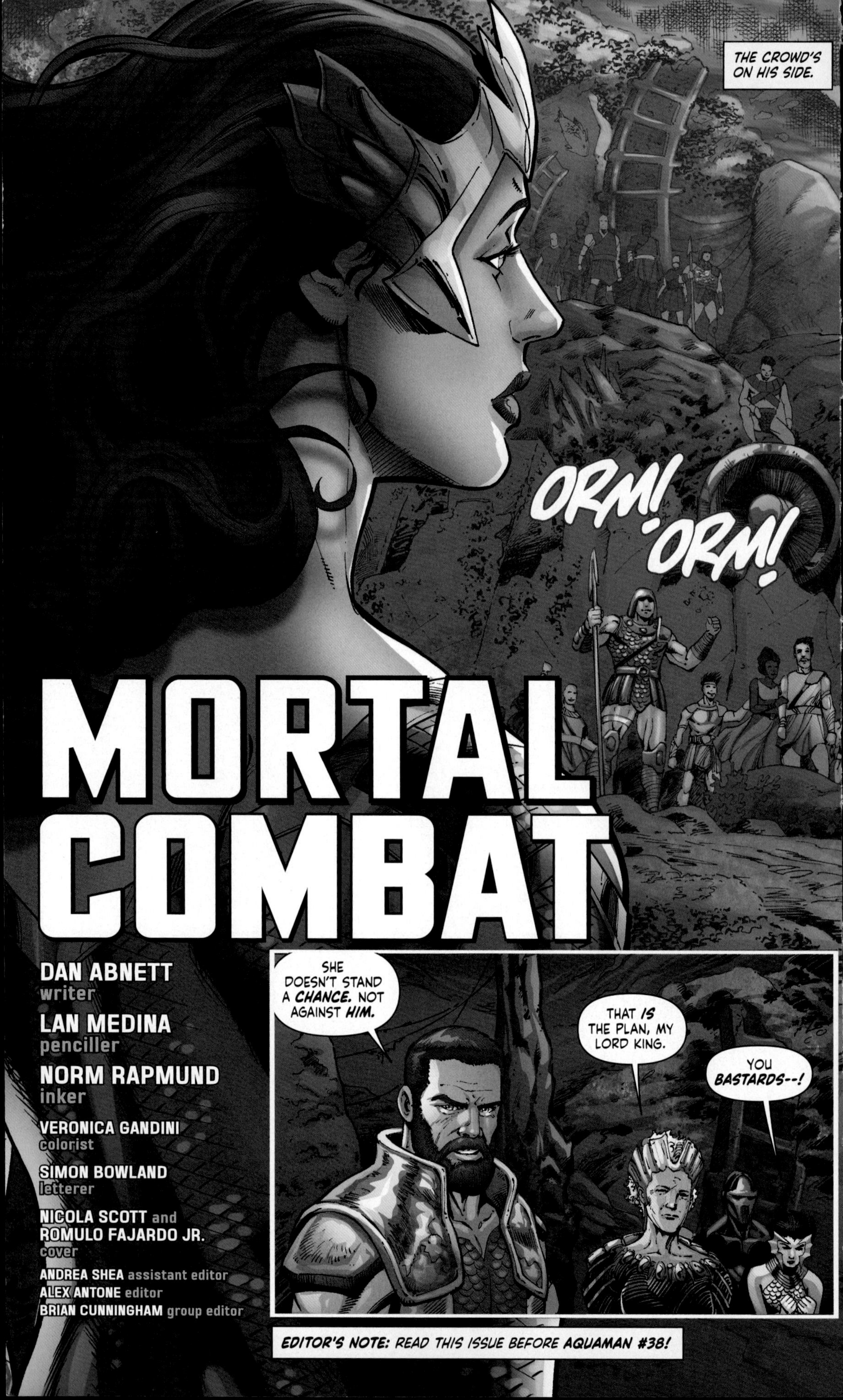
THE CROWD'S ON HIS SIDE.
ORM! ORM!
MORTAL COMBAT
DAN ABNETT writer
LAN MEDINA penciller
NORM RAPMUND inker
VERONICA GANDINI colorist
SIMON BOWLAND letterer
NICOLA SCOTT and ROMULO FAJARDO JR. cover
ANDREA SHEA assistant editor
ALEX ANTONE editor
BRIAN CUNNINGHAM group editor
SHE DOESN'T STAND A CHANCE. NOT AGAINST HIM.
THAT IS THE PLAN, MY LORD KING.
YOU BASTARDS--!
EDITOR'S NOTE: READ THIS ISSUE BEFORE AQUAMAN #38!

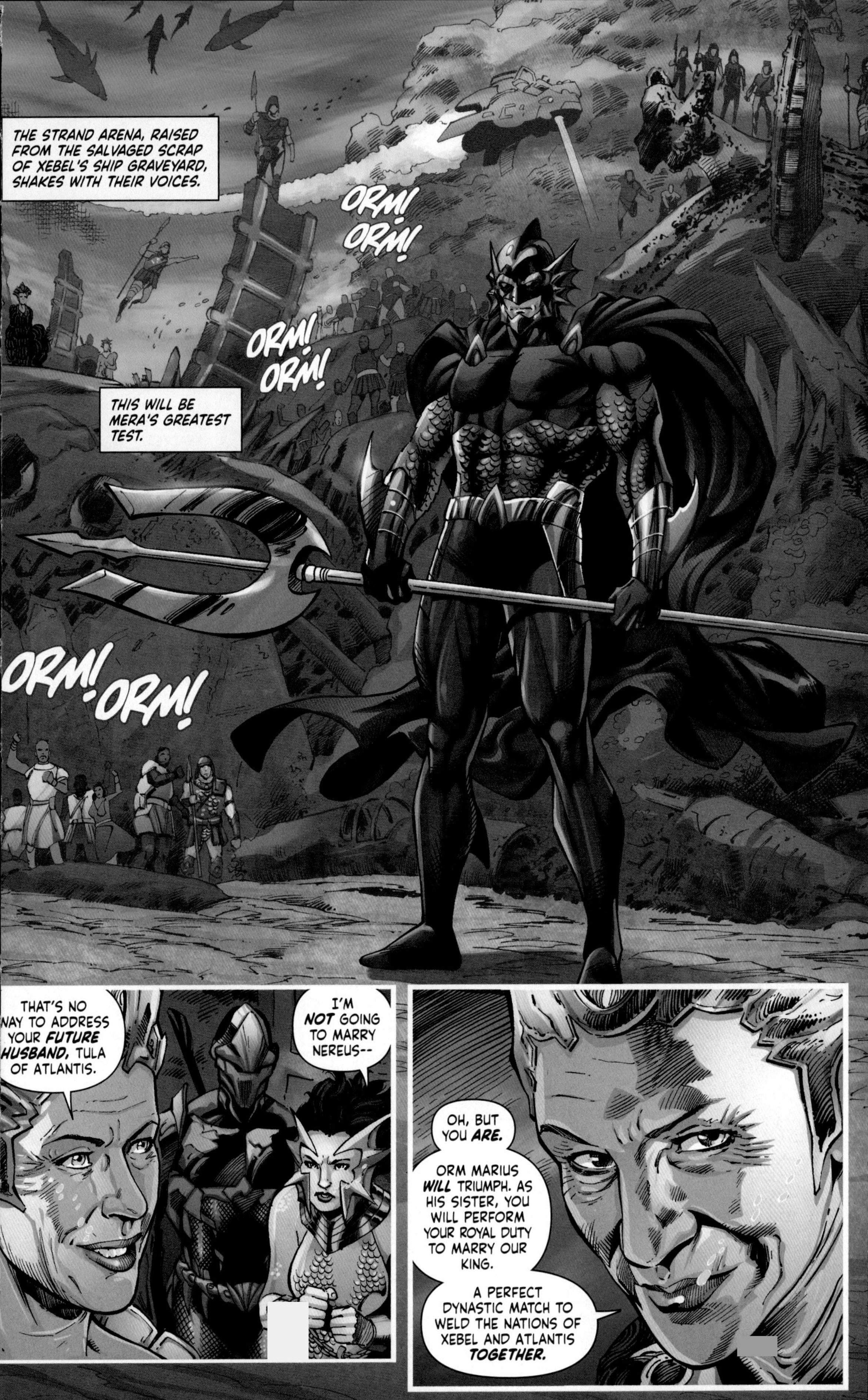
THE STRAND ARENA, RAISED FROM THE SALVAGED SCRAP OF XEBEL'S SHIP GRAVEYARD, SHAKES WITH THEIR VOICES.
ORM! ORM!
ORM! ORM!
THIS WILL BE MERA'S GREATEST TEST.
ORM! ORM!
THAT'S NO WAY TO ADDRESS YOUR FUTURE HUSBAND, TULA OF ATLANTIS.
I'M NOT GOING TO MARRY NEREUS--
OH, BUT YOU ARE.
ORM MARIUS WILL TRIUMPH. AS HIS SISTER, YOU WILL PERFORM YOUR ROYAL DUTY TO MARRY OUR KING.
A PERFECT DYNASTIC MATCH TO WELD THE NATIONS OF XEBEL AND ATLANTIS TOGETHER.

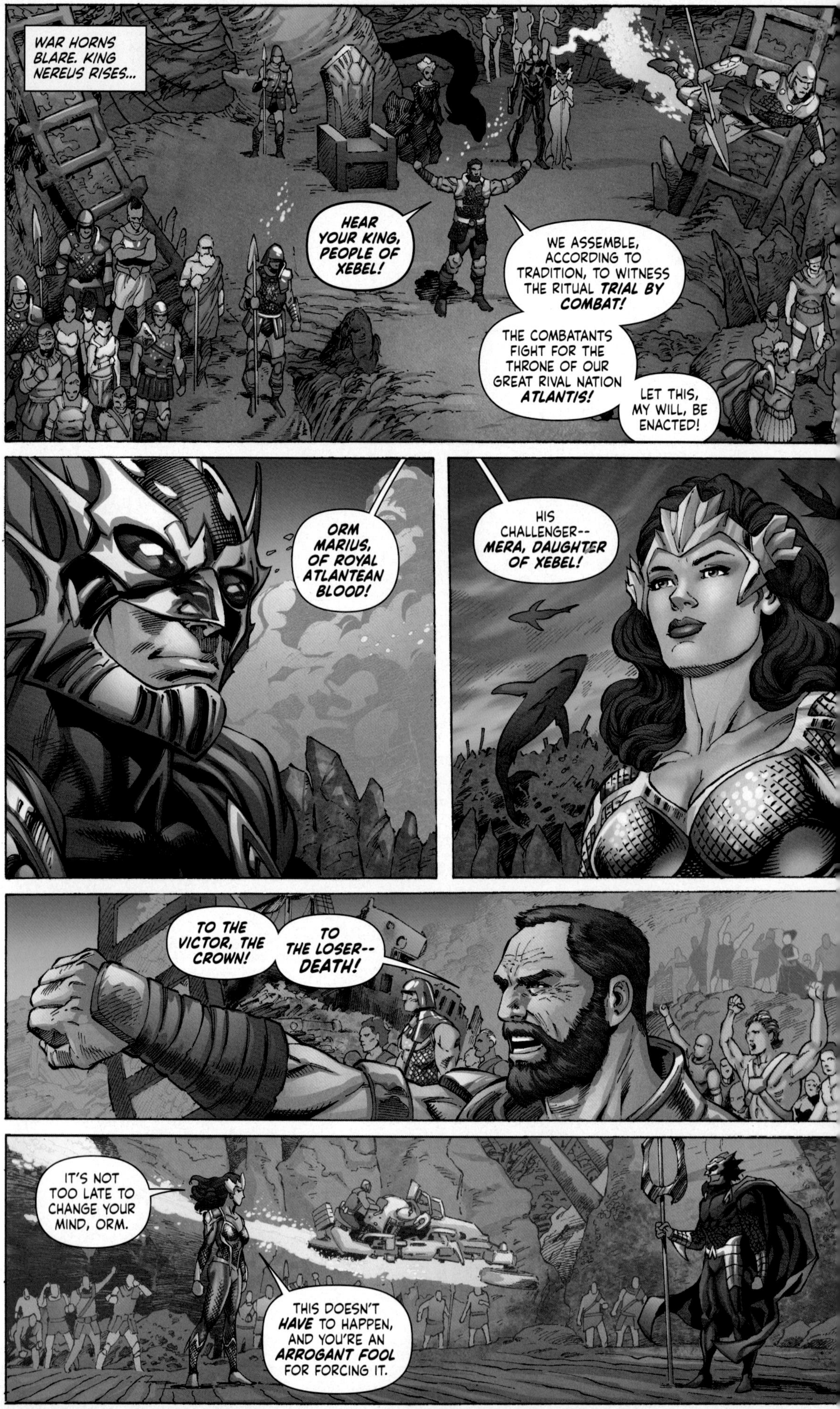

WAR HORNS BLARE. KING NEREUS RISES...
HEAR YOUR KING, PEOPLE OF XEBEL!
WE ASSEMBLE, ACCORDING TO TRADITION, TO WITNESS THE RITUAL TRIAL BY COMBAT!
THE COMBATANTS FIGHT FOR THE THRONE OF OUR GREAT RIVAL NATION ATLANTIS!
LET THIS, MY WILL, BE ENACTED!
ORM MARIUS, OF ROYAL ATLANTEAN BLOOD!
HIS CHALLENGER-- MERA, DAUGHTER OF XEBEL!
TO THE VICTOR, THE CROWN!
TO THE LOSER-- DEATH!
IT'S NOT TOO LATE TO CHANGE YOUR MIND, ORM.
THIS DOESN'T HAVE TO HAPPEN, AND YOU'RE AN ARROGANT FOOL FOR FORCING IT.

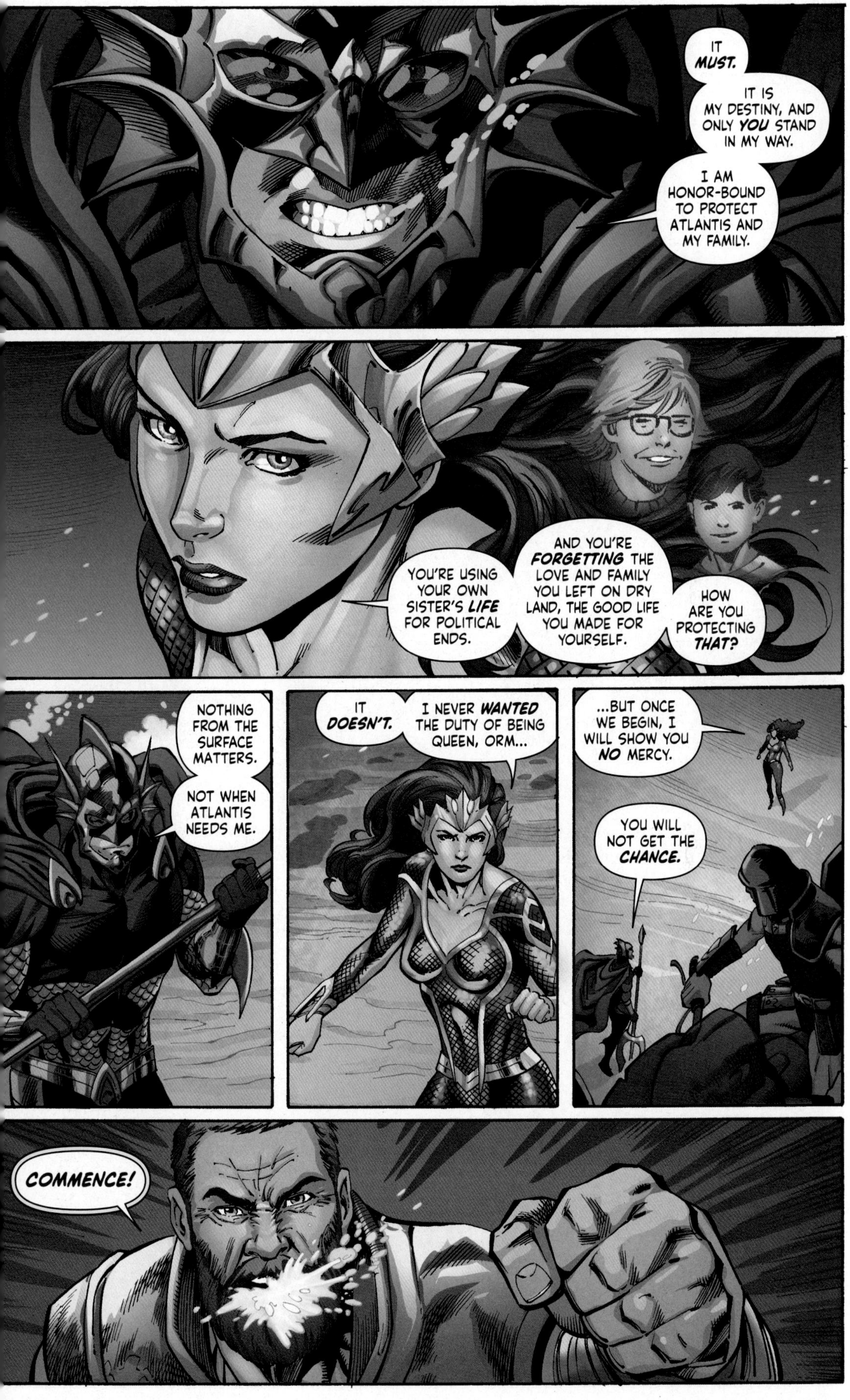
IT MUST.
IT IS MY DESTINY, AND ONLY YOU STAND IN MY WAY.
I AM HONOR-BOUND TO PROTECT ATLANTIS AND MY FAMILY.
YOU'RE USING YOUR OWN SISTER'S LIFE FOR POLITICAL ENDS.
AND YOU'RE FORGETTING THE LOVE AND FAMILY YOU LEFT ON DRY LAND, THE GOOD LIFE YOU MADE FOR YOURSELF.
HOW ARE YOU PROTECTING THAT?
NOTHING FROM THE SURFACE MATTERS.
NOT WHEN ATLANTIS NEEDS ME.
IT DOESN'T.
I NEVER WANTED THE DUTY OF BEING QUEEN, ORM...
...BUT ONCE WE BEGIN, I WILL SHOW YOU NO MERCY.
YOU WILL NOT GET THE CHANCE.
COMMENCE!

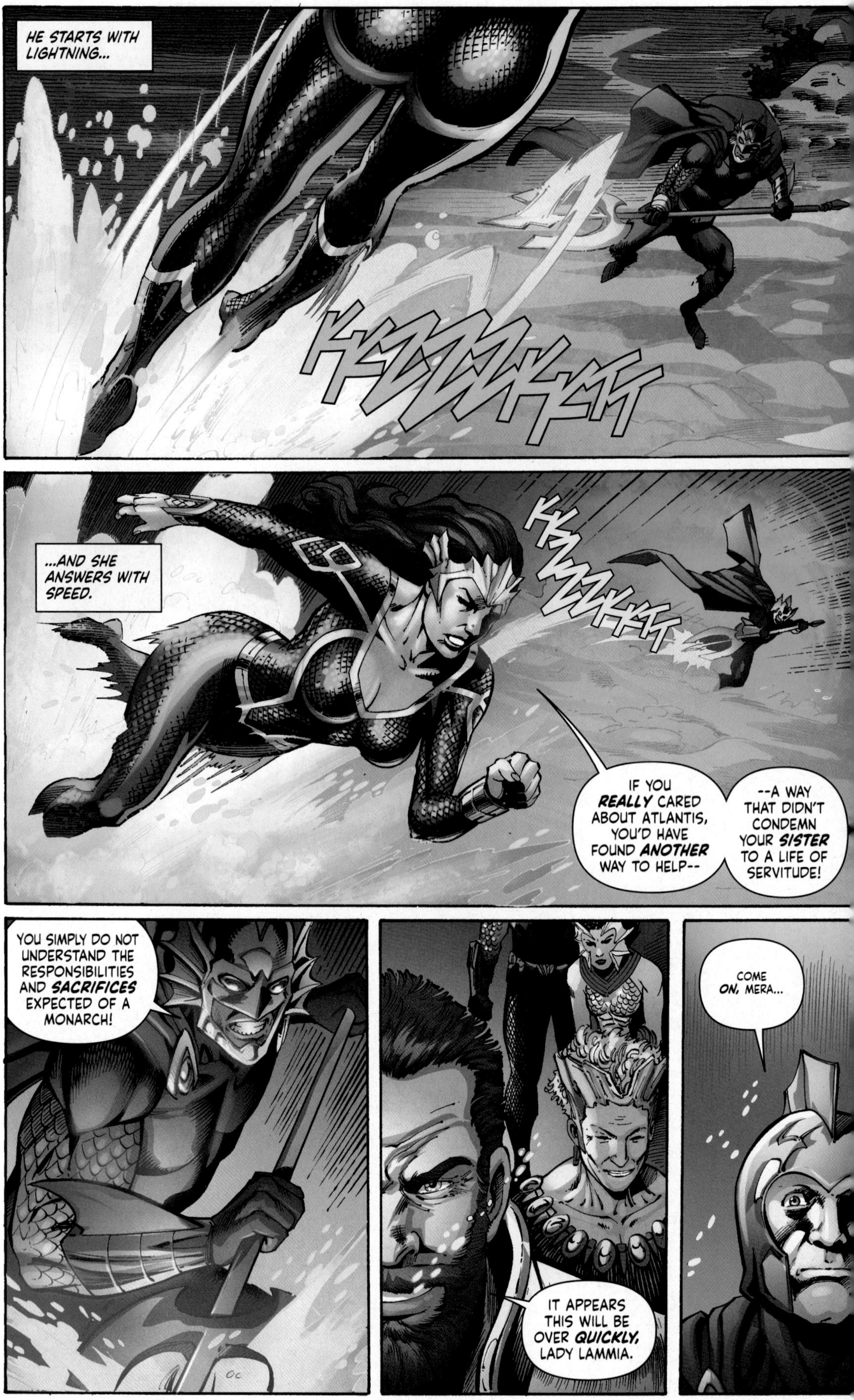

HE STARTS WITH LIGHTNING...
KKZZZKKKK
...AND SHE ANSWERS WITH SPEED.
KKZZZKKKK
IF YOU REALLY CARED ABOUT ATLANTIS, YOU'D HAVE FOUND ANOTHER WAY TO HELP--
--A WAY THAT DIDN'T CONDEMN YOUR SISTER TO A LIFE OF SERVITUDE!
YOU SIMPLY DO NOT UNDERSTAND THE RESPONSIBILITIES AND SACRIFICES EXPECTED OF A MONARCH!
IT APPEARS THIS WILL BE OVER QUICKLY, LADY LAMMIA.
COME ON, MERA...

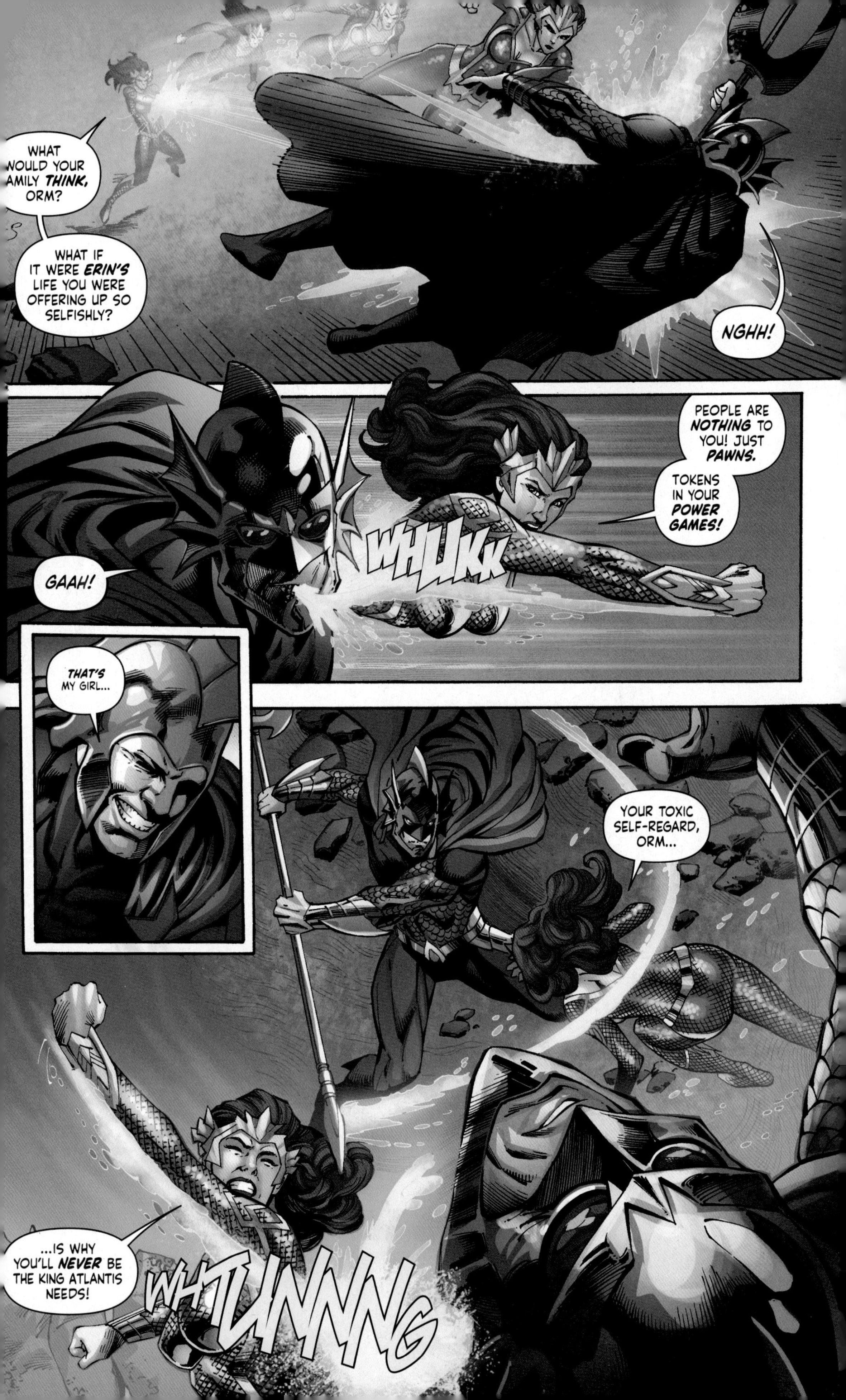
WHAT WOULD YOUR FAMILY THINK, ORM?
WHAT IF IT WERE ERIN'S LIFE YOU WERE OFFERING UP SO SELFISHLY?
NGHH!
PEOPLE ARE NOTHING TO YOU! JUST PAWNS.
TOKENS IN YOUR POWER GAMES!
WHUKK
GAAH!
THAT'S MY GIRL...
YOUR TOXIC SELF-REGARD, ORM...
...IS WHY YOU'LL NEVER BE THE KING ATLANTIS NEEDS!
WHUNNNG

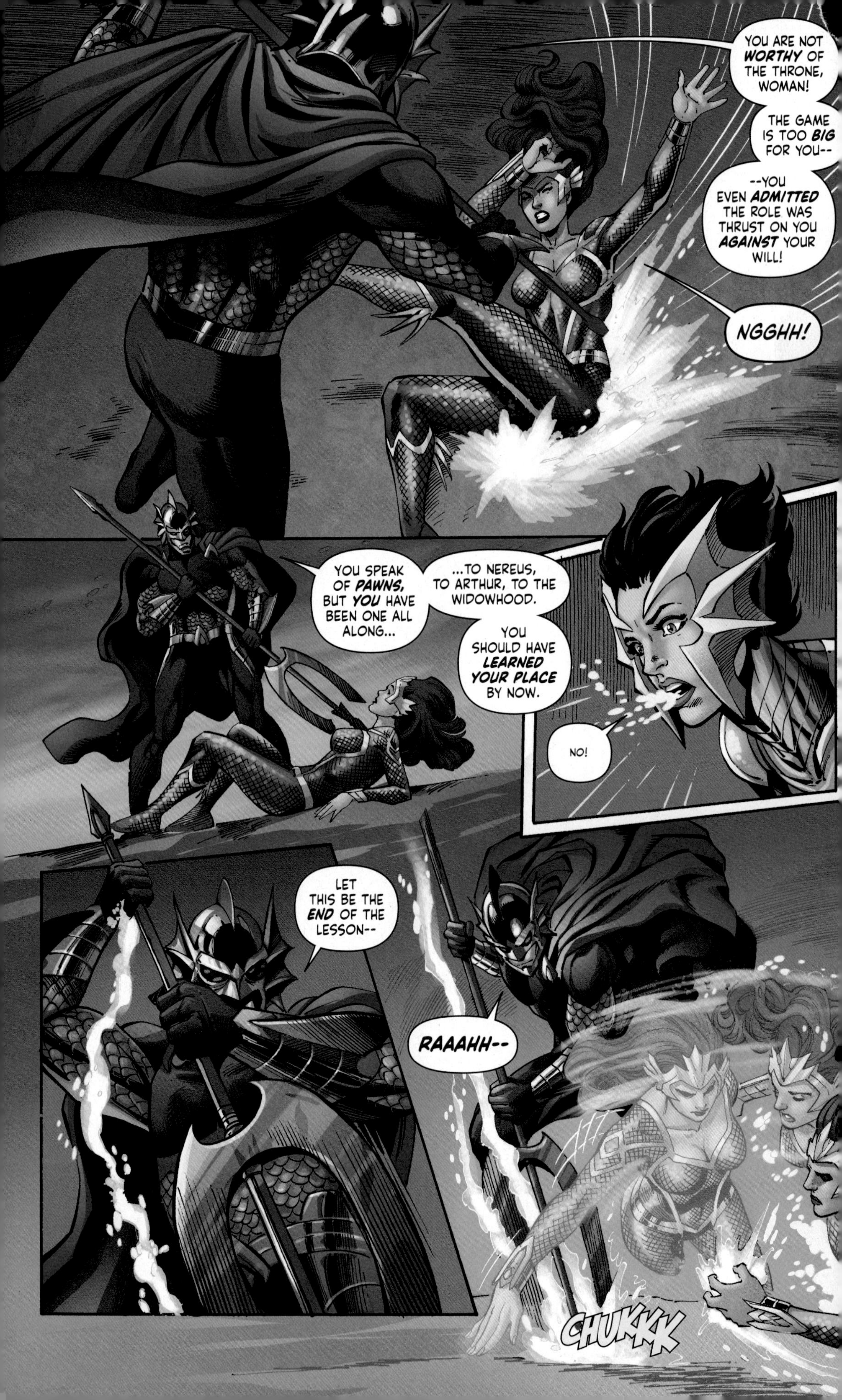

YOU ARE NOT WORTHY OF THE THRONE, WOMAN!
THE GAME IS TOO BIG FOR YOU--
--YOU EVEN ADMITTED THE ROLE WAS THRUST ON YOU AGAINST YOUR WILL!
NGGHH!
YOU SPEAK OF PAWNS, BUT YOU HAVE BEEN ONE ALL ALONG...
...TO NEREUS, TO ARTHUR, TO THE WIDOWHOOD.
YOU SHOULD HAVE LEARNED YOUR PLACE BY NOW.
NO!
LET THIS BE THE END OF THE LESSON--
RAAAHH--
CHUKKK

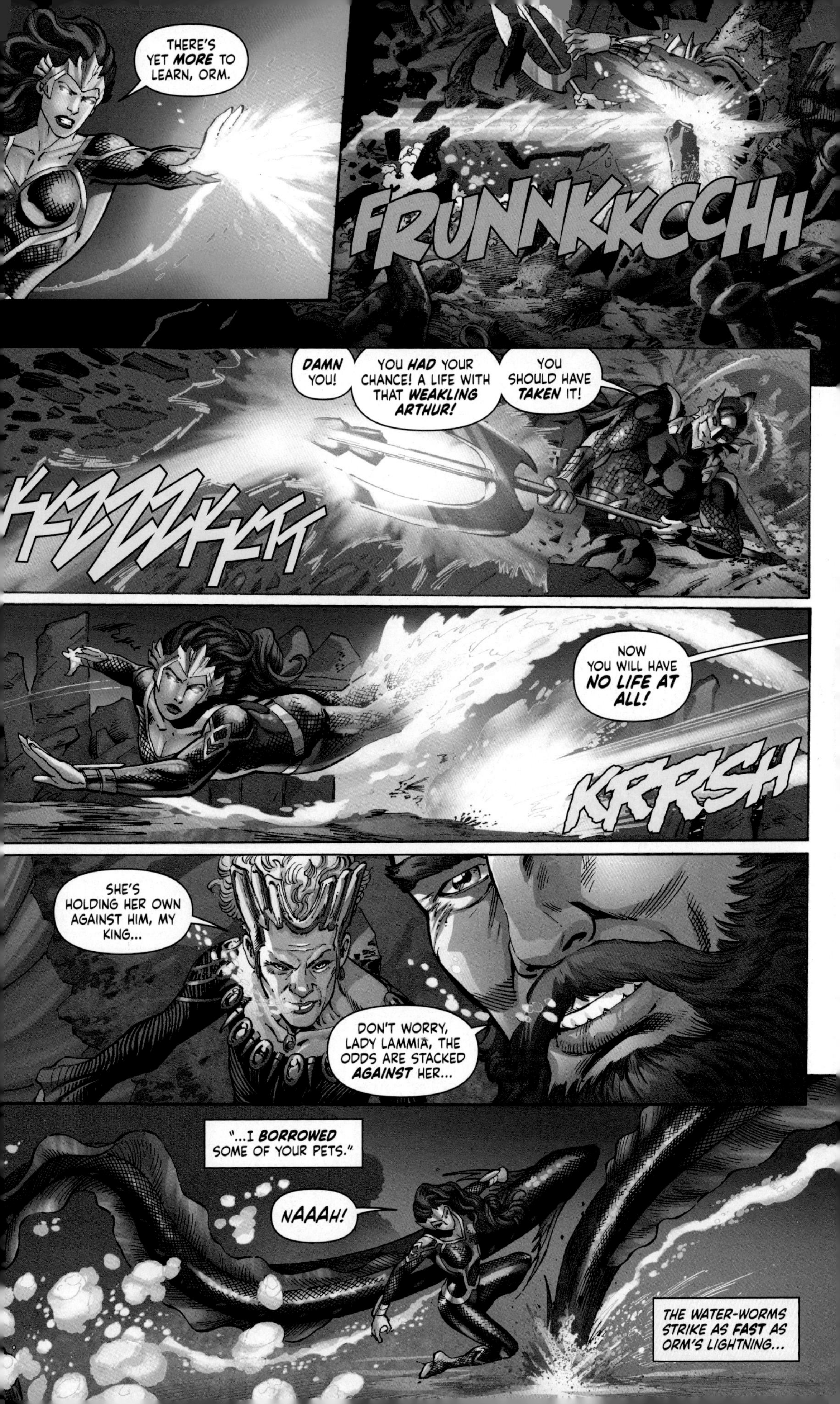

THERE'S YET MORE TO LEARN, ORM.
FRUNNKKCCHH
DAMN YOU!
YOU HAD YOUR CHANCE! A LIFE WITH THAT WEAKLING ARTHUR!
YOU SHOULD HAVE TAKEN IT!
KKZZZKKTT
NOW YOU WILL HAVE NO LIFE AT ALL!
KRRSH
SHE'S HOLDING HER OWN AGAINST HIM, MY KING...
DON'T WORRY, LADY LAMMIA, THE ODDS ARE STACKED AGAINST HER...
"...I BORROWED SOME OF YOUR PETS."
NAAAH!
THE WATER-WORMS STRIKE AS FAST AS ORM'S LIGHTNING...

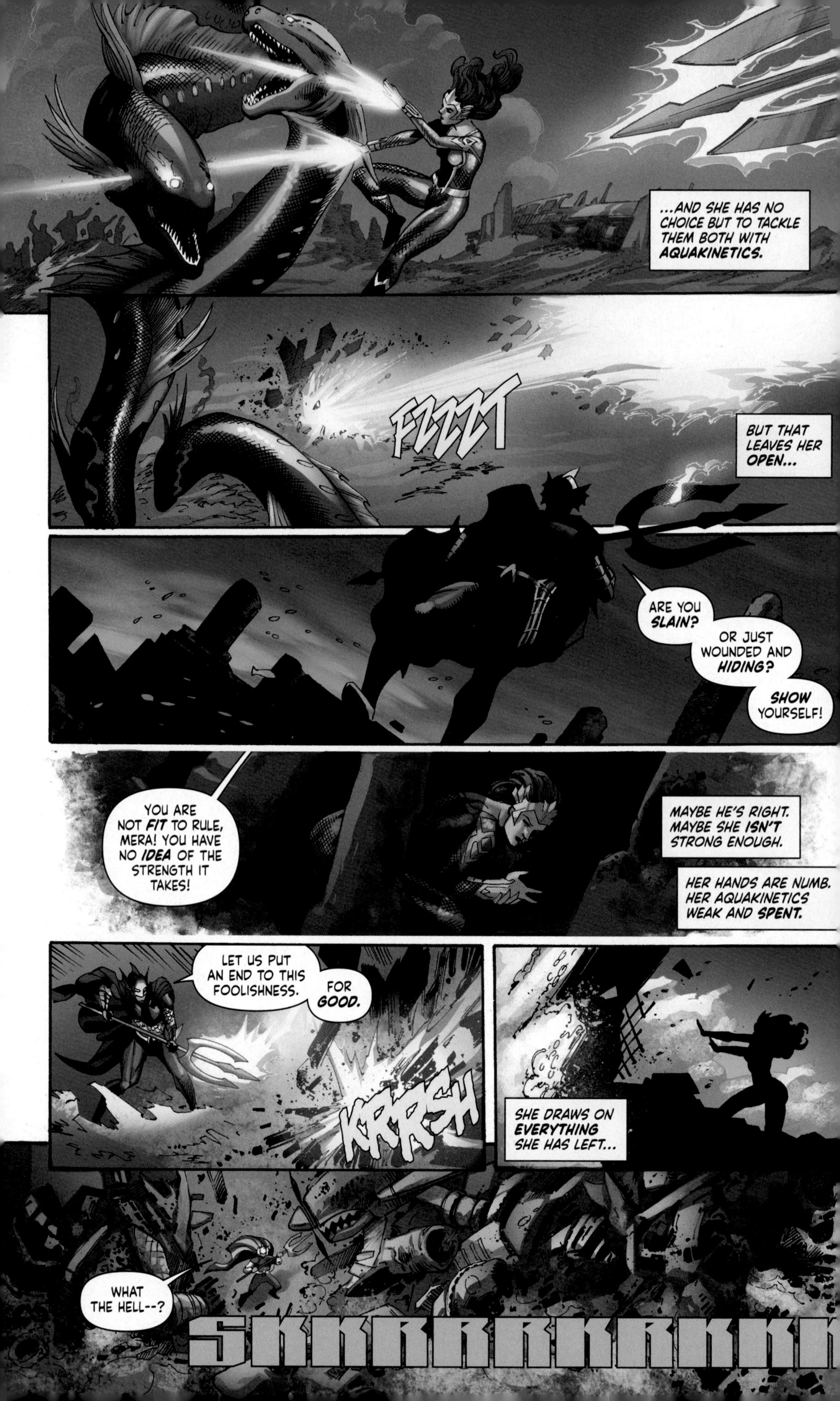

...AND SHE HAS NO CHOICE BUT TO TACKLE THEM BOTH WITH AQUAKINETICS.
FZZZT
BUT THAT LEAVES HER OPEN...
ARE YOU SLAIN?
OR JUST WOUNDED AND HIDING?
SHOW YOURSELF!
YOU ARE NOT FIT TO RULE, MERA! YOU HAVE NO IDEA OF THE STRENGTH IT TAKES!
MAYBE HE'S RIGHT. MAYBE SHE ISN'T STRONG ENOUGH.
HER HANDS ARE NUMB. HER AQUAKINETICS WEAK AND SPENT.
LET US PUT AN END TO THIS FOOLISHNESS.
FOR GOOD.
KRRSH
SHE DRAWS ON EVERYTHING SHE HAS LEFT...
WHAT THE HELL--?
SKRRRRRRRRR

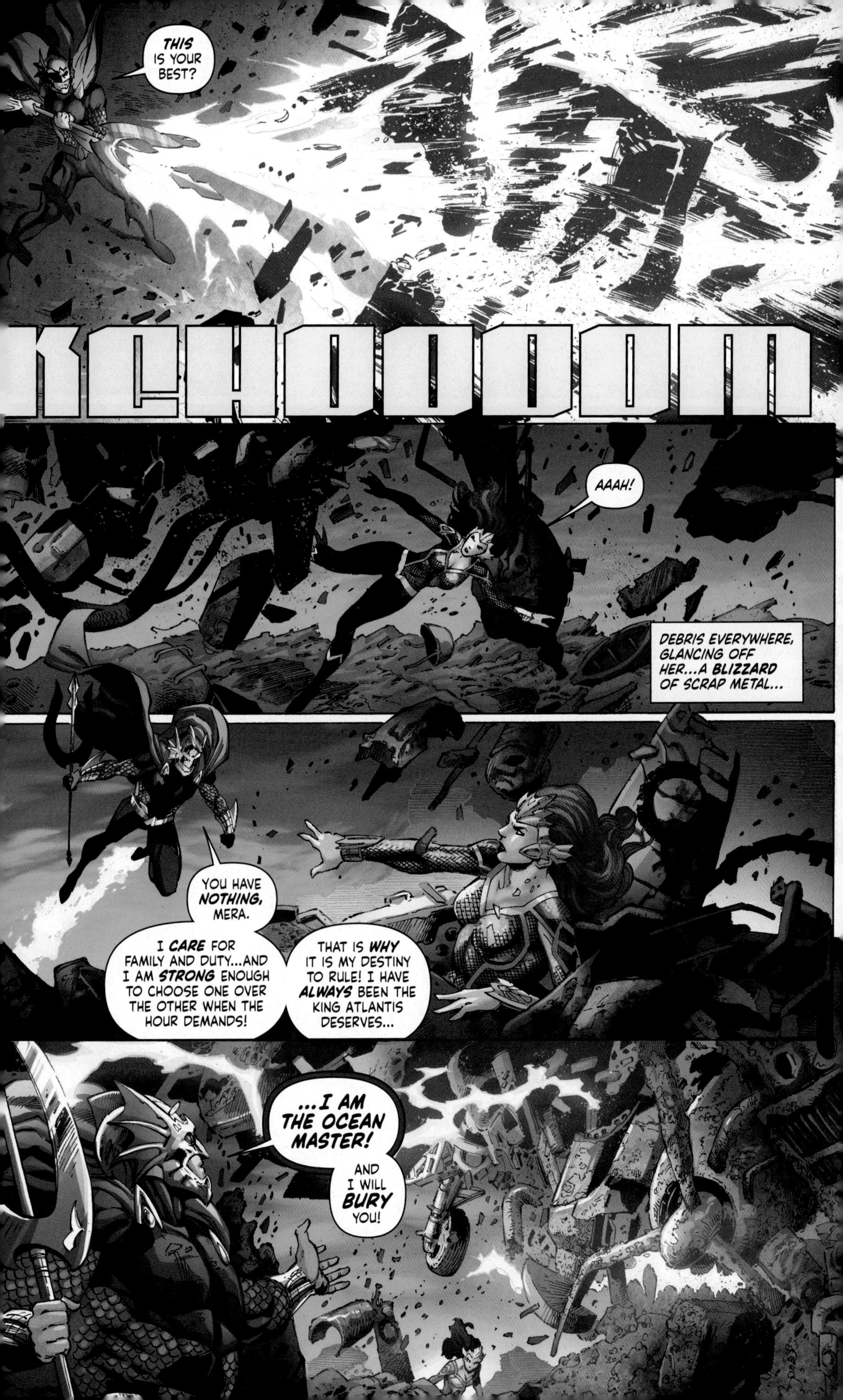

THIS IS YOUR BEST?
KCHOOOOM
AAAH!
DEBRIS EVERYWHERE, GLANCING OFF HER...A BLIZZARD OF SCRAP METAL...
YOU HAVE NOTHING, MERA.
I CARE FOR FAMILY AND DUTY...AND I AM STRONG ENOUGH TO CHOOSE ONE OVER THE OTHER WHEN THE HOUR DEMANDS!
THAT IS WHY IT IS MY DESTINY TO RULE! I HAVE ALWAYS BEEN THE KING ATLANTIS DESERVES...
...I AM THE OCEAN MASTER!
AND I WILL BURY YOU!

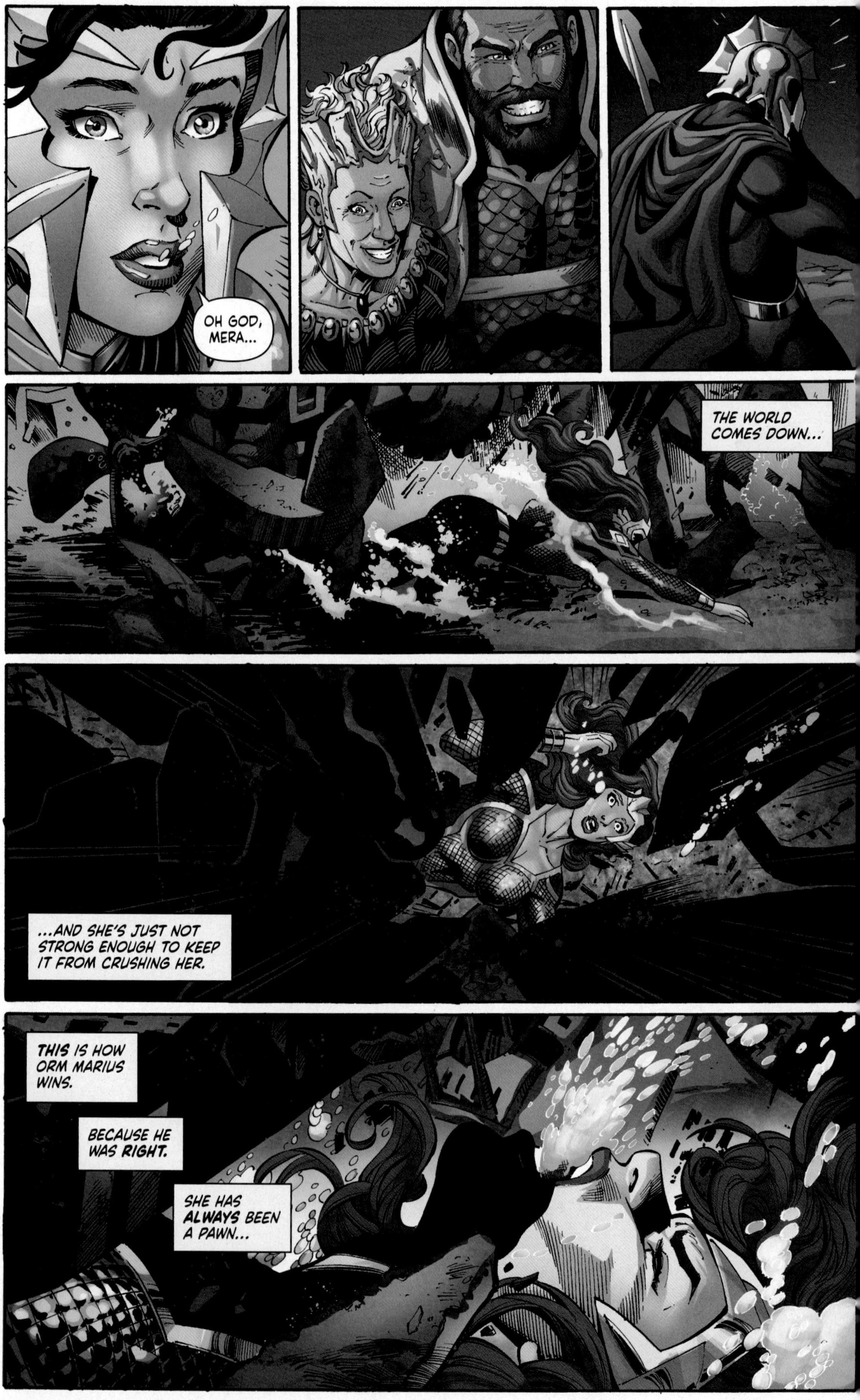

OH GOD, MERA...
THE WORLD COMES DOWN...
...AND SHE'S JUST NOT STRONG ENOUGH TO KEEP IT FROM CRUSHING HER.
THIS IS HOW ORM MARIUS WINS.
BECAUSE HE WAS RIGHT.
SHE HAS ALWAYS BEEN A PAWN...

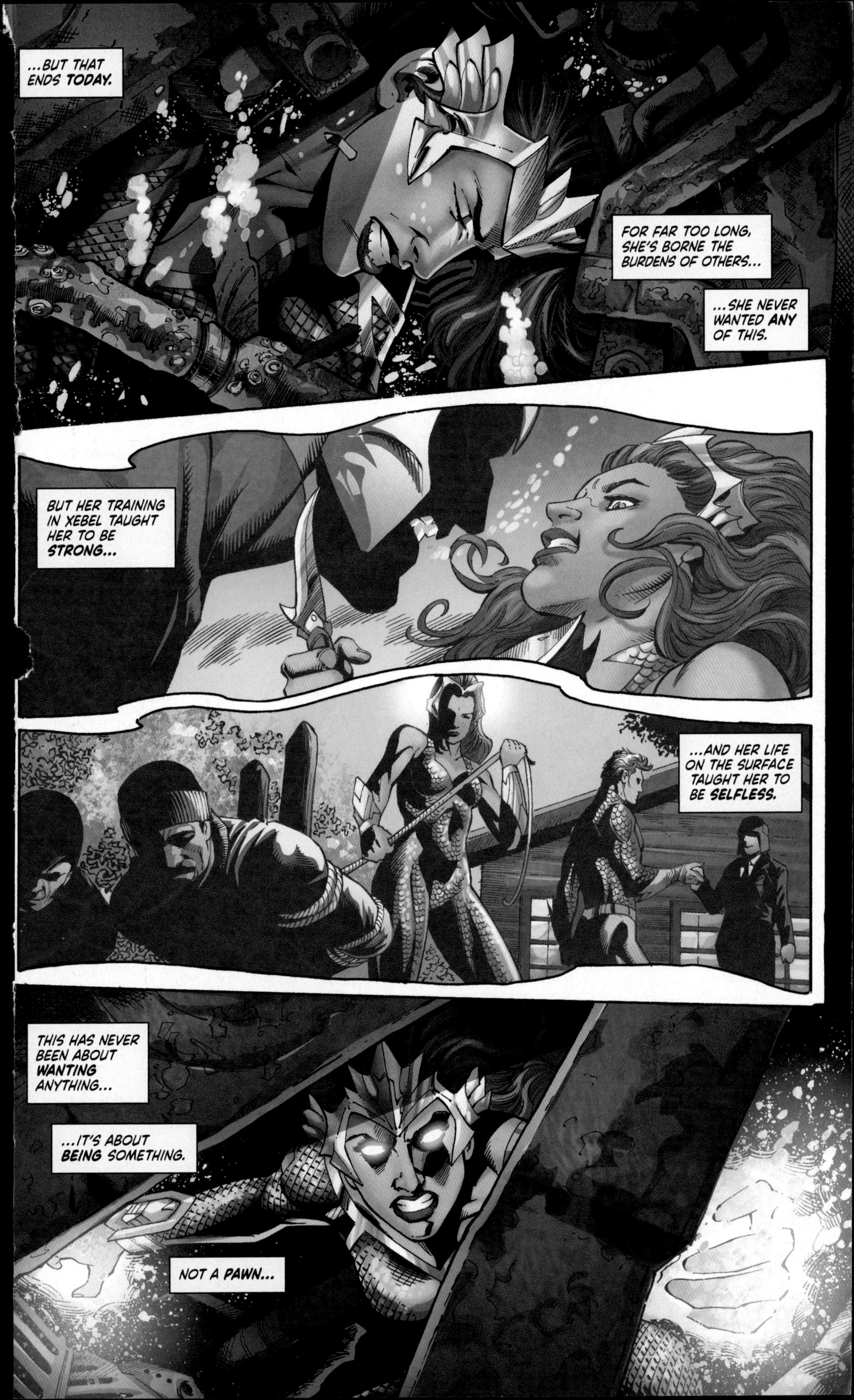
...BUT THAT ENDS TODAY.
FOR FAR TOO LONG, SHE'S BORNE THE BURDENS OF OTHERS...
...SHE NEVER WANTED ANY OF THIS.
BUT HER TRAINING IN XEBEL TAUGHT HER TO BE STRONG...
...AND HER LIFE ON THE SURFACE TAUGHT HER TO BE SELFLESS.
THIS HAS NEVER BEEN ABOUT WANTING ANYTHING...
...IT'S ABOUT BEING SOMETHING.
NOT A PAWN...

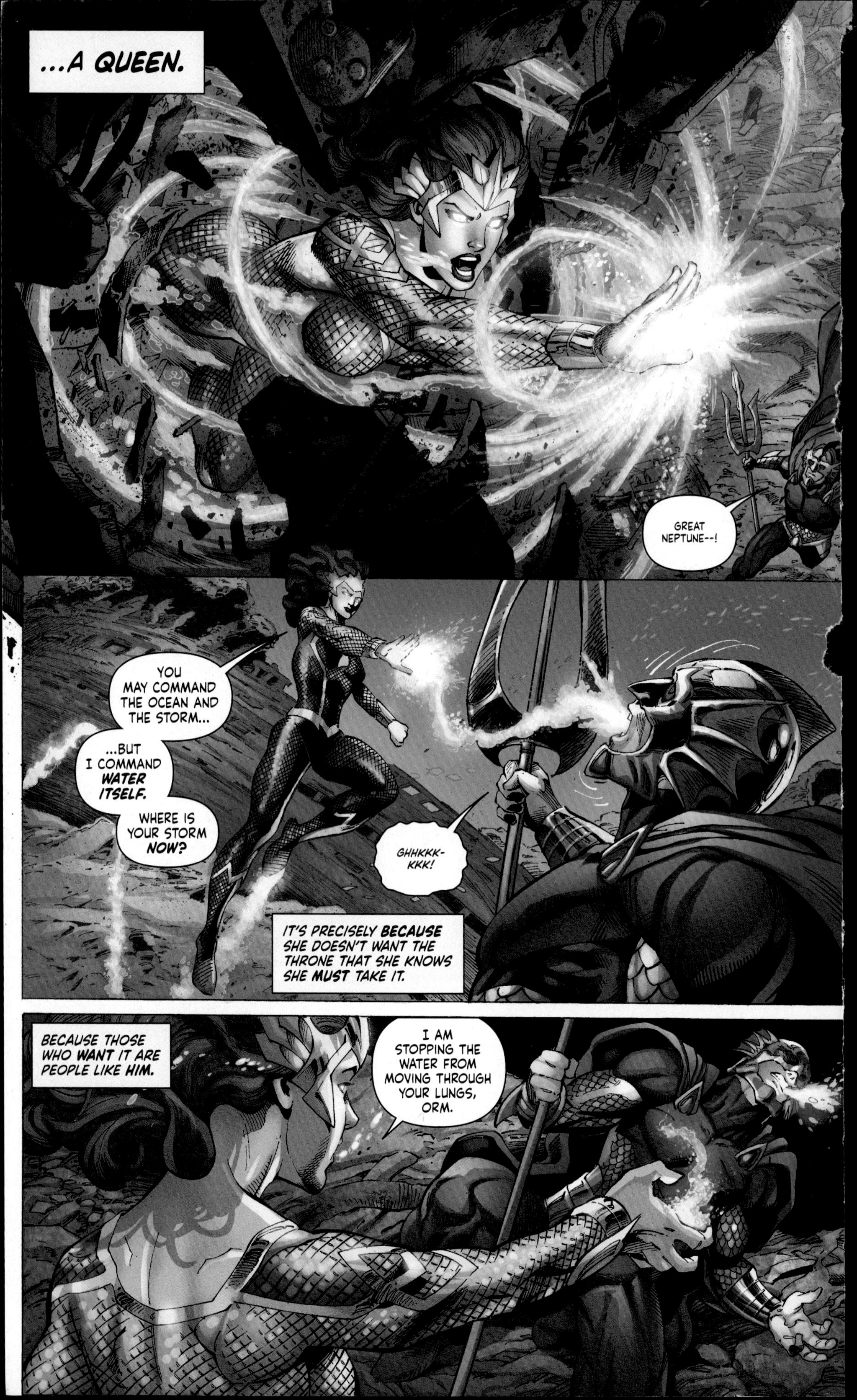
...A QUEEN.
GREAT NEPTUNE--!
YOU MAY COMMAND THE OCEAN AND THE STORM...
...BUT I COMMAND WATER ITSELF.
WHERE IS YOUR STORM NOW?
GHHKKK-KKK!
IT'S PRECISELY BECAUSE SHE DOESN'T WANT THE THRONE THAT SHE KNOWS SHE MUST TAKE IT.
BECAUSE THOSE WHO WANT IT ARE PEOPLE LIKE HIM.
I AM STOPPING THE WATER FROM MOVING THROUGH YOUR LUNGS, ORM.

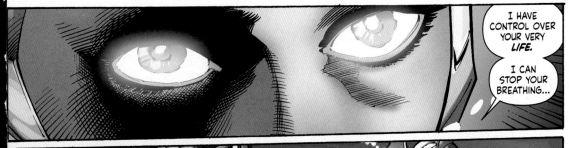

I HAVE CONTROL OVER YOUR VERY *LIFE.*

I CAN STOP YOUR BREATHING...

...I CAN TRIGGER A *STROKE.*

GHHKK...

I... WILL... N-NOT...

YOU'RE NOT THE KING ATLANTIS DESERVES.

HKKKK-KK-KK!

AND YOU *NEVER* HAVE BEEN.

SHE RELEASES THE CHOKE HOLD. DESPITE NEREUS' EDICT, SHE WON'T KILL.

SHE'S NOT A MURDERER LIKE ORM MARIUS.

BUT THE CROWD WANTS BLOOD AND A CLEAR VICTORY.

A GOOD FINISH, LERON SAID.

A DEMONSTRATION OF HER AUTHORITY, THEN... WHICH TO THE "OCEAN MASTER" IS A FATE WORSE THAN DEATH.

OCEAN MASTER... *SUBMIT.*

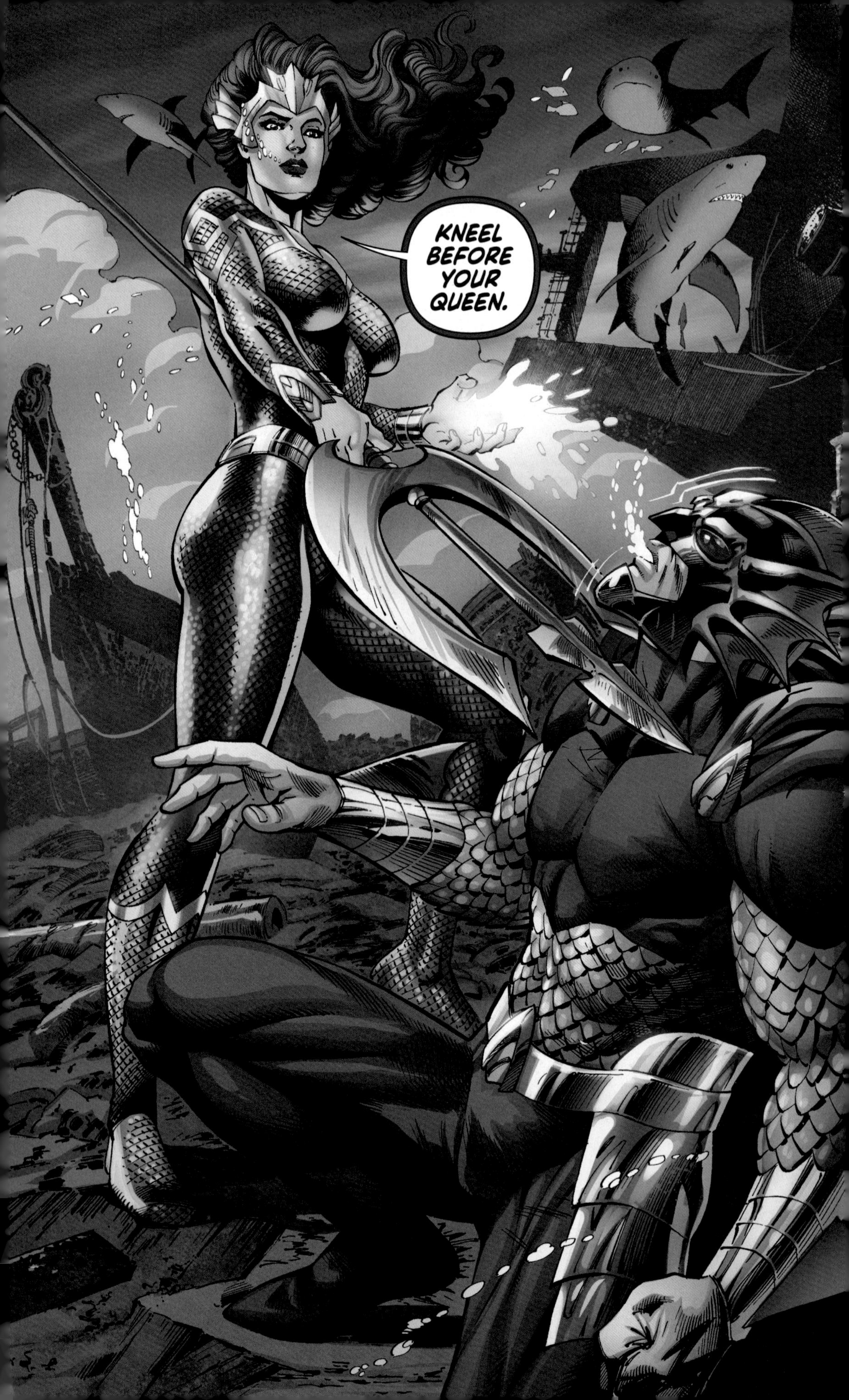
KNEEL BEFORE YOUR QUEEN.

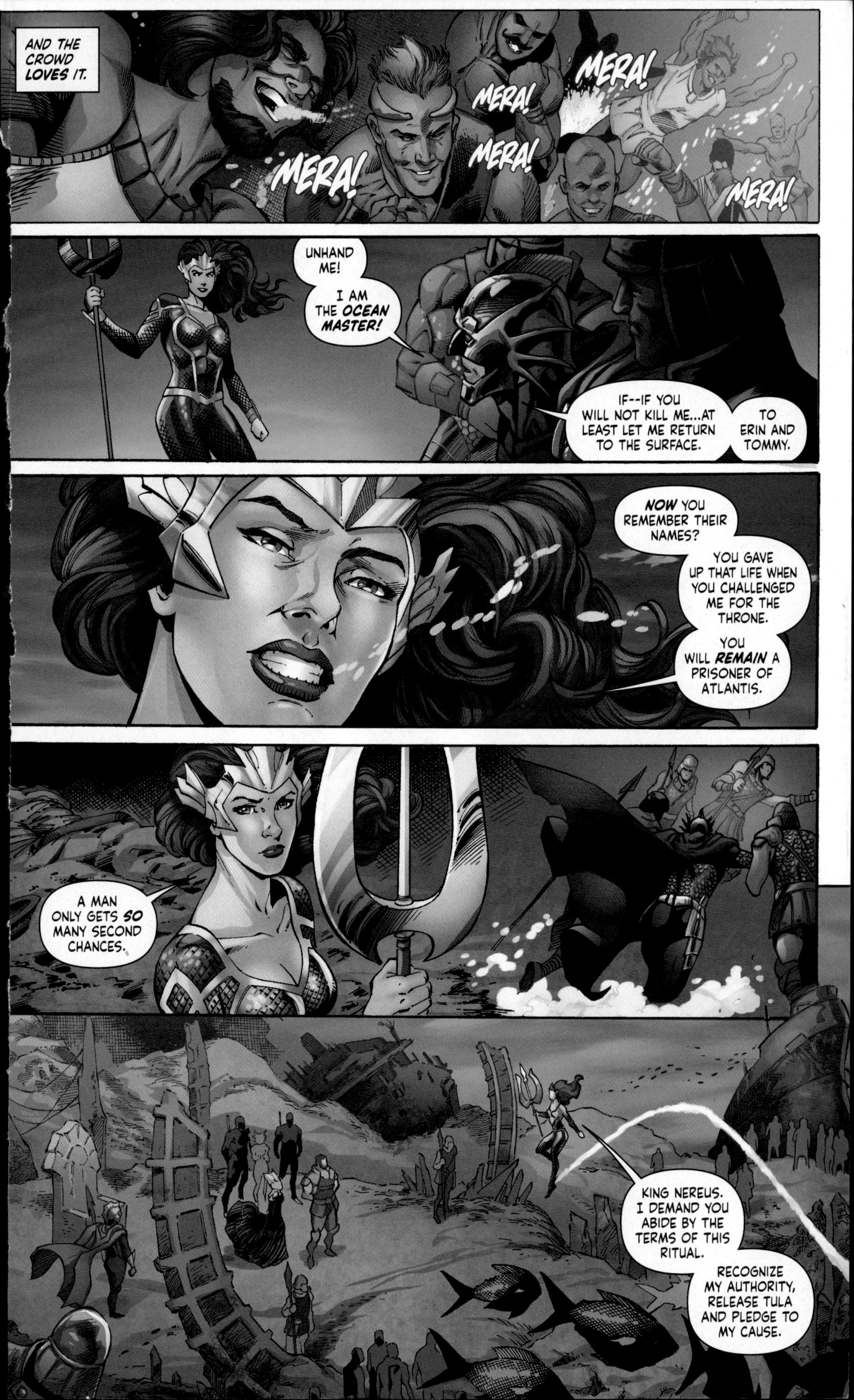
AND THE CROWD LOVES IT.
MERA!
MERA!
MERA!
MERA!
MERA!
UNHAND ME!
I AM THE OCEAN MASTER!
IF--IF YOU WILL NOT KILL ME...AT LEAST LET ME RETURN TO THE SURFACE.
TO ERIN AND TOMMY.
NOW YOU REMEMBER THEIR NAMES?
YOU GAVE UP THAT LIFE WHEN YOU CHALLENGED ME FOR THE THRONE.
YOU WILL REMAIN A PRISONER OF ATLANTIS.
A MAN ONLY GETS SO MANY SECOND CHANCES.
KING NEREUS. I DEMAND YOU ABIDE BY THE TERMS OF THIS RITUAL.
RECOGNIZE MY AUTHORITY, RELEASE TULA AND PLEDGE TO MY CAUSE.

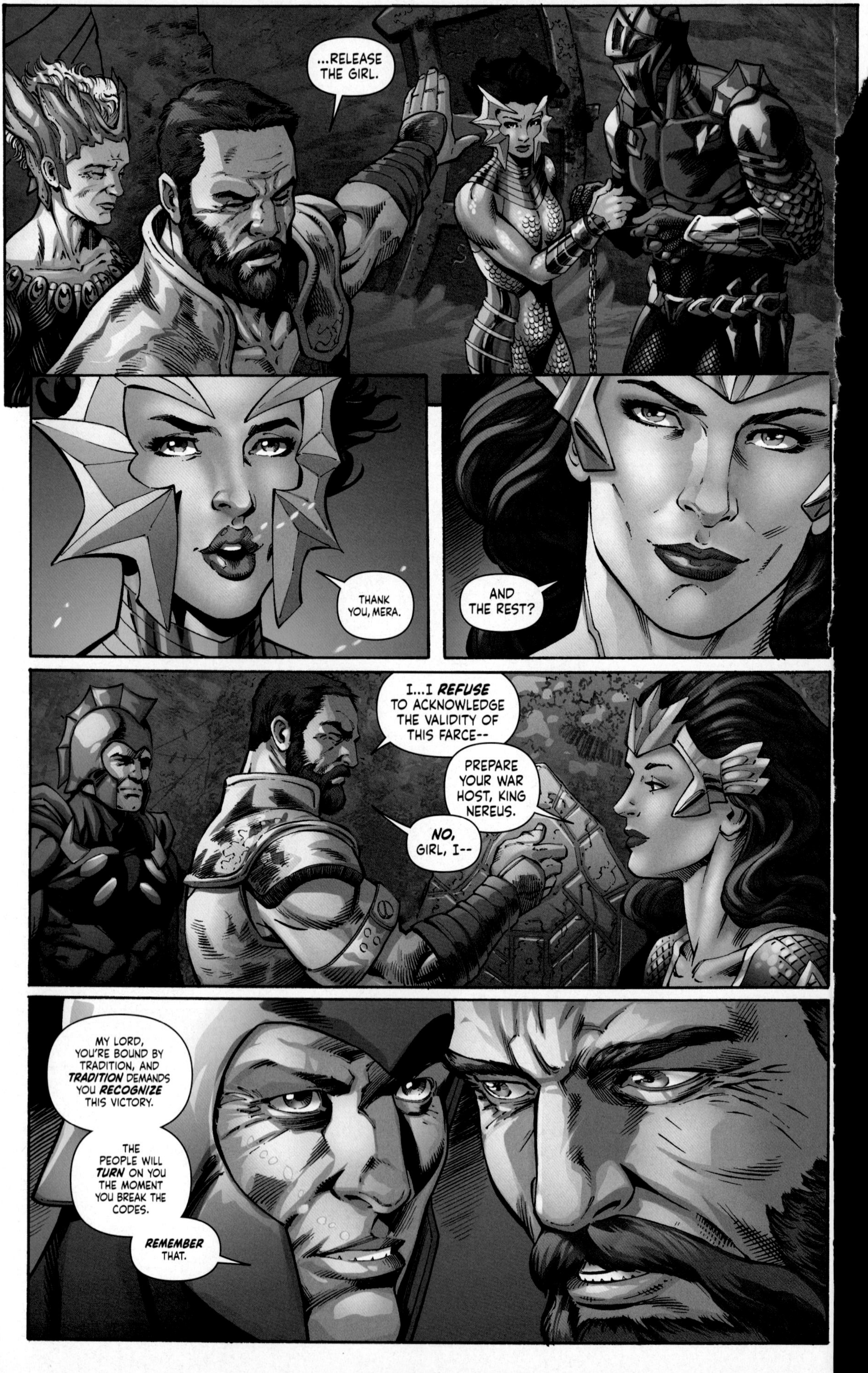
...RELEASE THE GIRL.
THANK YOU, MERA.
AND THE REST?
I...I REFUSE TO ACKNOWLEDGE THE VALIDITY OF THIS FARCE--
PREPARE YOUR WAR HOST, KING NEREUS.
NO, GIRL, I--
MY LORD, YOU'RE BOUND BY TRADITION, AND TRADITION DEMANDS YOU RECOGNIZE THIS VICTORY.
THE PEOPLE WILL TURN ON YOU THE MOMENT YOU BREAK THE CODES.
REMEMBER THAT.

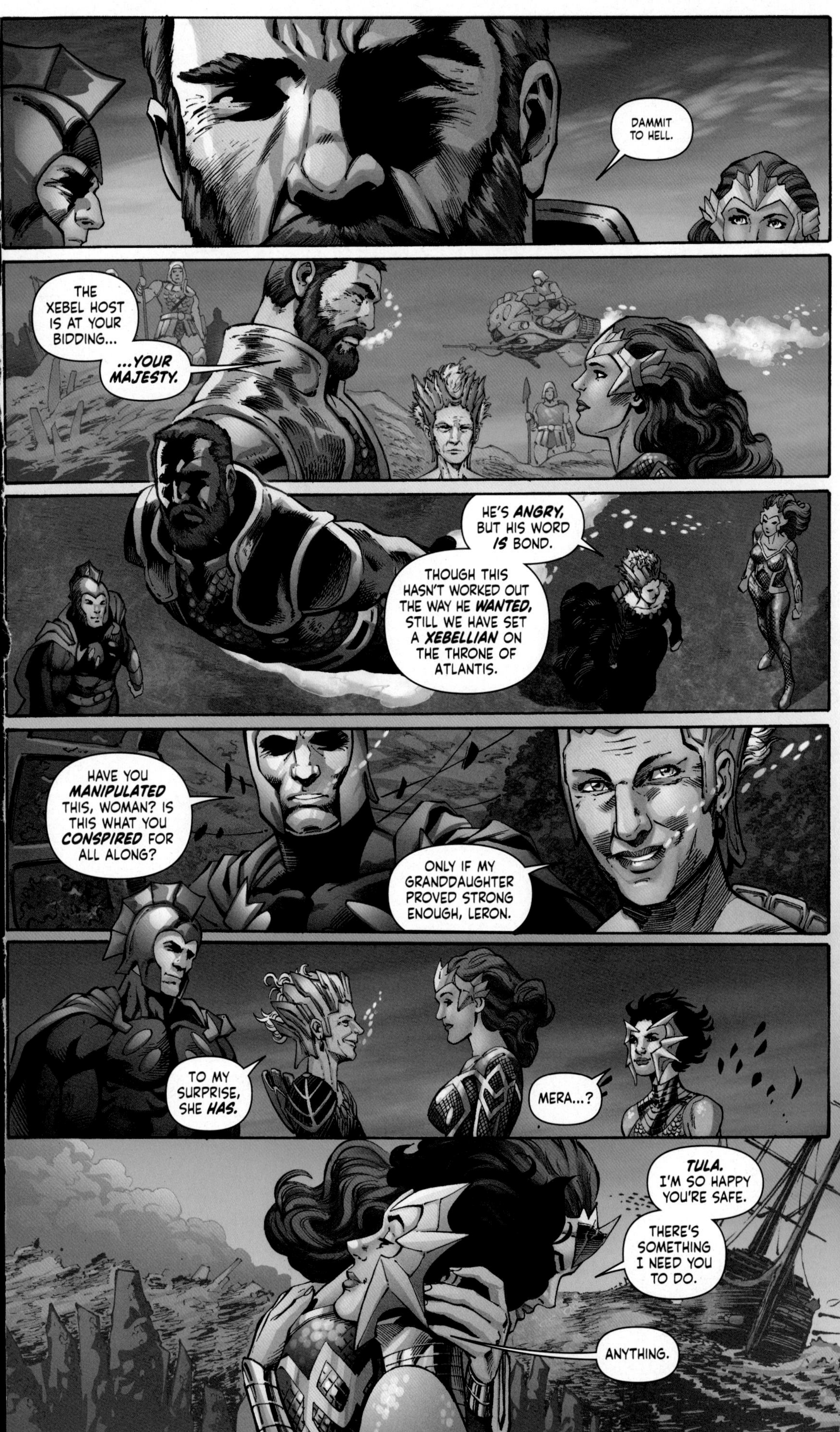
DAMMIT TO HELL.
THE XEBEL HOST IS AT YOUR BIDDING...
...YOUR MAJESTY.
HE'S ANGRY, BUT HIS WORD IS BOND.
THOUGH THIS HASN'T WORKED OUT THE WAY HE WANTED, STILL WE HAVE SET A XEBELLIAN ON THE THRONE OF ATLANTIS.
HAVE YOU MANIPULATED THIS, WOMAN? IS THIS WHAT YOU CONSPIRED FOR ALL ALONG?
ONLY IF MY GRANDDAUGHTER PROVED STRONG ENOUGH, LERON.
TO MY SURPRISE, SHE HAS.
MERA...?
TULA. I'M SO HAPPY YOU'RE SAFE.
THERE'S SOMETHING I NEED YOU TO DO.
ANYTHING.

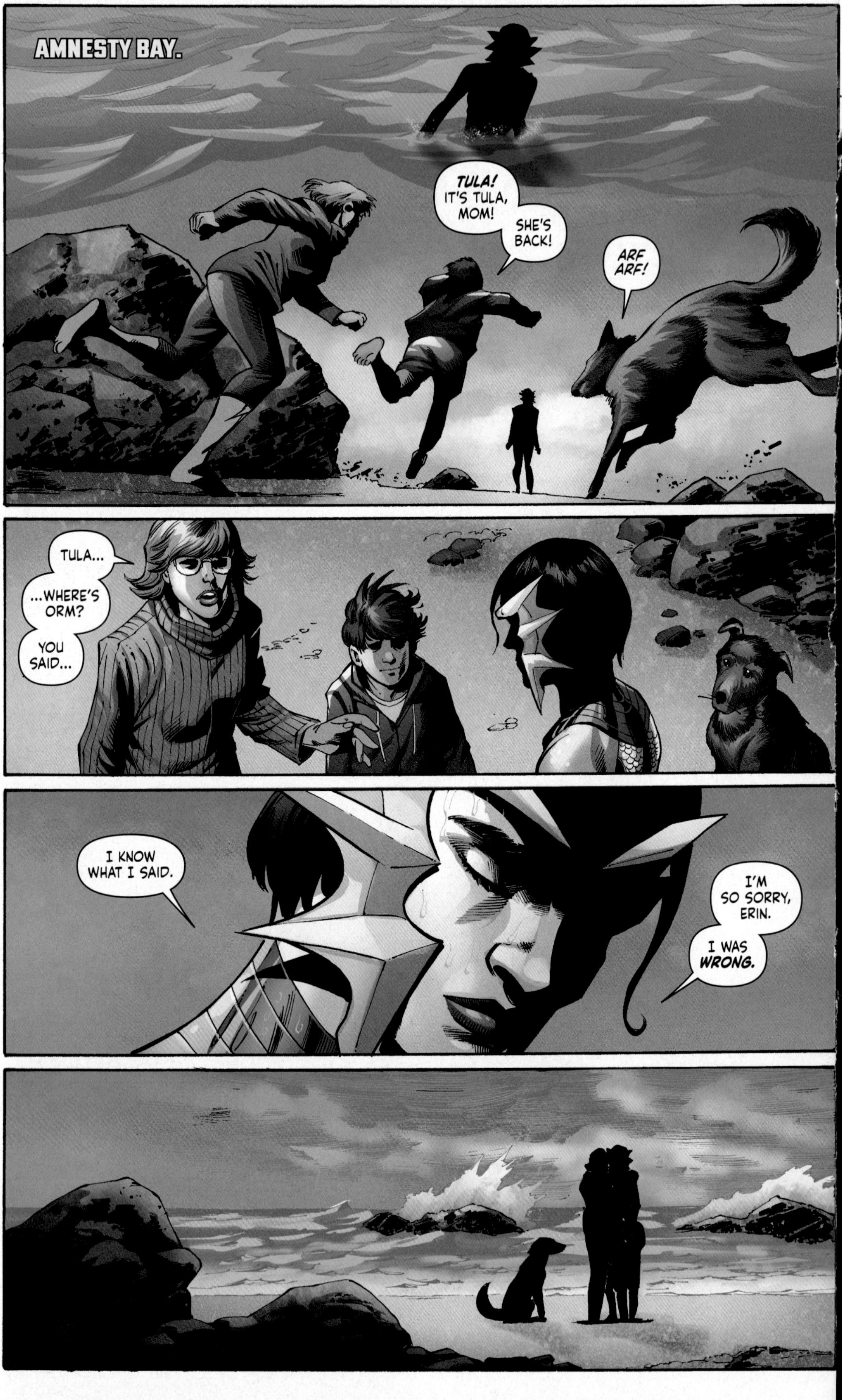
AMNESTY BAY.
TULA! IT'S TULA, MOM!
SHE'S BACK!
ARF ARF!
TULA...
...WHERE'S ORM?
YOU SAID...
I KNOW WHAT I SAID.
I'M SO SORRY, ERIN.
I WAS WRONG.

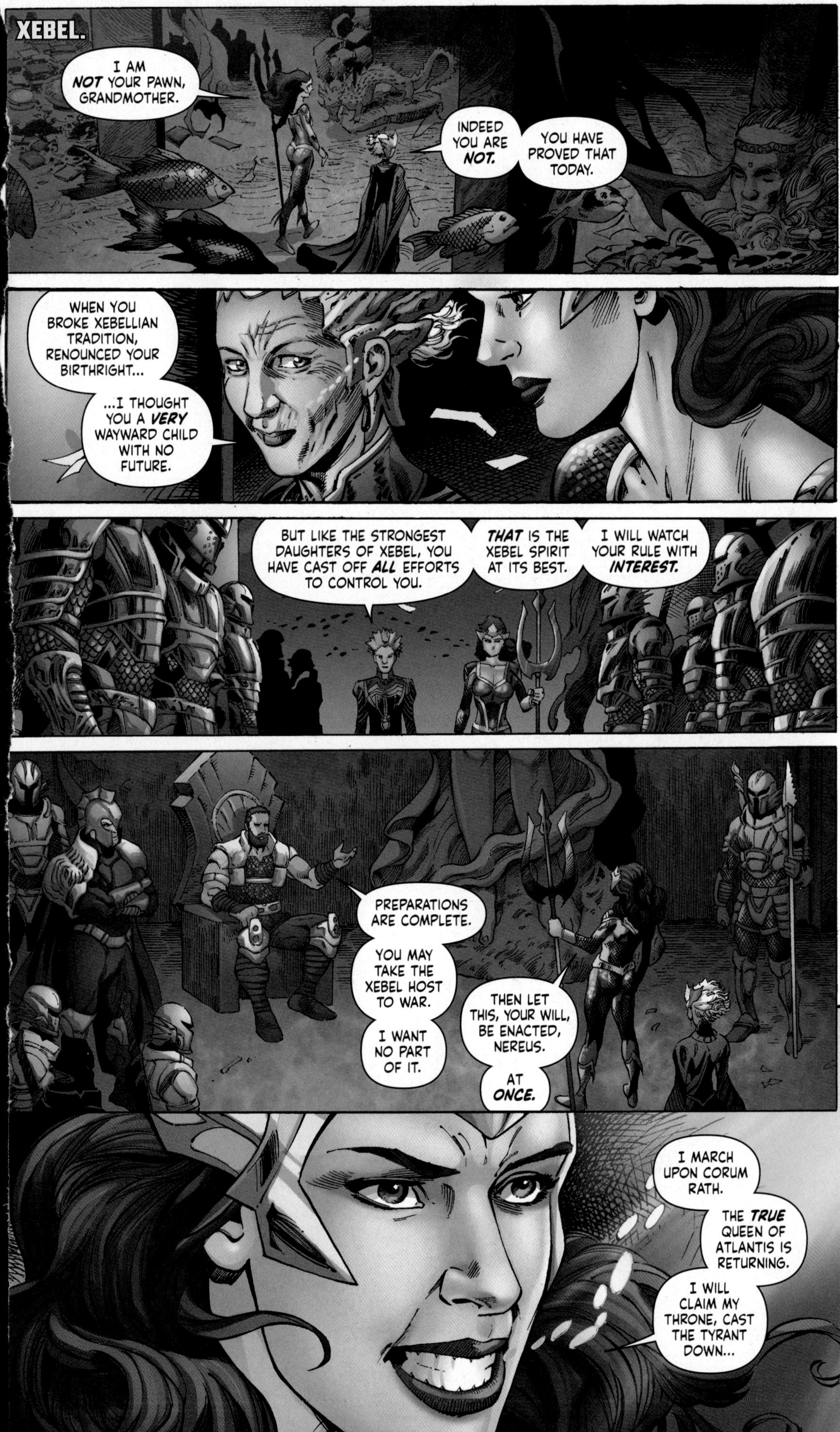
XEBEL.
I AM NOT YOUR PAWN, GRANDMOTHER.
INDEED YOU ARE NOT.
YOU HAVE PROVED THAT TODAY.
WHEN YOU BROKE XEBELLIAN TRADITION, RENOUNCED YOUR BIRTHRIGHT...
...I THOUGHT YOU A VERY WAYWARD CHILD WITH NO FUTURE.
BUT LIKE THE STRONGEST DAUGHTERS OF XEBEL, YOU HAVE CAST OFF ALL EFFORTS TO CONTROL YOU.
THAT IS THE XEBEL SPIRIT AT ITS BEST.
I WILL WATCH YOUR RULE WITH INTEREST.
PREPARATIONS ARE COMPLETE.
YOU MAY TAKE THE XEBEL HOST TO WAR.
I WANT NO PART OF IT.
THEN LET THIS, YOUR WILL, BE ENACTED, NEREUS.
AT ONCE.
I MARCH UPON CORUM RATH.
THE TRUE QUEEN OF ATLANTIS IS RETURNING.
I WILL CLAIM MY THRONE, CAST THE TYRANT DOWN...

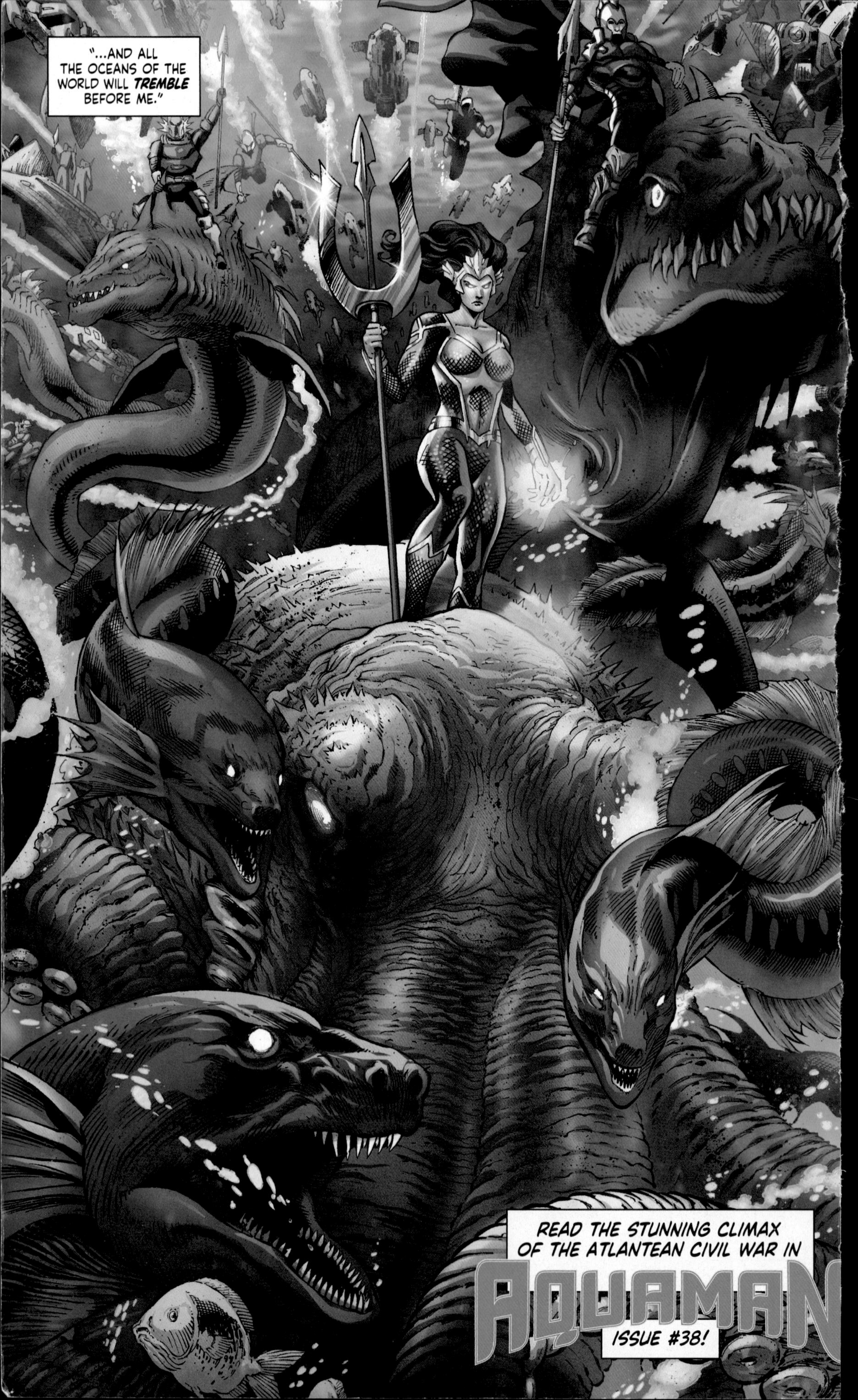
"...AND ALL THE OCEANS OF THE WORLD WILL TREMBLE BEFORE ME."
READ THE STUNNING CLIMAX OF THE ATLANTEAN CIVIL WAR IN
AQUAMAN
ISSUE #38!